JAVA PROGRAMMING
WITH VISUAL J++

JAVA PROGRAMMING
WITH VISUAL J++

Martin Rinehart

M&T Books
A Division of MIS:Press, Inc.
A Subsidiary of Henry Holt and Company, Inc.
115 West 18th Street
New York, New York 10011
http://www.mispress.com

Limits of Liability and Disclaimer of Warranty

The Author and Publisher of this book have used their best efforts in preparing the book and the programs contained in it. These efforts include the development, research, and testing of the theories and programs to determine their effectiveness.

The Author and Publisher make no warranty of any kind, expressed or implied, with regard to these programs or the documentation contained in this book. The Author and Publisher shall not be liable in any event for incidental or consequential damages in connection with, or arising out of, the furnishing, performance, or use of these programs.

All products, names and services are trademarks or registered trademarks of their respective companies.

First Edition—1997

Library of Congress Cataloging-in-Publication Data

       p.   cm.
    ISBN 1-55851-506-2

MIS:Press and M&T Books are available at special discounts for bulk purchases for sales promotions, premiums, and fundraising. Special editions or book excerpts can also be created to specification.

For details contact: Special Sales Director
                         MIS:Press and M&T Books
                         Subsidiaries of Henry Holt and Company, Inc.
                         115 West 18th Street
                         New York, New York 10011

10 9 8 7 6 5 4 3 2 1

Associate Publisher: *Paul Farrell*
Executive Editor: *Cary Sullivan*
Editor: *Michael Sprague*

Production Editor: *Patricia Wallenburg*
Copy Edit Manager: *Shari Chappell*
Copy Editor: *Karen Tongish*

TABLE OF CONTENTS

Part II: The Visual J++ Developer Studio

Chapter 6: Visual J++, A Guided Tour   141

Chapter 9: Frames, Windows, and Menus   223

Chapter 10: Entering Data   251

Chapter 13: A Thing of Beauty   343

Part III: Advanced Java Programming

Chapter 14: Exceptions Are the Rule   381

## PART I

BASIC JAVA PROGRAMMING

WHERE'S THE CESSNA?

This is a hands-on book. It's designed to be used in front of your computer. If you haven't installed Visual J++ yet, get that done before you continue. We'll be using Visual J++ right from the beginning. Each chapter begins by telling you where we're going. At the end, we wrap up with a summary of where we've been. Chapter 1 is where you'll get your first Java application compiled and running. Our goal is to say, "Hello, World!" with a Java application.

In this chapter we'll take a brief look at the awesome coding machine that Visual J++ is. Then we'll get busy turning off every option and toolbar we can get our hands on. We'll undock the docking windows; we'll undo everything except the power cord. When we've got Visual J++ stripped bare—nothing left but a few essentials—we'll start our first program. Before this chapter's done, you'll have written, compiled, and run your first Java program in the Visual J++ integrated development environment (IDE). Before we begin, let's take a look ahead.

The Journey's Plan

Visual J++ is a powerful machine for high-speed coding. It gives the Java ace the same visual programming power that Microsoft's other languages enjoy. It can really make Java programming a joy. But you're not a Java programmer. You need to learn the fundamentals of the Java language, the Java API, and so on. Visual J++ is a jet fighter, but you haven't learned the basics of flying Java yet. In Part I of this book, we start with the basics.

We'll begin in this chapter by stripping Visual J++ down to a very simple tool that is all a beginner needs. Then we'll write our first Java application. In the next three chapters we'll work on progressively more challenging portions of Java. You'll be writing many small applications to try the features that we're discussing.

Did I say *applications*? Yes, we'll postpone applets (an *applet* is an application that runs inside a Web browser, which is not quite as simple as an application) until Chapter 5. In that chapter we'll go over enough HTML programming so that you can convert your applications to applets running in your favorite Web browser. We'll build some nice Java-enhanced Web pages.

When you can write applets, we'll come back to Visual J++ and start to add back the powerful tools we turned off when we were getting started. This is the subject of Part II of this book.

We'll begin with a guided tour of the Developer Studio, looking at all the areas we've been ignoring. Then we'll dive into the pieces that help you write code at Mach 2. We'll use Wizards to generate code, dialog editors to program visually, and the debugger to trap any pesky critters that sneak in. Before we're done with this part, you'll add back all the Visual J++ pieces that we stripped out when you were beginning—and they'll make sense!

Finally, in Part III we'll look at some more advanced Java programming. For now, let's begin at the beginning.

Where's the Cessna?

I remember the first time I saw Visual J++. It had this complex array of windows, toolbars, and impressively powerful-looking things whose purpose was anything but clear. I was pretty sure that the code pilot who could fly this thing would be generating Java applets at about twice the speed of sound, probably without breaking a mental sweat. But I didn't know where to begin.

What I wanted was flying lessons, beginning at the beginning—in a one-engine Cessna trainer. Through trial and error, I discovered how to turn Visual J++ into a very minimal programming tool—just enough to enter code, compile it, and run it. It turns out that Visual J++ can be turned into a very passable Cessna without much work.

Let's begin at the beginning. What we want is something simple. We want to open a text file, type in a few lines of program, and then click a hotkey to build and run the program. Nothing more. We'll get there pretty quickly.

Start with the Taskbar

Your initial Visual J++ installation should look like Figure 1.1. Even if you're working on a 21-inch monitor, it looks busy. If you're trying to use your laptop, you're in serious trouble. Don't worry—we'll get this cleaned up in no time.

I assume you're using Windows 95. Even if you've got Windows NT, you should consider installing Windows 95, because that's the operating system that much of your target audience will be using. Windows 95 features the Taskbar and the ever-present **Start** button.

You'll start recovering necessary screen real estate by losing the Taskbar. Choose **Start/Settings/Taskbar...** to launch the Taskbar Properties tabbed dialog box shown in Figure 1.2.

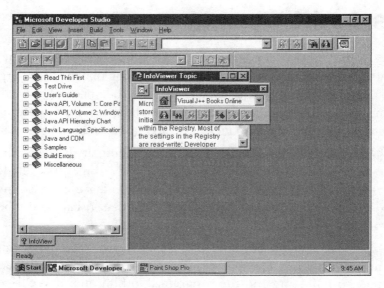

FIGURE 1.1   THE DEFAULT VISUAL J++ INSTALLATION.

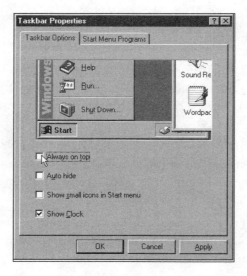

FIGURE 1.2   THE TASKBAR NOT ALWAYS ON TOP.

On the Taskbar Options page of this dialog box, uncheck the **Always on Top** option. With that done, the Developer Studio will hide the Taskbar when its window is maximized. (You can always click the main window's minimize button to reveal the Taskbar and **Start** button.)

Lose the Toolbars

Next, let's do something about the blizzard of toolbars facing us. Toolbars are wonderful, when you know what you're doing. Just click the right tool and the right thing happens. At the moment, however, we're just getting started. With a couple of exceptions (maybe **File Open** and **Save** make sense) you're looking at icons for processes you don't recognize.

So click the **View** menu and choose **Toolbars...**, as you see in Figure 1.3.

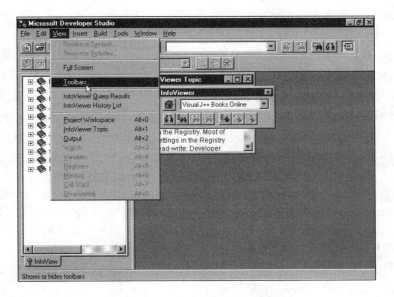

FIGURE 1.3 CHOOSING TOOLBARS.

This will launch the Toolbars dialog box that you see in Figure 1.4. You'll see that it has some interesting capabilities.

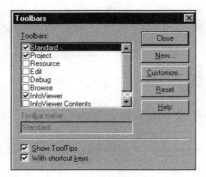

FIGURE 1.4 CLEARING THE TOOLBARS.

One of the best features of the Developer Studio is that you can really make it your own. You can pick your own toolbar buttons and arrange them to suit your own habits. For now, however, turning them all off will meet our needs.

Don't overlook that scrollbar in the right side of the toolbar window. There are more toolbars there than can be shown in the window. You have to scroll down to get them all.

When every toolbar is unchecked, click **Close** and you'll be back in the Developer Studio with a simpler, though still complex, arrangement.

Undock Your Windows

If you haven't played with Visual J++ at all yet, this is a good time to begin experimenting. Point at things and click the right mouse button. You'll see relevant menus pop up. In the InfoViewer, you'll see that **Docking View** is selected, as Figure 1.5 shows.

Click to unselect the docking view, and your InfoViewer window will be floated within your Developer Studio client area. Check your other windows' pop-up menus to be sure that no other docking view is selected, while you're at it.

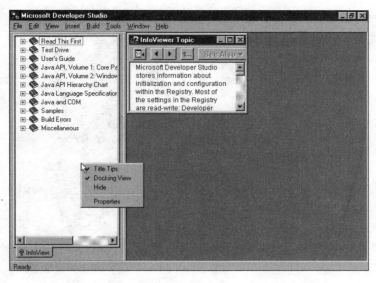

FIGURE 1.5 RIGHT-CLICKING TO VIEW A POP-UP MENU.

Close Almost Everything

Now we're ready to close everything. Don't just minimize your windows, close them. (Isn't Windows 95's upper-right **X** button handy? If you're 30,000 feet up and your trackball's missing, try **Ctrl-** (hyphen) to get the child window system menu and choose **Close**.)

When you've closed all the child windows, you'll have found the Cessna. You can probably figure out how to fly it without much help. Mine is shown in Figure 1.6.

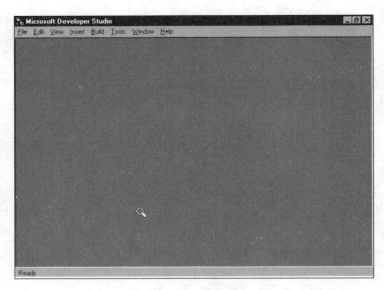

FIGURE 1.6   HERE'S THE CESSNA!

Now we're ready to write our first Java program.

Say "Hello, World!"

Ready to start writing Java programs? Here's what we're going to do:

- Enter code into a new text file.
- Save the file under a specific name.
- Create a new project workspace.
- Build the project.
- Execute the program as a stand-alone Java application.

All of this is a lot less trouble to do than to explain. Begin by choosing **File/New**. You'll get a pop-up menu, as Figure 1.7 shows. Choose **Text File** from this menu.

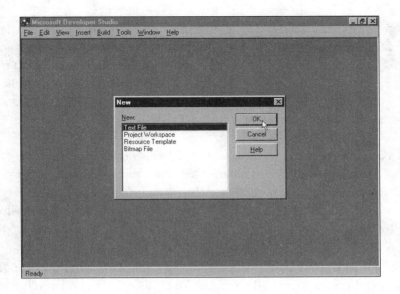

FIGURE 1.7   CREATING A NEW TEXT FILE.

You'll get an empty program editor window, with a file named **Text1** (or **Text2**, and so on, if you've already opened **Text1**). Enter the code in Listing 1.1.

LISTING 1.1   THE HELLO APPLICATION

```
class Hello
{
    static void main( String[] args )
    {
        System.out.println( "Hello, World!" );
    }
}
```

WARNING

Java, like C, is a case-sensitive language. Its case-sensitivity will probably drive you nuts at first. Even the file names are sensitive to case. If you want the class `Hello` to compile successfully, you'll need to put it in the file **Hello.java**. It won't work in **HELLO.JAVA** or **hello.java**. Similarly, `System.out.println` is not `system.out.Println` or any other capitalization scheme.

If you know C, you can probably read this code. It starts by creating a class. (All Java code is object-oriented; everything's done in classes.) Then it defines a function `main()` that has one working line, a call to `System.out.println()`. You've probably already figured out what that will do.

All these listings are on the disk included with this book. You'll find this one in **01-01**. Until we get going in the later chapters, I strongly recommend that you type all the code. You'll learn a lot, and you'll find your mistakes interesting.

Got that code typed into your file? Good. Now let's save it. Choose **File/Save As** to give it the correct name. You'll see the File Save dialog box, shown in Figure 1.8. Mine defaulted to writing code into **\MSDEV\BIN**, which is where the binaries for the Developer Studio are kept; it's not a good place to store your code.

I'm storing my Java source, as you see in the figure, in **\Msdev\projects**. (This is where Microsoft expects many of the samples supplied with Visual J++ to be developed. Your life will be easier if you store yours here until you finish this book and get on to your own projects.)

Make sure your file name is **Hello.java**—capital *H* and lowercase for the rest, please. This has to match the name of the class in the program file.

Got that? Good. Now we're ready to build our first project. You can't build anything until you create a project workspace, but Visual J++ is very helpful about that. Go ahead and choose **Build/Build Hello**. You'll get the Needs Workspace dialog box shown in Figure 1.9.

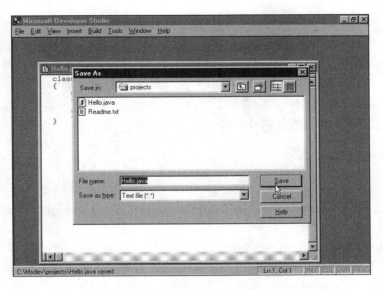

FIGURE 1.8 STORING YOUR PROJECTS IN \MSDEV\PROJECTS.

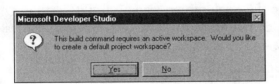

FIGURE 1.9 VISUAL J++ HELPS BUILD A WORKSPACE.

All you need to do to create a workspace for your Hello project is click **Yes**, or press **Enter**. Visual J++ will do the rest. It will open a Project Workspace window for you and then open the Output window to compile your program. As you might guess, the build will compile all the files in a multifile project, if it sees that you've modified the source code since your previous build.

Ready to run your program? Try **Ctrl+F5** to execute (from the menus, that's **Build/Execute**). You'll get the dialog box shown in Figure 1.10.

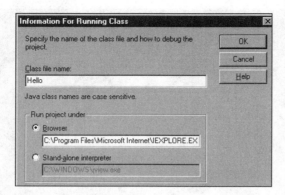

FIGURE 1.10 SPECIFYING HELLO.CLASS FOR THE COMPILED CODE.

You can omit the *.class* extension for the compiled file; that's the default. Make sure your capitalization is *Hello* before you accept this entry.

Be sure to choose the Stand-alone interpreter. Our code won't run as an Applet. We'll get to applets in Chapter 5. If you generate an applet by mistake, Internet Explorer will be launched to run it (even though it won't work). Close the Explorer and choose **Build/Settings**. From the Debug tab you can change from applet to application. Then use **Ctrl+F5** again and you'll be back in business.

Now, drum roll please; your Output window shows and then a new window is opened for **JVIEW.EXE**, the Java application stand-alone run-time system. It will open and say "Hello, World!" just as you hoped. (After it does this, it closes. Don't look away or you'll miss it.)

Congratulations. You've written and run your first Java application. Now let's get a bit smarter before we finish this chapter. Close everything but the Output window and your source code window. Arrange them so that you can see both, as Figure 1.11 shows.

Now make a trivial change in the output string. Try something like, "Hello again, World!" Don't rebuild; just press **Ctrl+F5** to execute. You'll get a `Files need to be built` message box, as you can see in Figure 1.12.

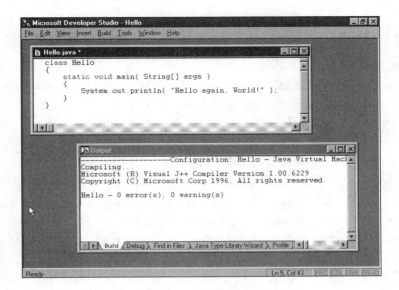

FIGURE 1.11 A WORKING APPLICATION ARRANGEMENT.

FIGURE 1.12 VISUAL J++ OFFERS ANOTHER HAND.

You can click **Yes** or press **Enter**. You can press **Enter** while you are waiting for Visual J++ to check to see if a build is needed. I just press **Ctrl+F5**, then **Enter**. This is an effective "rebuild anything that needs to be rebuilt and then run the latest version, please" command.

Try it yourself, changing the output message slightly between builds. Got it? I think you're going to like Visual J++ programming.

Summary

When we started, we had an intimidatingly complex programming tool facing us. Our first job was to simplify it. We turned off everything that was turned on, which simplified Visual J++ from a jet fighter to a one-engine Cessna, which is what we want to learn to fly simple Java programs.

Then we wrote a minimal "Hello, World!" program. Mostly letting Visual J++ work for you, you saved it; you created a project workspace; you built the **.class** executable code, and you ran it as a stand-alone application.

Finally, you set up a simple two-window arrangement, where you can edit code in one window then press **Ctrl+F5** and **Enter** to watch the revised code run in the other window. We've built our Cessna and learned to use it.

In Chapter 2, we'll meet a lot more of the Java language and you'll begin to understand Java programming.

Java Basics

In this chapter we'll look at the basic parts of the Java language. If you are a C programmer you'll find it is almost identical to C. We'll have boxes that highlight the differences, so you C programmers can just skim through, checking the boxes.

We'll start by creating a new workspace and setting up operations in full-screen mode. You'll see that this is even more minimal than the way we created our first application in Chapter 1.

After we get set, we'll review the structure of Java programs. We're going to go more deeply into structure in Chapter 3, but we'll start with enough here so that the examples in this chapter make sense.

After looking at the language's structure, we'll review the basic data types that are at Java's most elementary level. We'll try most of them in sample programs.

After we've introduced the basic data types, we'll put them to use in expressions, doing calculations and making comparisons. Last, we'll look at the statements that Java uses.

You'll see that Java is a very small, simple language. While it's more completely object-oriented than C++, in its small size and simplicity it is more like C than C++.

Setup

Setup Is for C Programmers

There will be a box, like this one, at the start of each section. If you know C, check these boxes. If you're not a C programmer, they're not for you.

Java is derived from C++, but many of its basic features will be familiar to C programmers. This setup section, however, is about the Developer Studio and should be read by everyone.

Ready to start programming? We'll begin by creating and populating a new project. Then we'll work on an optimal Visual J++ setup for the work that we're going to be doing.

Creating the Project

Let's start by creating a "Testing" project. Choose **File/New** and then choose **Project workspace**. Visual J++ will launch the dialog box you see in Figure 2.1.

Again, be sure to type *Testing* with the same capitalization everywhere you use it.

Now let's create a new text file for our source code. You can use **Ctrl+N** to do this more quickly than you can with the menus. (I like to keep my fingers on the keyboard while I'm writing code.) Choose **Text file** and enter the code in Listing 2.1.

Before you start typing, realize that Visual J++'s text editor is intelligent. It understands Java programming. If you *don't* touch the **Tab** key (and don't use the spacebar where the tabs go), the editor will insert the correct indentation for you. Let Visual J++ work for you.

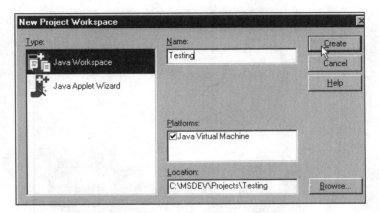

FIGURE 2.1 CREATING A NEW PROJECT.

LISTING 2.1 A BASIC TEST PROGRAM

```
// Testing.java

class Testing
{
    void main( String args[] )
    {
        System.out.println( "Testing!" );
    }
}

// end of Testing.java
```

When you have typed this in, press **F12**, the shortcut for **File/Save As**. Name the file **Testing** (let Visual J++ supply the default **.java** extension), and save it. Now press **Ctrl+F5**, and you'll see a problem.

Visual J++ will tell you that there is no source to compile. It will then ask you what class file you would like to use. Tell it **Testing** again (and let Visual J++ supply the correct **.class** extension). Now let's address the error.

The problem is that you haven't put your source code into the workspace. Tap **Alt+I**, then **I** (for **Insert/Files** into Project) and you'll see the dialog box shown in Figure 2.2.

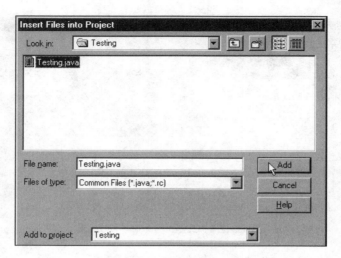

FIGURE 2.2   ADDING THE SOURCE TO THE PROJECT.

Click on the source file and its name will be typed into the File Name field for you. (If you type it yourself, you'll need to type the extension as well as the name—a small nuisance.) Click **Add**, and your project has a new file. The Project Workspace dialog box will appear set to its File View tab. **Ctrl+F4** closes the active child window, which is how I keep the Project Workspace window from intruding. It's always available (press **Alt+0**), so I don't usually leave it on my screen.

Now go back to **Ctrl+F5** and **Enter**. This time you should compile, link and run in the JVIEW standalone Java interpreter.

Getting Visual J++ Set Up

In the rest of this chapter we'll be working with a small program to test different pieces of the Java language. Let's do this in an optimal way. Begin by launching Visual J++'s full-screen mode. From the keyboard, pressing **Alt+V** followed by **U** will toggle full-screen mode.

In full-screen mode, the only thing you see is Visual J++'s client area, where you can keep your source and output windows open. The menus are still available from the keyboard. Try **Alt+V** to pull down the View menu again, and you'll see that it's there for you whenever you want it. This is very useful for working at the keyboard.

The **Esc** key will return you from full-screen mode to normal, but only eventually. It first escapes from dialog windows and from windows such as the Output window. (Output will come back with a press of **Alt+2**, by the way. This is useful when you've inadvertently closed it.) The build and execute process opens the Output window automatically, so you don't need to worry about this one. I prefer to use **Alt+V** followed by **U** for toggling full screen because it doesn't have any side effects.

Structure

Java Structure Is C Structure

If you know C's structure, you know Java's structure. You can skip this section altogether, but you'll probably want to try the examples.

In Chapter 3 we'll be going into Java structure in depth. Here, we're only going to look at what we need to do basic Java programming. Let's begin with the braces that Visual J++'s built-in editor seems to understand.

Braces and Blocks

All Java code lives in blocks delimited by curly braces. Our sample program has one block that encloses the complete Testing class. Within the class, another block encloses the `main()` function. (In this book, I'll always follow a function name with parentheses. Here, `main()` is a function.)

You have to use blocks to define classes and functions. You can also use blocks whenever you like. Try to run the buggy code in Listing 2.2.

LISTING 2.2 A SAMPLE WITH ERRORS

```
// Testing.java

class Testing
{
    void main( String args[] )
    {
        System.out.println( "Testing!" );

        int temp = 1;
        float temp = 1.1;
    }
}

// end of Testing.java
```

The compiler will complain that the variable temp is already defined when you attempt to redefine it. Variables exist only within the block that defines them. Putting the two temp variables into blocks fixes the problem. Listing 2.3 shows code that uses two temp variables.

LISTING 2.3 BLOCKS ELIMINATE THE CONFLICT

```
// Testing.java

class Testing
{
    void main( String args[] )
    {
        System.out.println( "Testing!" );
        {
            int temp = 1;
        }
        {
            double temp = 1.1;
        }
```

```
        }
}

// end of Testing.java
```

By the way, using a useless name, like `temp`, is bad programming practice, and using it for two different types of data is an even worse practice. This example illustrates our point about blocks, not good code style.

Variables

Variables store values, as you've seen. A variable needs a name and a data type. The name is any combination of letters and digits, starting with a letter. You can also use the underscore character and the dollar sign as alphabetic characters in a name. These examples create names for 16-bit integer values:

```
short row;
short last_output_row;
short mouse_x_location;
```

Statements

We've been using statements in our work this far. In Listing 2.3 we have a class statement, a function definition statement, a function call statement calling `println()` and two variable definition statements. We'll learn more about each of these shortly. For the moment, we're looking at statements' relationship to the structure of the program.

First, the whole program we're using this far is a single statement: a class definition statement. In Chapter 3 we'll define more classes in a single program. The class statement begins with a curly brace and ends with a curly brace. The indentation style used here shows you plainly how this is structured.

Similarly, the function definition statement that defines `main()` is the only statement in the class definition. It ends with a closing curly brace.

Statements that don't have statement blocks end with a semicolon. Like C, Java does not pay attention to the lines in your source code. To the Java compiler, a line end is no different from a space or tab character. Collectively, these are called *whitespace*, and they can be used freely to enhance program readability.

You can write multiple statements on a single line, if you wish. Listing 2.4 shows an example of this.

LISTING 2.4 MULTIPLE STATEMENTS ON A SINGLE LINE

```
// Testing.java

class Testing
{
    void main( String args[] )
    {
        System.out.println( "Testing!" );
        int row = 1; int col = 2;
    }
}

// end of Testing.java
```

Experienced programmers generally don't put multiple statements on a single line as a matter of good style. In the example in Listing 2.4, the two statements are closely related (assigning a location in a dialog box, perhaps) so the example is acceptable.

One final note on statements. Like C, Java lets you format your source code almost any way you like. You could write every program on a single line, never including a carriage return. Or you could write your programs with a single word on each line, running down the screen endlessly.

The style I'm using in these examples is only one possibility, but it's one that is generally considered a good programming style, and it's one that the built-in Visual J++ text editor understands and will support.

Comments

You've probably guessed that the first and last lines of each of our listings are comments, not part of the code. You can use the double slash to start a comment anywhere on a line. These are two common examples:

```
// this is a comment
int i = 1; // this is another comment
```

Here's another example that works, but I don't recommended it.

```
int // this will compile
i   // but it's very
=   // stupid!
100;
```

You can also enclose text in /* . . . */ delimiters. While the // comment starts with the // and extends to the end of the line, /* . . . */ comments begin and end with the slash-star and star-slash delimiters. This makes them very handy when you have multiple-line comments, as in this example:

```
/*
    These lines are
    all part of a
    single comment.
*/
```

Be careful when you do this. These comments do *not* nest. This will fail to compile, even though it looks good:

```
/*
    This shows that
    comments don't nest.
    /*
        This looks like a nested
        comment, but it's just
```

```
        part of the same comment.
    */

    The star-slash above this line ended the comment!
    The compiler will choke here!
*/
```

The first star-slash pair ends the comment. The second star-slash pair is an error.

Data Types

Java's classes define data types. In our examples, the String that is part of the definition of main() is a String class object. (By convention, you capitalize the first letter of any Java class.)

In this section, however, we're not going to look at objects. We're looking at the basic data types that underlie all our programs.

Java's Data Isn't C's Data

C programmers will find Java's data types familiar but in many ways different. Read this section carefully.

You'll not see the word *pointer* here. Java doesn't have pointers. (It handles pointers internally, of course, but it never shows the programmer a pointer.)

In particular, note that short and long are data types, not modifiers. You can have a short integer, but never a short int. Short and int are separate data types.

Boolean

Boolean variables have two possible values, true and false. These values, true and false, are also keywords that can be used in assignments to boolean variables. Listing 2.5 shows how this works.

LISTING 2.5   PRINTING BOOLEAN VALUES

```java
// Testing.java

class Testing
{
    void main( String args[] )
    {
        boolean good = true;
        boolean bad = false;

        System.out.println( "Is this good?" );
        System.out.println( good );
        System.out.println();
        System.out.println( "Is this good?" );
        System.out.println( bad );

    }

}

// end of Testing.java
```

Enter and run this for yourself. You'll see that Java answers the first question with true and the next with false.

By the way, isn't it convenient that println() knows how to display different types of data? If you want to learn what other types println() supports, select just the function name in your editor window (hold **Shift** down and use the arrow keys to highlight just the word *println*—this is much more precise than trying to use a mouse drag) and press **F1**. You'll get help on the selected item. (My version of the documentation forgot to include the short data type, which println() will also handle.)

Although it's getting ahead of ourselves, let's replace the constants with relational expressions, which evaluate to boolean results. Listing 2.6 shows this.

LISTING 2.6 ASSIGNING TO BOOLEAN VARIABLES

```
// Testing.java

class Testing
{
    void main( String args[] )
    {
        boolean good = 2 > 1;
        boolean bad = 1 > 2;

        System.out.println( "Is this good?" );
        System.out.println( good );
        System.out.println();
        System.out.println( "Is this good?" );
        System.out.println( bad );
    }
}

// end of Testing.java
```

Try this yourself and you'll see that 2 > 1 is true and 1 > 2 is false. Reassuring, isn't it?

Integer

There are four integer types:

byte —8-bit integer
short —16-bit integer
int —32-bit integer
long —64-bit integer

Integers are signed. The short type, for example, stores values up to positive 32K-1, and down to negative 32K. Test them for yourself by entering and running the code in Listing 2.7.

LISTING 2.7   TEST THE FOUR INTEGER TYPES

```
// Testing.java

class Testing
{
    void main( String args[] )
    {
        byte b = 123;
        short s = 12345;
        int i = 123456;
        long l = -1234567890;

        System.out.println( b );
        System.out.println( s );
        System.out.println( i );
        System.out.println( l );
    }
}

// end of Testing.java
```

That should work fine. Now change the byte's value from `123` to `128` and see what happens. The compiler tells you that it's an error. It says `cannot implicitly convert 'short' to 'byte'`. A byte stores values from -128 to 127. 128 won't fit in a byte, so it compiles 128 as a `short` numeric constant. If you had assigned that value to an `int` or a `long`, it would have converted the `short` constant to a constant of the appropriate type. Going from a larger to a smaller data size doesn't work, of course.

Character

Character data, `char`, is entered in single quotes. `Strings`—objects of the `String` class, not a basic data type—are entered inside double quotes. These two are different:

'a'—A character constant

"a"—A string object

There are some characters that would otherwise be a problem. These can be entered by preceding them with the backslash character. These are the main ones:

\n—Newline

\t—Tab

\b—Backspace

\\—Backslash character

\'—Single-quote character

\"—Double-quote character

You can also enter any character as a hexadecimal constant (e.g., \xHH where H is a hex digit). For example, \x1B is character 27, the **Esc** key. If your requirements are multilingual, you can also enter Unicode characters.

Listing 2.8 shows a char variable and some char constants put to use. It also introduces the print() function, which is used when you want to continue a print line.

LISTING 2.8 WORKING WITH CHARS

```java
// Testing.java

class Testing
{
    void main( String args[] )
    {
        char c = 'a';
        System.out.print( '\'' );
        System.out.print( c );
        System.out.print( '\'' );
        System.out.println( " is the char" );
```

```
        }
    }

// end of Testing.javaFloating Point
```

Java supports IEEE floating point data. The float type is 32 bits long, and the double type, the default, uses 64 bits. You have to start a floating point constant with a digit, and you need to include a decimal point. You can optionally include a D or F suffix, to specify the data size. You can also use an E and an exponent. These are examples:

```
float f = 1.1F;
double d = 1.1;
double d = 1.1D;
double tiny = 0.1E-12;
```

You can't assign 1.1 to a float. You have to use 1.1F for a float. (1.1 defaults to double.)

Arrays

You can make an array of any of the basic types by including subscripting brackets:

```
short[] my_list = new short[10]; // list of 10 shorts
```

You can put the subscripts after the type or after the variable name, if you prefer:

```
short[] my_list = new short[10]; // these are the same
short my_list[] = new short[10];
```

The common subscript notation references an individual array element:

```
. . . my_list[3]; // one member of the my_list array
```

Array subscripts start with zero. a[0] is the first element of array a. a[1] is the second element, etc.

Now we'll jump way ahead of ourselves to show an array example. You can probably decipher most of this code already. Listing 2.9 computes and displays the series 1, 3, 6, 10, 15....

LISTING 2.9   COMPUTING AN INCREASING SERIES

```java
// Testing.java

class Testing
{
    void main( String args[] )
    {
        int[] list = new int[10];

        list[0] = 0;
        byte i = 1;

        while ( i < 10 )
        {
            list[i] = list[i-1]+i;

            System.out.print( i );
            System.out.print( ' ' );
            System.out.println( list[i] );

            i++; // add one to i
        }
    }
}

// end of Testing.java
```

When you declare an array, you simply tell the compiler that you want an array. You need the new operator to actually get space for a specific number of array elements.

You can repeat the brackets if you want to have multiply dimensioned arrays:

```
int[][] arr = new int[5][10]; // a 5 by 10 array
```

You can also omit the last subscript if you just want the compiler to create an array of arrays. This lets you build ragged arrays (ones with varying-length rows). Listing 2.10 shows an array shaped like a triangle. Before you assign a value to an array with the new operator, its value is null, which is also a keyword.

LISTING 2.10 AN ARRAY OF UNEVEN LENGTHS

```
// Testing.java

class Testing
{
    void main( String args[] )
    {
        int[][] ragged = new int[10][];

        byte i = 0;

        while ( i < 10 )
        {
            ragged[i] = new int[i+1];

            byte j = 0;
            while ( j <= i )
            {
                ragged[i][j] = i*j;
                System.out.print( ragged[i][j] );
                System.out.print( ' ' );

                j++; // add one to j

            }
            System.out.println();
            i++; // add one to i
        }
    }
}
```

```
}

// end of Testing.java
```

By leaving off the last dimension of `ragged` when it is first created, you let yourself decide on the length of each row, one at a time. You create each row with another use of the `new` operator.

Expressions

It's a Lot Like C

C programmers will recognize almost all of the Java syntax from C, but look at three new operators: `>>>`, `instanceof`, and `+` (in string expressions). Also remember that the boolean data type is not an integer. Boolean operators apply only to boolean values.

We've been using expressions in every example this far. In Java, as in C, even an assignment operation is considered an expression. We've used very simple expressions so far, so we've not needed to think about the order of execution, which is our first topic in this section.

You can write an expression anytime you need a data value. Expressions can be simple or complex:

```
x = y + 2; // simple
x = (y > 2) ? x + y : (14-y) * z;
```

Whitespace isn't needed to separate operators and operands, but it certainly helps make your expressions more readable:

```
x = (y + 2) * (z - 3);

    // above and below are the same from the
    // compiler's point of view

x=(y+2)*(z-3);
```

Evaluation, Precedence, and Parentheses

Parentheses group operations, explicitly defining the order of execution of expressions that have multiple operations. Consider these examples:

```
4 - (2 - 1) // 4 - (1) which is 3
(4 - 2) - 1 // (2) - 1 which is 1
```

C and Java have similar precedence tables that define which operator will be applied first if you do not explicitly parenthesize your expressions. As a matter of good programming style, however, you should always parenthesize explicitly. If you do, you'll never worry about the precedence or associativity of your operators, and your programs will always do exactly what they say.

Arithmetic Operators

There are eight arithmetic operators. The basic add, subtract, multiply, and divide operations are specified with +, -, * and /. Integer division truncates (7/4 is 1). The modulus operator, %, produces the remainder after integer division (7%4 is 3). The minus sign can be used as a unary (one-sided) operator to specify arithmetic negation: 3 * (-x) is 3 times negative x.

Finally, the ++ and -- operators increment (add one) and decrement (subtract one), respectively. If they are used to the left of a variable, they are applied before that variable is used in another operation. If they are applied to the right, the variable's value is used in the expression, and the increment or decrement is done afterward. This illustrates the effect:

```
int i = 3;
System.out.println( ++i ); // increments i, then prints 4
System.out.println( i++ ); // prints 4, then increments i
System.out.println( i ); // prints 5
```

Used on the left, these operators are called *pre-increment* and *predecrement*. On the right, they are called *postincrement* and *postdecrement*. They can be used in combination to write very tricky, obscure (and possibly buggy) code. They can also be used alone to write readable code. The following example shows two ways of achieving the same result:

```
arr[i++] = ... ; // better written as follows

arr[i] = ... ;   // assign first
i++;             // then increment i
```

You can mix operands in arithmetic expressions. If you mix integers and floating values, the integer is converted to a floating value. If you mix different sizes, the smaller value is converted to the larger type before applying the operator.

Bitwise Operators

You can operate directly on the bits in a data value with the bitwise operators. There are four logical bitwise operators. Each performs the indicated operation on each pair of bits from the two operands. (Bits zero in both operands are used to set bit zero in the result; bits one in both operands are used to set bit one in the result, and so on.) These examples use 4-bit numbers (not a real Java type) to illustrate the operations:

```
~i  // ones complement ( ~5 is 10: ~0101 is 1010 )
i&j // bitwise and ( 7 & 2 is 2: 0111 & 0010 is 0010)
i|j // bitwise or  ( 2 | 4 is 6: 0010 | 0100 is 0110)
i^j // bitwise xor ( 3 ^ 5 is 6: 0011 ^ 0101 is 0110)
```

There are three bit-shifting operators:

```
i << 3  // shift the bits in i 3 to the left
i >> 2  // shift the bits in i 2 to the right
i >>> 1 // shift the bits in i to the right, filling with 0
```

In Java, all integers are signed, so the plain right shift operation is an arithmetic shift: if the most significant bit (leftmost bit) is set, shifting right fills with 1s, not with 0s. These examples illustrate this:

```
int i = -1; // i is all 1 bits
i = i << 2; // i is -4
i = i >> 2; // i is -1 again
```

Boolean Operators

Boolean operators apply only to boolean values. These are the fundamental logical operations, as these examples show:

```
!   // unary negation (if b is true, !b is false)
&&  // logical and (a && b is true if, and only if, a is
    // true and b is true
||  // logical or (a || b is true if either operand is true, or
    // if both operands are true
```

Comparison Operators

The comparison operators all yield a boolean result based on comparison of their operands. They are:

```
a == b // true if values are equal
a != b // not equal

a < b  // true if a is less than b
a <= b // less than or equal
a >= b // greater than or equal
a > b  // greater than
```

Assignment Operators

Assignment via the = sign is an operation you can use as part of an expression. It is good coding style to limit use of the equal sign to the leftmost operator, as in:

```
i = expression;
```

The equal sign combines with other operators when the operation is on a variable and the result is assigned to the same variable. For example, you can add 3 to x, storing the result in x, in these equivalent ways:

```
x = x + 3;   // same as the following

x += 3;      // add 3 to x, store result in x
```

The binary arithmetic operators all combine with equals (+=, -=, *=, /=, and %=) this way. These bitwise operators also can be combined with equal: &=, |=, ^=, <<=, and >>=.

Other Operators

We've used the `new` operator to create arrays. We'll use it in Chapter 3 to create other objects, too.

The cast operation lets you force conversions that the compiler otherwise wouldn't perform. For example, you may know that an integer variable is holding a value small enough to fit in a byte. You could assign it to a byte this way:

```
int i = 16;
byte b;

b = (byte) i;
```

This cast operation directs the compiler to discard the most significant bits of the larger value.

The ternary operator is used when you want to perform an evaluation like this pseudocode:

```
if (some condition)
    use this value when true;
    use this value when false;
```

It is written this way:

```
<condition> ? <true value> : <false value>

    // example:

tax = (subtotal > 0) ? (tax_rate*subtotal) : 0;
```

The `instanceof` operator returns a boolean value. It's `true` if an object is an instance of a class. We'll cover this in Chapter 3.

Although strings are implemented as a class, the + operator is defined to concatenate strings. The += operator also can be used with a string.

Labels and Statements

It's Almost C

It's tempting to say that Java's statements are just like C's statements, but that's not quite accurate. There are two differences.

You need a boolean value when you have conditions in Java. In C, you've probably used integers but thought of them as if they were booleans, so the two languages will look alike. Remember to use true boolean variables, and you'll think you're still writing C.

The other difference is in the switch statement. The switch variable can be a char or any integer type, which is significantly more powerful than C.

We've been using expressions terminated by semicolons. That is one type of statement. We've also met the braces that create a block statement. In this section, we'll cover the surprisingly short list of additional Java statements.

Labels

You can place a label in Java code just as you can in C code. You provide a name followed by a colon. I've never used this feature in C, C++, or Java and I don't intend to ever start using it.

Conditional Statements

The `if` statement executes code conditionally. Its simplest form is:

```
if ( <condition> ) <statement>
```

```
    // example:

if ( x > 0 ) x--;
```

The `<condition>` can be any expression that evaluates to a boolean result. The `<statement>` can be any statement, including another `if` statement or a block statement. This is a good style for executing multiple statements if a condition is true:

```
if ( condition )
{
    statement;
    statement;
    . . .
}
```

An optional `else` clause can continue the `if` statement, providing code to execute when the condition is false:

```
if ( condition )
{
    do this when
    condition is true
}
else
{
    do this when
    condition is false
}
```

As with the `if`, any statement can follow the `else`, including the block statement in the preceding example, or another if statement as the next example shows.

```
if ( condition ) do this;
else if ( another condition ) do something else;
else default to this;
```

Assume that your program provides a menu and your user picks among
Yes, No, or **Maybe,** assigning a char result to the variable `choice`. You
then want to call a function, based on the user's choice. This code could do
it:

```
// char choice is 'Y' or 'N' or 'M'

if      ( choice == 'Y' ) yes_func();
else if ( choice == 'N' ) no_func();
else                      maybe_func();
```

For longer lists of choices, you'll want to use a `switch` statement.

Switches

You use a `switch` when a variable could take one of several values. The
code to execute is selected based on the variable's value. Look at an example:

```
// char choice is 'Y' or 'N' or 'M'

switch ( choice )
{
    case 'Y': yes_func(); break;

    case 'N': no_func();  break;

    default:  maybe_func(); break;
}
```

As in C, each `case` clause specifies a single constant value, which is compared to the `switch` variable's value. Execution begins with the code following a matching `case`. Execution continues until a `break` statement. (I
make it a rule to type the `break` statement first, and fill in the code later.
Ask any experienced C programmer to tell you about the weird bugs you
get when you forget a break in a `switch`.)

The switch variable can be a `char` or any of the integer types. More precisely, the `switch` works on an expression. The most common expression in a `switch` is just a variable, as our example shows.

Loops

We used `while` loops in Listings 2.9 and 2.10. As you probably guessed, the code in a `while` loop is executed as long as some condition is true. In this example, the loop code will execute ten times (the i variable will count up from zero through nine):

```
short i = 0;

while ( i < 10 )
{
    // other statements here;

    i++;
}
```

This loop is called a *top-tested* loop because the condition is written at the top and is tested before executing the loop code. If the condition tests false before entering the loop, the loop code will not be executed.

If you want your loop to always execute at least once, you would use a *bottom-tested* loop, as the next example shows:

```
short i = 0;

do
{
    // statements here;
    i++

} while (i < 10);
```

The execution is exactly what the syntax suggests. The statement following do (which is almost always a block statement, as shown here) is executed and then the condition is tested. If the condition evaluates to `true`, the statement following do is executed again. Execution continues until the condition evaluates to `false`.

The third loop available in Java is the `for` loop. Taken straight from C, the `for` loop is not as straightforward as our first two loops, but it is so handy it will probably the one you use most often. Here's an example:

```
int i;

for ( i = 0; i < 10; i++ )
{
    statements here;
}
```

The parentheses following the keyword `for` enclose three items, separated by semicolons. The first is an initialization statement. The second is a boolean expression, and the third is a statement to execute after executing the body of the loop. As you might guess, the body of the loop is executed while the boolean evaluates to `true`.

You can define a variable in the initialization part of the `for` statement. If you do that, the variable will be local to the `for` statement, including the statement (or block statement) that follows the `for`. This illustrates the point:

```
for ( int i = 0; i < 10; i++ )
{
    System.out.println( i ); // this is OK
}

System.out.println( i ); // Error! "i"'s history, here
```

The `for` loop is top-tested, like the `while` loop.

Any of the loops can include `break` or `continue` statements. The `break` forces an exit from the loop. The `continue` jumps back to the beginning of the loop. Here's a chapter-writing routine that uses these statements:

```
while ( chapter_not_finished() )
{
    write_text();

    if ( summary_completed() ) break;

    if ( example_needed() )
    {
        write_code();
        continue;
    }

    if ( figure_needed() )
    {
        set_up_shoot();
        shoot_screen();
        crop_as_needed();
    }
}
```

Subroutines

The preceding example calls subroutines such as `write_text()`. Because all Java is written in classes, all subroutines will be class methods, which we'll cover in Chapter 3. The point is that a call to a subroutine is a valid component of an expression (if the routine returns a result of a type that is allowed in the expression; a subroutine call can be an entire expression, and that means that a subroutine call can also be an entire statement if you terminate it with a semicolon.

Other Statements

A few additional statements are supported by Java. We'll cover the ones related to classes, interfaces, and packages in Chapter 3. Chapters 14 and 15 will introduce the exception- and thread-related statements.

Keywords

As in C, you cannot use a Java keyword except as Java intends. You can't, for example, use one as a variable name. Table 2.1 lists the keywords in Java.

TABLE 2.1 KEYWORDS AND RESERVED WORDS

abstract	boolean	break	byte	byValue*
case	cast*	catch	char	class
const*	continue	default	do	double
else	extends	final	finally	float
for	implements	import	inner*	instanceof
int	interface	long	native	new
null	operator*	outer*	package	private
protected	public	rest*	return	short
static	super	switch	synchronized	this
throw	throws	transient	try	var*
void	volatile	while		

These keywords are reserved but not yet implemented.

Don't try to memorize Table 2.1. If you inadvertently use one of these words as a variable name, your compiler will catch the error.

Summary

We began by creating a new workspace and code appropriate for testing small examples. By now, you should be comfortable with the Cessna-sized subset of Visual J++ that we're using.

After that, we went into the basic structural elements of Java. These included using braces to create block statements and to define classes and functions.

We went on to look at the basic (non-object) Java data types. These are integer, floating point numbers, characters, and boolean (true/false) values. They can all be organized in arrays. Integer types are byte (8-bit), short (16-bit), int (32-bit), and long (64-bit). Floating types are float (32-bit) and double (64-bit).

We use these data types to build expressions. We discussed Java's operators. These include arithmetic operators, bitwise operators, boolean operators, comparison operators, assignment, and other operators.

We went on to look at the labels and statements from which Java programs are built. There are only a few statements here. The `if` and `switch` statements handle conditional processing. `while`, `do` and `for` loops, along with `break` and `continue` statements, handle looping. We'll look at a few more in later chapters.

We finished with a look at Java's keywords, both implemented and reserved for future use. Don't waste time memorizing them because your compiler definitely knows them all.

In Chapter 3, we're going to use these language basics to start doing some object-oriented programming.

CLASSES, INTERFACES AND PACKAGES

Although all our programs have begun with a class definition, we haven't really used objects yet. We'll begin object-oriented coding in this chapter. We'll start with multiple methods, or *subroutines* in a procedural language.

We'll use classes and create objects, which are members of our classes. You'll see the ways that Java supports controlled access, making some classes available to others while allowing you to designate others completely private.

We'll look briefly at the other features of "compilation units" (call them *files*, for now): interfaces and packages.

Interfaces give you most of the benefits of multiple inheritance but none of its complexity. *Packages* provide convenient ways for you to group compilation units into useful pieces. Java itself makes extensive use of packages.

We'll begin with an introduction to Java's object-oriented programming concepts.

Object-Oriented Programming

While Java introduces some of its own concepts, it uses C++'s basic object terminology. A group of similar objects is called a *class*. The individual *object* is a member of the class.

Other programming languages call the class an *object* and call our objects *instances* of the object. I bring this up in case you discuss object-oriented programming with others—it's wise to start the conversation with a definition of terms, or you can end up talking at cross purposes.

Data Members

We can associate data items with either the object or the class. Consider an application's menus. We would have a menu class, and each menu would be an individual object. Now consider the color of the menus.

If all the menus are going to be the same color, you would make the menu color a data member of the class. This would make programming a customization dialog box simple. The user could select a color for the menus (among other things). Your menu drawing code would read this color every time it drew a menu. All the menus would be consistent.

If you wanted each menu to have its own color, you would make the color a member of each menu object. Instead of the class having a color data item, each menu object would have its own color data item. Your menu drawing code would read the menu object's color, not the class's color.

Methods

Numerous writers have explained that an object encapsulates both data and code, which we call *methods* of the object. Forget it. That's no way to implement an object-based programming system.

Methods are associated with classes, not object instances. The subroutine that manipulates an object is a member of the class. One menu-drawing routine, for example, serves the menu class. The data members of the menu class and the individual menu object are both data that this routine can use.

In procedural programming, a method is a subroutine. Subroutines are sometimes divided into functions, which are subroutines that return a value, and procedures, which are subroutines that don't return a value. In C, all subroutines are called *functions*. Those that don't return a value are said to return *void*. IN Java, the void keyword is used as it is in C to indicate that a subroutine does not return a value.

But passing and returning values are much less important in object-oriented programming. In the syntax of a language, you access the method the same way you access its data members. Here are three menu examples:

```
menu.number_of_options  // a data member
menu.color              // another data member
menu.draw()             // a method member
```

Assuming that your design lets individual menus have as many options as they need, the number_of_options datum is part of the menu object. If you chose to have the menus all be the same color, the menu.color datum could be associated with the class. (If you later changed your design, giving each menu its own color, you'd just change the class definition and recompile to give each menu its own color.)

The menu.draw() method is a member of the class. As always, the parentheses distinguish code from data. If you have a method, you know that there is just one copy of the method for the whole class. It will process individual menu objects just as procedural subroutines could process individual data records or structures.

Inheritance

Inheritance is one of the most powerful and, formerly, confusing aspects of object-oriented programming. It got confusing because of some particularly inappropriate terminology, which Java lays to rest.

Most object systems begin with a very fundamental building block. In Java, it's the class Object. (Note the capital letter. By convention, class names in Java start with a capital letter. Class and object members and other variables start with a lowercase letter, again by convention.) Object class objects need to "know" some very simple things:

What size am I?

How do I find the space I need?

How do I free that space when I'm disposed of?

Each class that inherits from Object *extends* (another Java keyword) the class by adding additional data and method members. In much of the object literature, a class that extends (i.e., inherits from) another is called a *subclass*, which led to no end of confusion. Those subclasses are actually supersets of the classes they extend. A subclass is a superset? That's a good way to confuse people. You won't see the word *subclass* in any other paragraph of this book. It wouldn't hurt if it were lost everywhere else, too.

You extend a class by adding new data members, methods, or both. The new, extending class is said to *inherit* the data and methods of the extended class. Because every class in Java extends Object, every object will know its own size and have methods to allocate and free its needed space.

A Box class could inherit from Object, adding data such as height and width, screen location, border type, color, and methods such as draw(). A Menu class could extend the Box class by adding data members such as number_of_options. It might also have an array of Option objects.

If Menu extends Box, Menu-class objects all have the data and method members of the Box class, including a height and width, screen location, and so on. Each Box object is a subset of each Menu object. The Menu is a superset of the Box.

The Menu class would also need a method to show itself on the screen. You might want a menu.draw() method. A method in an extending class that has the same name as a method in an extended class is said to *override* the method. Consider the following fragment, based on this example:

```
// bx is a Box class object
// mn is a Menu class object
```

```
// the Menu class extends the Box class

bx.draw(); // calls the Box class draw() method
mn.draw(); // calls the Menu class draw() method
```

Overriding methods in extended classes is a good idea when the basic idea of the method is the same. As your application expands, you may have a `Tear_off_menu` class, for example, that extends the `Menu` class. `Tear_off_menu.draw()` would override `Menu.draw()`, adding the tear-off functionality.

Writing classes that are reasonably small and that extend other classes in modest increments is a good idea. You could put the tear-off functionality into the `Menu` class, but then every application you wrote with a `Menu`-class object would include tear-off functionality. Do you want that overhead in a small utility?

The `Box` class's functionality could be coded as part of the `Menu` class, too. But writing a separate `Box` class means you have a base to extend for the `Dialog` class, for the `Window` class—even for the `Button` class. `Box` objects' characteristics can be used in lots of other, more complex objects.

With that background, let's get on to programming a simple class with multiple methods.

Multiple Method Programming

Our code so far has looked just like procedural code, wrapped in an unused class statement. You're about to find out that Java is, in fact, truly an object-oriented language. Let's begin by trying some procedural code.

Listing 3.1 introduces a second function, `say()`, in the `Testing` class. It looks like it might display five nice lines, doesn't it? But it won't work.

LISTING 3.1 PROCEDURAL CODE WON'T WORK

```
// Testing.java

class Testing
{
```

```
void main( String args[] )
{
    for ( short i = 0; i < 5; i++ )
        say( i ); // THIS WON'T WORK!
}

void say( short s )
{
    System.out.print( "The value is ");
    System.out.println( s );
}
}

// end of Testing.java
```

Are you getting a `NullPointerException` error? (If not, you've made extra mistakes. Track them down before you read on.) We're getting this exception on the call to `say()`. Why?

First, there are no pointers in Java, so how could we mess one up? Second, we're passing a `short` argument to a function that takes a `short` parameter. What's the problem?

Calling Object Methods

The problem is that there is a sophisticated set of pointers just beneath the surface of Java. Once you get used to its requirements, you'll seldom meet them. But right now, we've just met one head on.

You can't just call a method. You have to call an object's method. No, I'm not contradicting what I said earlier about methods being members of the class, not of the object. The syntax we want is:

```
object.method( [params, if req'd] )

// Example:

//mn is a Menu object

mn.draw()
```

The reason is that most methods work on an object. The menu class's draw method needs the data members of a particular menu to draw that menu, for example. (It needs to know where it goes, how big to make it, how many options, etc.) In your code you'll write `mn.draw()` as if the `draw()` method is a member of a particular `Menu` object. What is really happening is that Java is calling the `Menu` class's `draw()` method, passing it a particular menu as a hidden parameter:

```
// You write this:
    mn.draw();

// Java does this:
    Menu.draw( mn );
```

Internally, Java passes the method a pointer to the object it should act on. If you have no object, you have a `NullPointerException`, even in a simple little method such as our `say()` example.

To correct the problem, you need to create a `Testing` class object and then use it when we call our method. You create objects with the `new` operator, similar to the way you initialize arrays. Listing 3.2 shows a corrected program.

LISTING 3.2   CORRECTLY CALLING AN OBJECT'S METHOD

```
// Testing.java

class Testing
{
    void main( String args[] )
    {
        Testing t = new Testing(); // Make object

        for ( short i = 0; i < 5; i++ )
            t.say( i ); // OBJECT.METHOD()!
    }

    void say( short s )
```

```
        {
            System.out.print( "The value is " );
            System.out.println( s );
        }
}
```

```
// end of Testing.java
```

This version creates a single object, called t, of the Testing class. Then you can call t.say(), applying the say() method to a particular object. In this example, that's a bit foolish, because the say() method happily ignores the object you've created. Let's add a data member to the Testing class and then have the say() method use that member.

You assign data members to the class or to objects by defining them inside the class statement but outside the method definitions. (Variables defined in method definitions are local variables used by the method.) By default, these data members are members of the individual object. Prefacing the type keyword with the keyword static makes them class members.

Listing 3.3 shows the data member init_val created for each object of the Testing class. It's assigned a value in the main() function and then used in the say() function. Try some more data members and objects on your own.

LISTING 3.3   CREATING AND USING A DATA MEMBER

```
// Testing.java

class Testing
{
    short init_val; // a data member

    void main( String args[] )
    {
        Testing t = new Testing();
        t.init_val = 100; // ASSIGNED HERE!
```

```
        for ( short i = 0; i < 5; i++ )
            t.say( i );
    }

    void say( short s )
    {
        System.out.print( "The value is " );
        System.out.println( init_val + s ); // USED HERE!
    }
}

// end of Testing.java
```

Before we get on to arguments and parameters (which we're using already), let's look at one more example. It may surprise you that Listing 3.4 is correct. It splits the output lines into a say() method that reports the value is and a value_say() method that adds the actual value, showing how one method can call another.

LISTING 3.4 A METHOD CALLS A SUB-METHOD

```
// Testing.java

class Testing
{
    short init_val; // a data member

    void main( String args[] )
    {
        Testing t = new Testing();
        t.init_val = 100; // ASSIGNED HERE!

        for ( short i = 0; i < 5; i++ )
            t.say( i );
    }

    void say( short s )
    {
```

```
        System.out.print( "The value is ");
        value_say( s );
    }

    void value_say( short s )
    {
        System.out.println( init_val + s ); // USED HERE!
    }
}

// end of Testing.java
```

When a method correctly receives the hidden pointer to an object, it passes this pointer along to submethods that it calls. Java handles it, so you don't need to worry about it.

Arguments and Parameters

First, for those of you who have little tolerance for stupidity, I want to talk about those two names, *argument* and *parameter*. When a function is called, the value provided is an argument. When the function uses the value, it's a parameter. Imagine a baseball game in which the pitcher throws arguments and the catcher catches parameters. Sounds optimal to you?

Passing By Value and Reference

At any rate, simple arguments are passed by calling programs as values. Our `main()` method passes a numeric value on each of five trips through its loop. The value is received by the `say()` method. Manipulating it in `say()` wouldn't change the value of the argument in `main()`.

On the other hand, complex arguments are passed by reference (or address, if you prefer). Arrays and objects (even the simplest ones) are considered complex arguments for this purpose. In general, an object can be used anywhere a primitive data type can be used, but in this usage, there is that important difference.

If the method changes a data member in the object, it will change the data member. There's only one object—it's shared by the calling and the called methods. Similarly, if the method changes an array element, the array element is changed. There's only one array, shared by caller and callee.

Type Mismatches

In our example, we've passed a `short` argument and caught it with a `short` parameter. What happens if the types don't match?

The same rules that apply to expressions apply here. (That's not surprising when you realize that arguments can actually be expressions. The simple variables we're using here are a trivial expression.) You can pass a shorter datum to a larger parameter, and it will be expanded to fit. Similarly, you can pass in integer to a floating point receiver, and it will be converted correctly.

It's an error to try to force these conversions backward, however. You can't shrink a datum or convert floating point to integer automatically. The compiler thinks this is a mistake. If you really want to do this (suppose you have an `int` but you know its value will fit into a `short`), you can use a `cast` in the argument expression, like this:

```
// int i; short s;

. . . foo( (short) i); . . . // cast forces conversion

void foo( short s ) { . . . }
```

When you use a `cast` this way you're saying, "Compiler, get out of my way. I know what I'm doing." Make sure that you mean it before you say it.

Programming with Objects

We're already programming with objects, but now we're going to use them in more object-oriented ways. We'll begin with constructors, the methods that create objects.

Constructors

We've already used the new operator to create a Testing class object. That's an example of using a default constructor. First, the Testing class inherits from the Object class. When we discuss inheritance in the next section, you'll see that you can specify any class you want to extend. If you don't specify one, your class extends Object.

The Object class has a default constructor that simply grabs the space it needs. If you don't provide a constructor for your class (we didn't), your object will use the Object constructor, which will grab the space it needs.

If you want to take charge of the initialization, provide your own constructor. That's a typeless method whose name matches (case-sensitive match) the name of the class. Listing 3.5 shows a constructor for the Testing class that assigns a value to init_val.

LISTING 3.5 A SIMPLE CONSTRUCTOR FOR TESTING

```java
// Testing.java

class Testing
{
    short init_val; // a data member

    void main( String args[] )
    {
        Testing t = new Testing();

        for ( short i = 0; i < 5; i++ )
            t.say( i );
    }

    Testing() // constructor
    {
        init_val = 100; // ASSIGNED HERE!
    }

    void say( int s )
```

```
    {
        System.out.print( "The value is ");
        value_say( s );
    }

    void value_say( double s )
    {
        System.out.println( init_val + s ); // USED HERE!
    }
}

// end of Testing.java
```

Note that the constructor is `Testing()`. The `new` operator calls the constructor. Unlike methods that are called with a hidden pointer to an object, the constructor returns a hidden pointer to the object it creates.

Suppose that we don't always want `init_val` equal to 100? Constructors can have parameters that accept arguments. In Listing 3.6 I've changed the constructor to one that accepts an argument and assigns `init_val` appropriately.

LISTING 3.6 PARAMETERIZING THE CONSTRUCTOR

```
// Testing.java

class Testing
{
    short init_val; // a data member

    void main( String args[] )
    {
        Testing t = new Testing( (short) 1000 );
                            // NEW VALUE!

        for ( short i = 0; i < 5; i++ )
            t.say( i );
    }
```

```
    Testing( short ival ) // PARAMETERIZED constructor
    {
        init_val = ival; // PARAM ASSIGNED
    }

    void say( int s )
    {
        System.out.print( "The value is " );
        value_say( s );
    }

    void value_say( double s )
    {
        System.out.println( init_val + s ); // USED HERE!
    }
}

// end of Testing.java
```

`Testing()`—if a method name starts with a capital letter, you know it's the class constructor—is now called with an argument, a short value that will be assigned to the `init_val` data member in the constructor. (Try it without the cast and see what happens. Is that a compiler bug? Wouldn't it be better if the compiler looked at the size of the constant, instead of making us do that?)

You add parameters to the constructor method just as you do with any other method. They're given a type and a name inside the parentheses that follow the method name.

Constructors can be arbitrarily complex. Some pop up complex dialog boxes, for example. If you can write the code, you can put it in your constructor.

Destructors

There are no destructors in Java. (C++ programmers have to write their own destructors, so they're probably looking here to see how that's done in Java.)

When an object goes out of scope, its space is freed. If the object has complex data members (i.e., arrays, objects, arrays of objects, or whatever) their space is recovered by Java. You don't have to do it.

If you want to do something special before your object disappears, put the cleanup code (or call a cleanup method) in just before your object goes out of scope. An object will disappear at the brace that closes the block in which it was created:

```
type meth
{
    Someclass sc = new Someclass( ... );
        // sc created here

    ... more code

} // object sc is discarded at this brace
```

Overloaded Methods

In older languages, you could have only one parameter list for a subroutine of a particular name. In newer languages, you can assign lots of different parameter lists to the same name. Our `println()` method is a good example of an intelligently overloaded function. It's got one version that accepts a `String` object, another that prints a `char`, another for a `short` datum, etc.

The full identifier for a method is a combination of its name and its parameter list. Consider these three distinct methods: `foo()`, `foo(int i)`, `foo(int i, int j)`. If you call the `foo()` method, the compiler calls `foo()`. If you called `foo(1,2)` the compiler would call `foo( int i, int j )`.

Let's use this to override the `Testing` constructor. A nice programming practice is to provide constructors that use their own defaults, and other constructors that let you provide your own values. Listing 3.7 shows how this is done.

LISTING 3.7   OVERLOADING THE CONSTRUCTOR

```java
// Testing.java

class Testing
{
    short init_val; // a data member

    void main( String args[] )
    {
        Testing t1 = new Testing( (short) 1000 );
        Testing t2 = new Testing(); // DEFAULT version

        for ( short i = 0; i < 5; i++ )
        {
            t1.say( i ); // SHOW BOTH
            t2.say( i );
        }
    }

    Testing() // DEFAULT provided here
    {
        init_val = 100;
    }

    Testing( short ival )
    {
        init_val = ival;
    }

    void say( int s )
    {
        System.out.print( "The value is " );
        value_say( s );
    }

    void value_say( double s )
    {
```

```
        System.out.println( init_val + s ); // USED HERE!
    }
}
```

```
// end of Testing.java
```

We've got two constructors now, `Testing()` and `Testing( short )`. You can use either one. Getting confident? Try writing one that accepts an `int` and uses a cast to assign it to a `short`. Your grade is B if you make it work. You get an A if your code tests to be sure that the `int` actually fits in a `short`. (Just print a message if it doesn't fit. We'll get to exceptions in Chapter 14.)

Multiple Classes

You can create multiple classes. As you probably know from experience (or have guessed from what we've done so far) substantial applications are built with lots of different objects from lots of different classes. Java's API, which we'll meet in Chapter 4, is a set of prewritten Java classes. In this section we'll see how different classes can work together.

Multiple Classes in One File

We'll begin by adding a second class to our **Testing.java** file. Obviously, only one class in a file can have the same name as the file. When we get to protection, we'll see that the class that matches the name of the file is the only one that can be `public`, that is, accessed from other files. The other classes in a single file are only there to help the main class.

Listing 3.8 shows a second class, called `Supporting` (which is the role it plays) added to a simplified version of the `Testing` class. Create and run one of your own along these lines.

LISTING 3.8 ADDING A SUPPORTING CLASS

```
// Testing.java
```

```
class Testing
{
    short init_val; // a data member

    void main( String args[] )
    {
        Testing t1 = new Testing();
        Supporting s1 = new Supporting( 10000 );

        for ( short i = 0; i < 5; i++ )
        {
            int total = s1.sup_val + t1.init_val + i;
            t1.say( total );
        }
    }

    Testing() {     init_val = 100; }

    void say( int s )
    {
        System.out.print( "The value is " );
        System.out.println( s );
    }
}

class Supporting
{
    int sup_val;

    Supporting( int sv ){ sup_val = sv;      }
}

// end of Testing.java
```

Note that I've written both `Testing()` and `Supporting()` as one-liners. While white space is a cheap resource, horizontal lines on the screen are a scarce resource. (Don't you always end up wishing your editor window was a few lines longer?) I save horizontal lines when I think readability isn't hurt too much.

Here, data members from one object of each class are used to compute the total, inside `main()`'s loop. Note that our `Supporting` class is pretty small. If you're used to creating structures in other languages, this will suggest how you get the same result in Java. Just add as many data members to the class as your structure has members. Toss in a constructor method to make it easy to assign to these data members, and you're in business.

When we get to protection, you'll see that taking a little more trouble here will produce a more robust result, but that can wait its turn.

Multiple Classes in Multiple Files

Chances are, you'll build your applications from multiple public objects: objects that you can access from more than one program. To make them public, you'll need to add the keyword `public` (we're peeking ahead to the protection topic) and put the public class names with the file.

Let's create a reference object to see how this works. Our reference class will have a static (attached to the class, not to each object) array of reference values. These might be tensile strengths of different metals, for example. The live version of this class might perform statistical analyses on the results of experiments to find these values. We're going to keep this data in a separate class so that other classes can conveniently refer to these results and so that we can update them as our experiments generate additional data.

For our sample, we'll just assign the value 1000.0 to the first reference, 2000.0 to the next, and so on. These numbers make testing simple.

The new class in a new file is shown in Listing 3.9. Press **Ctrl+N** for a new file, choose **Text file** and enter the code. You'll see a weird, `static` block statement in it—we'll talk about that in a minute. When you've entered the code, save it as **Ref.java** (**F12** is quicker than **Alt+F, A**).

LISTING 3.9 A NEW CLASS IN A NEW FILE

```
// Ref.java

public class Ref
```

```
{
     static double[] ref_vals;

     static
     {
          ref_vals = new double[100];

          for ( int i = 1; i <= 100; i++ )
               ref_vals[i-1] = i * 1000.0;
     }

}
```

```
// end of Ref.java
```

Just because you're looking at a file doesn't mean that Visual J++ knows that it should be part of your project. (It could be your grocery list, for all it knows.) You have to insert it into your workspace. Use **Alt+I, I** to launch the Insert Files Into Project dialog box. Visual J++ will launch the Project Workspace window (the one that **Alt+0** launches) in File view, to show you that it obeyed orders. **Ctrl+F4** will close that child window.

Now, what's that block statement labeled `static`? It's the one exception to the rule that all code is in methods. `static` class members are attached to the class, not to individual objects. This block of code is available to initialize class `static` variables. It could have its own local variables, but it can't refer to any data members other than the class's `static` (class-wide) members.

Listing 3.10 shows a modified version of the Testing class that references the ref_vals[] in the Ref class.

LISTING 3.10 USING REF'S DATA IN TESTING

```
// Testing.java

class Testing
{
     short init_val; // a data member
```

```
void main( String args[] )
{
      Testing t1 = new Testing();
      Supporting s1 = new Supporting( 10000 );
      Ref r = new Ref();

      for ( short i = 0; i < 5; i++ )
      {
            double total = s1.sup_val + t1.init_val + i;
            total = total + r.ref_vals[i];
            t1.say( total );
      }
}

Testing() {      init_val = 100; }

void say( double d )
{
      System.out.print( "The value is " );
      System.out.println( d );
}
}


class Supporting
{
      int sup_val;

      Supporting( int sv ){ sup_val = sv;          }
}

// end of Testing.java
```

I've changed a lot of values to doubles. You can study this meticulously, but that's not efficient. Type the obvious changes, and let your compiler find the ones you've missed. It's very good about data type matching.

What is `Ref  r`? That's an object of the `Ref` class, of course. I created it so I could access `r.ref_vals`. You can also refer to class statics using the class in place of an object. In this case it would be `Ref.rev_vals[i]`.

Ready to try inheriting? That's our next topic.

Inheritance Is Extension

C++ was the original villain that reused the `static` keyword to distinguish class-wide data members from object data members. Java picked up this vice. Couldn't we think of a better word? I'd prefer an extra keyword to a misapplied word.

Sometimes, however, Java really looked at C++ to see what it did wrong that should be, could be, and would be fixed. Inheritance is a perfect example. The `extends` keyword expresses precisely what one class does when it inherits from another.

Let's create a class that extends the `Testing` class, adding another data member. Real classes usually add a lot more than just one data member, but adding one shows exactly how it's done. If you'd feel better adding three, or twenty-three, go right ahead.

Listing 3.11 shows another version of `Testing` that illustrates inheritance. The class `Extending` replaces the `Supporting` class.

LISTING 3.11 TESTING ADDS AN INHERITING CLASS

```
// Testing.java

class Testing
{
    short init_val; // a data member

    void main( String args[] )
    {
        Extending
            e = new Extending();

        for ( short i = 0; i < 5; i++ )
```

```
            {
                    double total = e.init_val + e.ext_val + i;

                    e.say( total );
            }
        }

        Testing() {      init_val = 100; }

        void say( double d )
        {
                System.out.print( "The value is ");
                System.out.println( d );
        }
    }

class Extending extends Testing
{
        int ext_val;

        Extending()
        {
                super();
                ext_val = 1000;
        }
}
// end of Testing.java
```

The important point is that the `Extending` object has an `init_val` data member, because `Testing`, the class it extends, has this data member. If another class extended `Extending`, it would inherit both `init_val` and `ext_val` members.

Overriding Methods

Sometimes you want to replace a method with the extending class. For example, `Menu.draw()` might override `Box.draw()` in a `Menu` class that extended a `Box` class. This helps keep the code simple:

```
// display routine passed param "obj" — an object

obj.draw();
```

In this fragment, the code calls the object's `draw()` method, presumably to have the object appear on the screen. It does not need to tell menus to draw with the `Menu.draw()` method, pushbuttons to draw with their method, etc. It depends on each object having a `draw()` method that works for the object.

Listing 3.12 adds a `say()` method to the `Extending` class. When you add this method, you'll see that `e.says()`—calling the `says()` method for an `Extending` class object—calls `Extending.says()`.

LISTING 3.12 OVERRIDING THE SAYS() METHOD

```
// Testing.java

class Testing
{

    short init_val; // a data member

    void main( String args[] )
    {
        Extending e = new Extending();

        for ( short i = 0; i < 5; i++ )
        {
            double total = e.init_val + e.ext_val + i;

            e.say( total );
        }
    }

    Testing() {      init_val = 100; }

    void say( double d )
    {
```

```
        System.out.print( "The value is " );
        System.out.println( d );
    }
}

class Extending extends Testing
{
    int ext_val;

    Extending() { ext_val = 1000; }

    void say( double d )
    {
        System.out.print( "Extend says " );
        System.out.println( d );
    }
}
// end of Testing.java
```

The report you'll get from **JVIEW.EXE** is that Extend says….

this and super

Sometimes you'll need to explicitly choose either the current object's class or the class it extends. The keywords this and super handle this job. C++ programmers will recognize the this pointer and some of the power of the scope resolution operator here. Java retains about 80% of the power of C++ in this area, with about 20% of the complexity.

Consider these method calls:

```
// in a Foo-class method; Foo extends Bar

paint(); // call Foo.paint for current object

this.paint(); // ditto, but more explicit
super.paint(); // call Bar.paint() method
```

Try this yourself. Add this line to the Extending.say() method:

```
super.say();
```

That will call the `Testing.say()` method, so you'll see the original and the newer displays interwoven. Be careful not to try `this.say()` in `Extending.say()`. That will cause infinite recursion—and *infinite recursion* really means it runs until the stack overwrites something critical and then who knows? I hope you're backed up.

Access Limitations

Classes, data members, and methods can have an access-limiting qualifier prefixing their specification. The three access qualifier keywords are `public`, `protected`, and `private`.

Within a class, all methods can access all other methods and data members. *Access* refers to the ability of outside classes to access the class and its members. Access limitations imposed at the member level *do not* override the class's limitations. A `private` class's members cannot be accessed from outside the class even if they are declared `public`.

These are some sample access specifications:

```
public class Pubclass { ...
private class Privclass { ...

protected int protint ...
private void privmeth( ...
```

Access specifications are fully described in the Java language definitions, which you'll find in the online documentation. These get complicated. (Let's see, if this is a `protected` data member in an extended `public` class in the same package but not the same compilation unit, that means....) There are three specifications; three grammatical units; extending and nonextending classes; and classes, data members and methods to think about. There are 54 combinations of these items. There's an easier way to write Java than trying to memorize all the rules.

I'll prescribe a set of reasonable access specifiers that are generally accepted as good programming practice. Follow these recommendations while you are getting started. Once you understand Java application and applet programming, you can modify this prescription to suit your requirements.

Class Access

Only the class that has the same name as the source file is available for `public` access. It's not necessary, but I suggest you label that one explicitly as public. The other classes are `private`, and again, I suggest that you also add this designation explicitly.

I always qualify my classes (one `public`, the rest `private`) in my own code, but I've left that out thus far to focus on other matters. From now on, you'll see these qualifiers appear.

Data Member Access

I almost always use `protected` access for data members. A `protected` member can be accessed within the *package* in which they are declared, depending on their class's access. (C++ programmers will note that this is much wider access than `protected` C++ members.) Access to `protected` members is further restricted to the compilation unit for `private` classes.

Provide methods for accessing and updating data members by outside classes, if this access is needed.

Now, let me explain *almost*. Sometimes I want a true `public` data structure. If this is really what you want, don't be afraid to put `public` data into a `public` class. If you find yourself doing this frequently, however, I'd start to worry.

Method Access

I usually omit access qualification from methods. They default to `public`, which means that they have the class's access. If an outsider can access a class, it can access the class's methods.

Very often, however, it's inconvenient to write a single function that handles the method. (The `draw()` method may be extremely complex. For example, think about a chess game.) So a public method may rely on supporting submethods. I declare these supporting players as `private` methods because outsiders really have no business even knowing about them.

That lets me rewrite a method, completely revising the internal organization if I want to, without worrying about consequences to calling routines.

Interfaces

Interfaces are a class-like mechanism that Java provides for two reasons:

Interfacing with foreign APIs (e.g., with Windows)

Replacing multiple inheritance

This section will provide a brief introduction to interfaces. We'll be using them throughout the next several chapters, although we won't cover them thoroughly until we get to Chapter 15, where we work with the run-time threads package.

Defining an Interface

The compilation units we've written so far include multiple class statements. These can be followed with multiple interface statements, which look just like classes, except the keyword is *interface*. This is what the compilation unit looks like:

```
// optional comments
public class c1 { ... }
private class c2 { ... }
...

interface i1 { ... }
interface i2 { ... }
...
```

Like classes, interfaces declare methods. Unlike classes, the interface only declares that the method exists (and provides acceptable parameter lists). It does not provide the code for the method. (Assume you are interfacing to the Windows API. Microsoft has already written that rather large body of code. You don't rewrite it in your interface definition.)

Implementing an Interface

Your classes implement interfaces when they need to use them. The keyword is, sensibly enough, *implements*. This is a class that implements an interface:

```
public class c1 implements i1 { ... }
```

When a class declares that it implements an interface, it must, again sensibly, actually implement that interface. This means that it has to provide the definitions for the methods that the interface declares. If the interface it to a foreign API, the method code calls that API, perhaps after appropriately setting up needed arguments. (Return values might also need special handling.)

On the other hand, the implementing method could be written entirely in Java. The important point is that the implementing class provides the Java portion of the interface's method definitions.

Using an Interface

Unlike classes, interfaces are not actually used directly. It is the implementing class that is used. In effect, your classes (or someone else's classes) provide a wrapper that interfaces to the rest of your application or applet.

Now we're ready to look at packages.

Packages

Java introduces the concept of *packages*. Java's style—one public class per compilation unit—encourages the use of many smaller files, as opposed to a few large ones. As a veteran programmer, I heartily approve. I've found that I really like my code up to about 500 lines per file. I start to heartily dislike it after it hits a couple of thousand lines or so. but that can lead to a proliferation of small files that can become unwieldy as your applications (or even applets) grow. I'm going to get to Java syntax in a moment, but let me first speculate on the use of the term *compilation unit*.

So far, I've been reminding you that *compilation unit* is Java-speak for *file*. I don't think this is what Java's designers had in mind. Consider the following implementation.

Compilation Units Need Not be Files

When I build my perfect Java coding environment, the compilation units are going to be collected into logical groups. Let's use the word *package* to refer to this group. I'll have all the compilation units in a package collected into a single code database.

My editor will have a tree-structured front end that lets me drill down from the project into packages, then to compilation units, classes, and finally methods. It won't bother me with files. I'll tell it what to put where when I create something new, and then it will take over for me.

When I edit a method (or whatever), my ideal Java machine will recompile the affected compilation unit, which is exactly what the name suggests. By keeping the compilation units small, I'll eventually get a recompile that happens just about as fast as I can give a save command to my code editor.

By keeping my packages (sets of related compilation units) in separate files, it will be easy for me to send one off to my friend Jane when she wants to fiddle with it.

This isn't the way Visual J++ is organized, at the moment, but Java suggests that this is a logical organization.

For what it's worth, an equally valid organization would dump all my code into two databases: a shared team database and a private one where I could experiment freely. The same drill-down logic could work in my editor. I'd still think about compilation units and packages, and the computer would worry about files.

All this is to help you stop thinking about operating-system–defined files as the way Java collects its source code. It collects small compilation units into larger packages. Microsoft (and its competitors) put these into disk files any way they choose.

Once you get the concept, the implementation is dead simple.

Package Syntax

If you want your compilation unit to be part of a package, you simply name that package with a `package` statement. It's the first nonwhite, noncomment statement in your compilation unit. This one defines its compilation unit as part of my button package:

```
package my_button_pack;
```

All compilation units labeled with this `package` statement are part of this package. You've got to appreciate this bit of design. It could hardly be simpler.

Using Packages

The directory (which may be a subdirectory, of course) containing your packages is defined by the CLASSPATH environment variable. From this directory, you create subdirectories for each package. The names correspond to the package names. For instance, all the compilation units in `my_button_pack` will be in the subdirectory `my_button_pack\`.

With that setup, Java knows where to look for each package. When you want to use something in a package, prefix the package name and a period to whatever component you are using:

```
my_button_pack.Yes_btn yes_button = . . .
```

If you were going to refer frequently to that button class, you could add an `import` statement that would eliminate a lot of typing. This is what you would do:

```
import my_button_pack.Yes_btn
```

```
. . .
Yes_btn yb1 = . . .
Yes_btn yb2 = . . .
```

The `import` statement does not add code. It's not like a C or C++ `#include` directive. It just tells the compiler where to go to find the name `Yes_btn`.

If you wanted to import all of the class names in a package, use the * symbol, as in:

```
import my_button_pack.*
```

Again, this tells the compiler to make the names available, so you don't have to qualify any of them with `my_button_pack`.

Organizing Packages

Of course, a one-level tree doesn't go very far toward organizing real-world applications. You can use periods in your package name. These correspond to subdirectory-separating backslashes in your disk structure. For example, you might organize user-interface packages into one subdirectory (`ui`). That might divide into widgets and gadgets. Radio buttons might be a gadget package. It could look like this:

```
import ui.gadgets.rad_btn.*

// Package ui.gadgets.rad_btn is found in:

// \%CLASSPATH%\ui\gadgets\rad_btn
```

The * in the `import` statement applies only to the classes within a package. You can't do this:

```
import ui.* // ERROR: "*" only goes for classes
```

Universal Package Names

One package is implicitly imported: `java.lang`. It's as if all your compilation units began this way:

```
import java.lang.* // this happens automatically
```

This has given us access to (fully qualified):

```
java.lang.System.out.println( ...
```

The `java.` packages are supplied through Visual J++ by Sun. Sun has also specified the ultimate, net-wide package naming system. Today, I wouldn't want Visual J++ to have to find compilation units all over the Internet every time I compile an application. Tomorrow, though, who knows what speeds we'll reach?

Today you can use Sun's convention for spreading packages across a local network. It won't be long before we can spread packages across the Net.

Sun's convention is to reverse your organization's domain name and put it in front of your department, user name and package directory structure. For example:

```
// you are jane_doe@some_co.com, in the personnel department

// organize your packages for access this way:

// COM.some_co.personnel.jane_doe....
```

(Capitalizing COM (or ORG, NET, etc.) is part of the specification.)

Sun's really looking ahead with this one. Do you think we'll all be sharing each other's packages anytime soon?

Summary

We started this chapter with the basics of object-oriented Java programming. We saw that classes could have data members and methods; objects could have there own data members. Inheritance lets one class *extend* another.

We then went into programming with multiple methods. You learned that Java needs an object reference to call a method. The hidden pointer that Java uses is automatically passed to submethods. Arguments and parameters don't need to match if they conform to expression rules: a smaller datum can be promoted to a larger size, or an integer can be promoted to a floating-point type (but you can't go the other way without an explicit cast).

Then we went on to more object programming. We wrote constructors and saw that Java handled the problem of recovering object's space, so it doesn't need C++'s destructors. We also overloaded methods, using the same name in an extending class as we used in the extended class.

Then we went on to write programs with multiple classes in a single compilation unit and then in separate compilation units. We used the `extends` keyword for class inheritance, and we learned to use `super` and `this` to explicitly refer to the extended or extending class. We also adopted a convention for `public`, `protected`, and `private` access limitations.

Then we considered interfaces briefly. We'll make extensive use of interfaces as we go forward, but won't program them explicitly until we get to multithread programming in Chapter 15.

Last, we looked at packages. Java organizes small compilation units into larger packages. We saw that the `package` statement provides a very simple way of assigning compilation units to packages, and that the `imports` statement provides a convenient method for accessing packages. We'll begin using `imports` statements in almost every compilation unit, starting in Chapter 4.

We've covered a lot of ground here. You're probably pleased to have learned as much Java as you have, but a little frustrated by our friend `System.out.println()`. Well, you've learned enough to put `println()` out to pasture. In Chapter 4 we'll delve into the Java API, where you'll find dialog boxes, buttons, and the other goodies of a modern user interface.

4

THE JAVA API

Like C, Java is a very small language. Unlike C, however, early Java comes with a very substantial library of classes, which are called, collectively, the Java API. It includes both general-purpose programming classes, such as the `String` class, and user-interface–specific classes, such as the `Button` class.

When you write Java programs, you are writing to a pseudo–operating system known as the *Java Virtual Machine*. The Java user-interface (UI) classes are adapted by various implementors to run on Microsoft's Windows (3.x, 95, and NT) systems, Unix systems, Apple's Macs and a wide variety of other systems.

The disadvantage of a cross-platform UI is that it conforms to the lowest common denominator among the platforms. As you'll see, that denominator isn't very low. You'll probably miss your favorite Windows-specific feature but you'll be able to write very good applications, regardless.

In this chapter we're going to start with the non-UI portions of the API. We'll write a little code, learn to use the online documentation, and take a very brief tour of the categories of general-purpose classes.

Then we'll move on to the UI-specific classes. Again, we'll write a little code and take a brief tour. We won't write much UI code, because one of the major functions of Visual J++ is to generate this code automatically. That's the subject of Part II of this book. We will launch a cool dialog box, though. (It's simple!)

To make effective use of Visual J++ it won't be enough just to know how to use its visual tools. You'll need to know how to dive into the API documentation and the Visual J++–generated code. That's what this chapter will teach you.

Programming with the API

In the last chapter, you learned that you use an `import` statement to simplify naming classes, data members and methods of Java components in packages outside your current compilation unit. The one exception is the `java.lang` package. All the classes in `java.lang` (implicit: `import java.lang.*`) are imported.

We've already been programming with `System.out` methods located in the `java.lang` package. As with, for instance, `System.out.print()`, the other Java API classes and methods are just Java code that was written by earlier Java programmers. You use it just as you use your own Java code.

Let's start by writing a simple delay method. Java keeps time in milliseconds, starting from January 1, 1970. We'll get into the InfoViewer in the next section. You might make a mental note to use what you learn there to track down the `Date` class in the `java.util` package. You'll find out exactly how complex counting those seconds can be. Most PCs fake it.

A simple delay method will just note the current time and then keep checking the time until the specified period has elapsed. (A better delay program would turn control back to the operating system—with a `wake me up at` message, of course.)

Looking at the Time

The number of milliseconds elapsed since the start of 1970 is a 64-bit integer, returned by this function:

```
long java.lang.System.currentTimeMillis();
```

Java's `Date` class looks at this `long` for all date arithmetic. Each year has about 32 million seconds, or 32 billion milliseconds. That takes about 35 bits. Long integers are 64 bits. Positive longs use only the first 63 bits, so a long has 28 bits (63 - 35) to identify the year. Java's time/date scheme is simple and will outlive all of us by millennia.

Before we get to programming, let's take a moment to review our setup. For simple programs, I like to work with the source file and the output window open. Figure 4.1 shows my setup.

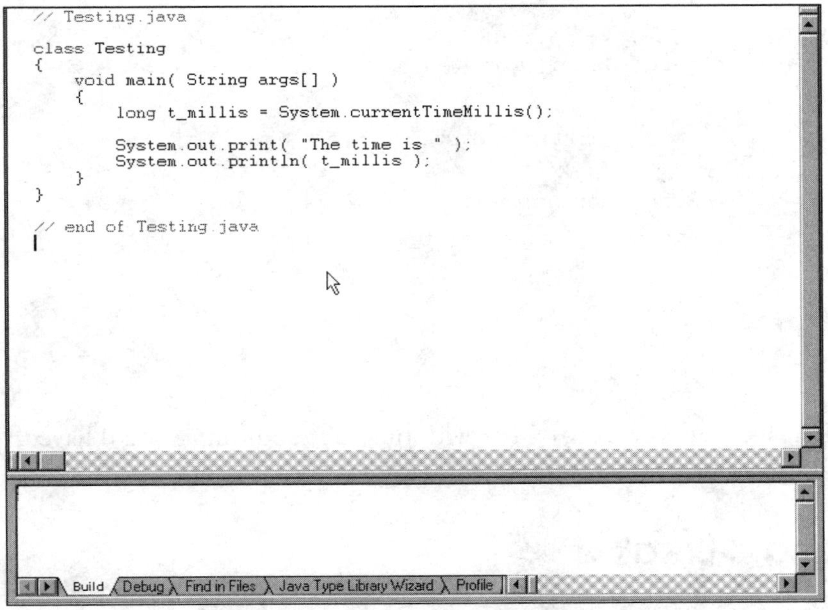

```
// Testing.java

class Testing
{
    void main( String args[] )
    {
        long t_millis = System.currentTimeMillis();

        System.out.print( "The time is " );
        System.out.println( t_millis );
    }
}

// end of Testing.java
```

`◄ ► Build ╲ Debug ╲ Find in Files ╲ Java Type Library Wizard ╲ Profile ║ ◄ ║`

FIGURE 4.1 SOURCE AND OUTPUT, BIG TIME.

How do you get this many lines for the source file? Start by choosing the docking view for the Output Window. You can do this by right clicking in the Output window and toggling **Docking View** on the popup menu. Next, click the maximize button in the source window.

As in Windows 3.x, **Alt+Spacebar** pops up the application's System menu. **Alt+Hypen** pops up a child window's System menu. On the System menu, **R** (Restore) returns to the nonmaximized state. **Alt+Spacebar**, **N** (minimize) will drop Visual J++ to just an icon on the taskbar. **Alt+Hyphen**, **X** or **R** will select the maximized or normal source code window. Learning these tricks helps your fingers get more work done on the code.

Listing 4.1 shows a program that will report the time, Java-style. As I write this, the time is 842110154660.

LISTING 4.1 A JAVA-STYLE CLOCK

```
// Testing.java

class Testing
{
    void main( String args[] )
    {
        long t_millis = System.currentTimeMillis();

        System.out.print( "The time is " );
        System.out.println( t_millis );
    }
}

// end of Testing.java
```

Replace your `Testing.java` with this code and run it. You'll have to look fast to see what your time is.

Taking a Break

Wouldn't it be nice if we could tell the program to pause for a few seconds so we could read the time? I'll bet you've been thinking that since you ran your first Java application. Well, now you have the tools to write a `delay()` method. Why don't you try that before you look at my version.

Listing 4.2 shows how I wrote `delay()`.

LISTING 4.2 PAUSING TO VIEW OUTPUT

```java
// Testing.java

class Testing
{
    void main( String args[] )
    {
        Testing t = new Testing();

        long t_millis = System.currentTimeMillis();

        System.out.print( "The time is " );
        System.out.println( t_millis );

        t.delay( 10000 ); // 10 second pause
    }

    void delay( int msecs ) // delay in milliseconds
    {
        long t = System.currentTimeMillis();
        while ( true )
            if ( System.currentTimeMillis() - t >= msecs )
                break;
    }
}

// end of Testing.java
```

Now, may I ask you a question? When did I write this? The answer is, "a few minutes after 842110154660," of course. If you knew the whole Java API, you could write two lines of code and you'd know what time and date 842110154660 represents in a more common, human-readable notation.

Because you don't know the whole API (you'll get to know it better as you work with it, but it's already so big that no one knows it all), let's work on the next best thing: knowing how to find what you need when you need it.

In Java, 842110154660 is a `Date` class value. Dates are a utility class. How can you use this information?

The API in the InfoViewer

You can search for a particular function with the help system, but the best way to look around is certainly with the InfoViewer. To open an InfoViewer window, press **Alt+0**.

If you have a workspace open, the InfoViewer is one of the tabs in the Workspace window. The others are the File and Class views of your workspace. You may need to click a tab to see the InfoViewer. If you don't have a workspace open, the InfoViewer is the *only* tab in the Workspace window.

I keep my InfoViewer in Docking view, as shown in Figure 4.2. This works very well with either a source window or with an InfoViewer topic window maximized on the right. If your source window is already maximized, the **Alt+0** behavior is particularly meaningful.

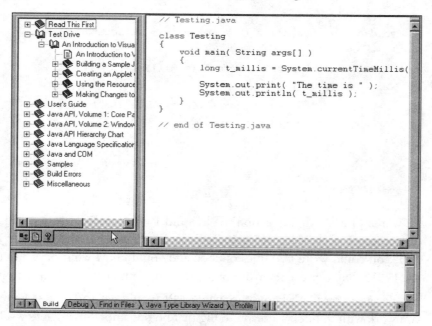

FIGURE 4.2 THE INFOVIEWER, DOCKED.

The Java API, Volume 2

Open your InfoViewer and take a look at the two volumes of Java API documentation. Let's dispose of Volume 2 first. Volume 2 documents the AWT, Java's Abstract Windows Toolkit.

In the documentation for package `java.awt` you'll find out everything about Java's UI classes. You won't need `java.awt.peer` yet. The `java.awt.image` package won't be necessary until you start working with graphics. (Not just displaying them—this is for the fun stuff. Morphing, anyone?). The applet package will be part of almost everything we do starting in the next chapter, but you'll seldom need to look at it; there's very little to document.

The Java API, Volume 1

Volume 1 has all the non-UI classes. It's where you'll find the `Date` class and hundreds more. Begin by clicking the plus sign next to Volume I. The list of packages is shown in Figure 4.3.

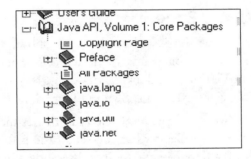

FIGURE 4.3 LOOKING INTO THE JAVA API, VOLUME 1.

The package names are intended to be self-explanatory. They are:

`java.lang`—Java language classes, such as String

`java.io`—input and output classes

`java.util`—utility classes

`java.net`—networking classes

I think that I mentioned that the `Date` class was in the utility package. Click `java.util`'s plus sign to take a look. There is method in the madness.

The classes are listed first, in alphabetical order, excluding the exception classes. The interfaces follow the classes.

The exception classes are listed last. We'll go over exceptions in Chapter 14. For now, you can ignore them and concentrate on the classes.

Drilling into a Class

Drill down into the `Date` class. You can single-click the plus sign or double-click the class name. If your rodent has wriggled off, pressing **Enter** also toggles a topic between expanded and contracted modes. In fact, the right/left arrows expand/contract an outline node. I prefer to use **Enter** because it will drill down into a page, which the arrows won't do.

The first level that opens in each class shows a page and two further drill-down topics: constructors and methods. We'll start by taking a look at the class's summary page.

The Class Summary Page

At the final drill-down level, (when the topic shows a page icon) you'll launch the InfoViewer Topic window automatically when you drill into the page. If your InfoViewer is in docking view, on the left, the Topic window will appear on the right. Mine is shown in Figure 4.4.

In the InfoViewer Topic window, **Ctrl+T** toggles the topic title. I leave it turned off because it repeats what you see in the InfoViewer window on the left. **Ctrl+Shift+T** toggles the toolbar. It is shown in Figure 4.4.

Actually, I leave the toolbar off, too. I know the hotkey combinations for the essential functions:

> **Ctrl+B**—Back (to former page)
>
> **Ctrl+S**—Synchronize with InfoViewer
>
> **Ctrl+Shift+N**—Next topic
>
> **Ctrl+Shift+P**—Previous topic

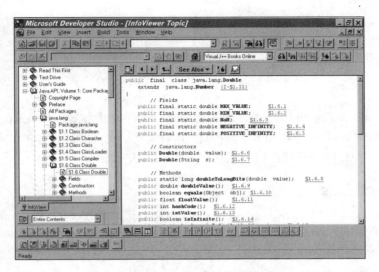

FIGURE 4.4   MAXIMIZED, UNTITLED INFOVIEWER TOPIC.

Now let's look at the page itself. Each class page starts with a very concise summary of the class's constructors and other methods. It seems overly dense at first. Once you know the class fairly well, you'll find it very fast for quick lookups.

Following the dense method summary is a description of the class.

Page down or mouse down with the scroll bar to take a look at the Date text. If you want, go ahead and read it all. You'll learn all about leap seconds, Universal Time, UTC time, and other stuff. We'll wait for you.

The Constructors

Back again? Go back to the InfoViewer window, and drill down into the constructors. You'll find another page. When you drill down into that page, you'll get a new page in the Topic window. (If you're big on short-cuts, you can use **Ctrl+Shift+N**, **Next page** in the Topic window to go from the class summary to the constructors page.)

You should usually start with a constructor because your code will start with one. As you can see, the constructors page is much less dense than the summary page. If you look around, you'll see that there is a nice variety of ways to create a `Date` object. If you have a value, such as 842110154660, one of the constructors is called with a `long`. A line of code like this one will build a `Date`:

```
Date wrote_it = new Date( 842110154660L );
```

You did notice the *L* at the end of that constant, didn't you? It won't work without it. The default integer type is `int`, 32-bit, which won't fit all those digits. (Is this a nice bit of rigor or a compiler design flaw?)

The Methods

Once you've built an object, the next step is to use it. Return to the InfoViewer window and drill down into the methods of the `Date` class. As you see, there are several.

One thing to bear in mind when you work with Java is that the API is big. At first that means you'll have a hard time finding what you need, but as you get used to it, it means that what you need is probably in there, waiting for you to use it. Spending a little time looking will often save a lot of time coding.

One of the methods, `toLocaleString()` has a promising title. Drill down into that one and see what the Topic window says.

It specifies the intent of the function to provide a `Date` representation that the user can understand. Put these two lines into a `main()` function and see what happens:

```
Date wrote_it = new Date( 842110154660L );
System.out.println( toLocaleString(wrote_it) );
```

The `toLocaleString()` method takes a date argument and returns a `String` object. One of `println()`'s acceptable arguments is a `String`.

If you've gone this far, you can run your code and answer the question I posed. Got it? You're becoming a Java-enabled programmer!

In the next section, we'll take a tour of the general-purpose API. I know that you really want to dive into the UI programming, so we'll be really quick about it. You can wander around in the InfoViewer at your leisure, whenever you like.

Touring the General-Purpose API

Here we'll take a very brief tour of the general-purpose API, stopping just long enough to give you some information about actually using the classes and methods you'll meet here. We'll begin with the `java.lang` package.

Language Classes

The vital `java.lang` package is imported by default. It contains all the functions you expect in a contemporary computer language. Do you need to know if a character is a digit or a letter? It's in here. Unlike most languages in use today, Java is purely object-oriented, so there's a small difference to consider, but we'll get to that in a minute.

The `java.lang` package includes classes that let you manipulate each of the base data types. For instance, the Character class lets you write character-type functions, but you can't use them the way we've been using methods such as `delay()`. Look at the error line in Listing 4.3.

LISTING 4.3 CHARACTERS CAN'T BE CONSTRUCTED

```
...
    void main( String args[] )
    {
        Testing t = new Testing();
        Character c = new Character(); // ERROR!

        System.out.println( c.isLetter( '*' ) );

        t.delay(2000);
    }
...
```

If you try this, you'll find that the `Character` class has no constructor. You can't instantiate a `Character` object. The class really serves to collect methods. (My version of Visual J++ includes a constructor in the documentation but not in the implementation. A later version should resolve this one way or another.)

If a method doesn't need an object instance, you can qualify it as a static method. Then you can call it with the name of the class, in lieu of an object of that class. If you drill down into the documentation of, say, Character.isLetter() you'll see that the function is public static boolean. The public keyword makes the default explicit. *Static* means that you don't need a Character class object to call the method.

Consider these:

```
Testing t = new Testing();
t.delay(2000);

    // same as this:

Testing.delay(2000); // delay() must be static
```

This is how you call Character methods:

```
char c = 'x';

Character.isLetter( c ); // true
Character.isLetter( '9' ); // false
```

Listing 4.4 shows another version of Testing, that illustrates the creation of your own static method and the use of the API's static methods.

LISTING 4.4 CALLING API METHODS WITH CLASS NAMES

```
// Testing.java

import java.util.*;

class Testing
{
    void main( String args[] )
    {
        System.out.println( Character.isLetter( '*' ) );
```

```
        Testing.delay(2000);

    }

    static void delay( int msecs )  // delay in milliseconds
    {
        long t = System.currentTimeMillis();
        while ( true )
            if ( System.currentTimeMillis() - t >= msecs )
                break;
    }
}
```

```
// end of Testing.java
```

Be sure to use the `static` keyword when you define your methods if you want to use them like this.

When you drill down into the `java.lang` classes, you'll see an additional topic, fields, added to the class. I'm not sure why they didn't call the data members something like *data members*. At any rate, you'll see the class's data members documented under this topic.

In addition to the base type classes (`Boolean`, `Character`, `Integer`, etc.) a number of other interesting classes are here. The `String` class handles string functions, of course. It's interesting because the string constant (i.e., the characters between double quotes) is implemented in the compiler. The designers elected to violate the syntactic simplicity here for ease of use. I'm glad they did.

The `String` object is a string constant. If you want to change the value of the object, use a `StringBuffer`. You can put data into a `StringBuffer`.

There are also classes related to threads and exceptions, such as `Thread` and `Throwable`. We'll go into these in Chapters 14 and 15.

Most classes here have a `toString()` method. You should provide one for your classes, too. It lets a function like `print()` accept any object and call its `toString()` method. This way, the `print()` method doesn't need to know about all the other objects you might dream up.

Input/Output Classes

The `java.io` package handles input and output, of course. You'll see that it handles input and output from the standard streams: `in`, `out`, and `err`. I'd have written a simple function that waits for a keystroke to call before each of our sample program's **JVIEW.EXE** output disappeared, but there's a problem.

If you drill into `System` in `java.lang` you'll see that it has data members `in` and `out`. `System.in` is an object of the `InputStream` type, which is listed here in `java.io`.

Drill down into `java.io.InputStream`. Look at its `read()` method. You'll see that `InputStream.read()` throws an `IOException`. You can't use a method that throws an exception if your calling code doesn't catch that exception. This is the subject of Chapter 14. It's not particularly complex, but you just can't do everything at once. Anyway, not many real applets use standard `in`, `out`, or `err` these days.

This package provides buffered streams, unicode-capable streams and file streams. It handles both sequential- and random-access files. Piped streams let you build pipes between different threads (see Chapter 15) in your applets and applications.

While we usually talk about the Java Virtual Machine's UI, the JVM also includes all system I/O. These classes insulate you from system dependencies.

Utility Classes

We've already used the `Date` class. The utility package has a number of other interesting classes, as well.

The `Dictionary` class lets you set up information structures where key values sort objects. It works with `Hashtable` objects.

For applications such as database querying, bit vectors are invaluable. The `BitSet` class provides bit vector capabilities.

The `Random` class provides streams of random numbers. It's similar in capabilities to the `random()` method in `java.lang.Math`.

Network Classes

Have we mentioned the Internet yet? You probably opened this book believing that Java was the language for programming Internet applications. You weren't wrong, but a little more precision is in order.

Java is a general-purpose programming language. Handling connections to the Internet is just like handling connections to other hardware devices. (Granted, the Net is vastly larger than any disk drive and certainly far more complex, but that's not the perspective of a computer language.)

Like all I/O in languages based on B (C's predecessor), Java moves these complexities out of the language and into subroutine packages. It's here in `java.net` that the Internet connection is made.

Need a socket to connect to http://www.your_co.com? Try this:

```
import java.net.*
...
Socket your_co = new Socket( "http://www.your_co.com" );
...
```

Like the `java.io` classes, many of these throw exceptions, so you'll need to get through Chapter 15 before you start using them.

Now let's move on to doing slick user interface work, with complex widgets and gadgets and next to no programming work.

Hand-Written UI Code

We're going to start with a very brief example of hand coding for the Abstract Windows Toolkit to create a Java Virtual Machine in action. This will be a very brief introduction to the topic because one of the main purposes of using Visual J++ is to help you do visual programming. That means you paint it; you don't hand code it.

On the other hand, there's a bit of a chicken and egg problem.

The first law of code generation is that the generating machine never gets the output precisely the way you wanted it. As Murphy says, "If anything can go wrong, it will." The corollary for machine-written code is, "Even if you have no imagination, it won't come out exactly like you imagined it."

If you're going to be happy with the output of Visual J++, you're going to need to tweak it here and adjust it slightly there. Visual J++ may do 90% or even 95% of the programming, but that last bit is critical. You have to know how UI code is written if you're going to do that work. So let's take a quick look.

In your InfoViewer, close Volume 1 and open Volume 2. Take a look at the classes in the `java.awt` package.

Lots of goodies in there, right? You've got buttons and checkboxes, dialogs and windows, entryfields and lists. You've got all the paraphernalia of a modern UI. The best part is that you've got all these UI components for Windows-based PCs, Apple Macs, and lots of Unix machines.

Begin by creating an AWT workspace.

Creating an AWT Workspace

Here's a challenge: create a workspace named `awt` and populate it with a file, **Awt.java**, with a skeleton class, ready for programming. If you don't like little challenges, try this: do it from the keyboard without leaving full-screen mode. Leave just the source open on top and a docked output window on the bottom. If you're up for it, try it without reading the rest of this section.

By the way (I presume I'm speaking to the more modest, methodical members of the audience), that challenge wasn't fair. Unless Microsoft revises the InfoViewer window, it can't be closed from the keyboard with the default setup.

In Chapter 6 we'll switch the **Alt+0** hotkey from the command that opens the Workspace window to the command that toggles the window. That should probably be the default. As it is, you press **Alt+0** to open the window, and then **Alt+0** becomes inoperative.

Of course, if you were really competitive, you'd try an end run. Press **Alt+T** (for the Tools menu), then **C** for Customize. You'll get to a tabbed form. Press **Shift+Tab** once or twice to get to the Keyboard tab. Then....

We've got work to do. **Ctrl+F4** closes the InfoViewer Topic window, if it's open. **Alt+0** closes the Workspace window (InfoViewer) on my machine, but not on yours (not yet, anyway). Grab the mouse, right-click the window, and choose **Hide** from the popup menu. Then **Alt+F**, **K** will close workspace. Now try **Ctrl+N** for a new file and choose Workspace.

Call it **awt**. Use **Ctrl+N** again, this time for a text file. After you type in a few lines, use **F12** to save it as **Awttest.java**. Make sure your class is named `Awttest`. Figure 4.5 shows where you should be at this point.

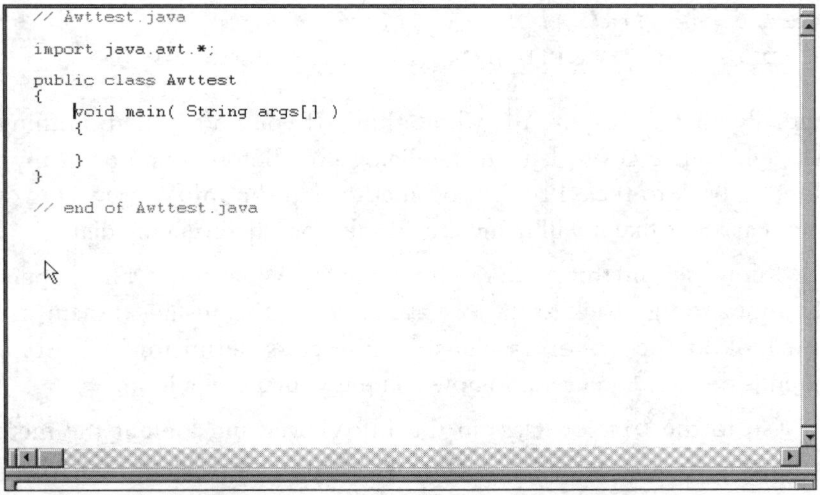

```
// Awttest.java

import java.awt.*;

public class Awttest
{
    void main( String args[] )
    {
    }
}
// end of Awttest.java
```

FIGURE 4.5   AWTTEST.JAVA READY TO PROGRAM.

By the way, my start and end comments are pretty minimal. You get extra credit for doing a better job.

Writing the AWT Program

We're ready to put the Abstract Windows Toolkit to use. How about a textfield, a scrolling picklist, an outline viewer, and a few other UI components, for starters? I'm serious.

The file-selection dialog box includes all those things. Let's program and launch one. Start by looking up the `FileDialog` class in `java.awt`.

According to the constructors documentation, a `Frame` object and a title `String` will be needed for parameters. Assuming we have a `Frame` named `f`, this should work:

```
FileDialog fd = new FileDialog(f, "Neat AWT Window!" );
```

Now, what about that `Frame` object? Again, if you look up the constructors for the `Frame` class, you'll find one that doesn't need any arguments at all. This couldn't really be simpler. The whole thing is:

```
Frame f = new Frame();
FileDialog fd = new FileDialog(f, "Cool AWT Window!" );
```

Actually, that's not quite the whole thing. If you do just that, nothing will happen. You've got to launch the dialog box. Before you look at my solution, go back to the `FileDialog` methods in the InfoViewer. Do you see one that looks like it will launch (or display or whatever) the dialog?

I don't see anything even remotely likely. What now? This happens all the time. You go back to the `FileDialog` (in this instance) main window and look at the `extends` clause in the class definition. `FileDialog` extends the `Dialog` class. So now you put yourself in a loop.

Go to the `Dialog` class in the InfoViewer and look at the methods. Does one look promising? Again, we're drawing a blank. So what does `Dialog` extend? We loop.

`Dialog` *extends* `Window`. Got a promising looking method here? Bingo! `Window.show()` looks like it ought to display a Window object. It's a void method that takes no parameters. Let's add that so we're up to the version of the code shown in Listing 4.5. Before you test it, let me warn you that you'll have to force an exit from **JVIEW.EXE**.

Windows will warn you that you're breaking the rules and that you "will lose any unsaved data," but that's OK. The problem is that we're not just launching the dialog box, we're also launching the AWT event loop, which is busy looping, as loops are wont to do. Just click the window's close button, and tell Windows that you really do want to shut it down.

LISTING 4.5 LAUNCHING A COOL AWT WINDOW

```
// Awttest.java

import java.awt.*;

public class Awttest
{
    void main( String argv[] )
    {
        Frame f = new Frame();
        FileDialog fd = new FileDialog(f, "Cool AWT Dialog");

        fd.show();
    }
}

// end of Awttest.java
```

When you run this program, you should get a really cool AWT dialog box, like the one that you see in Figure 4.6.

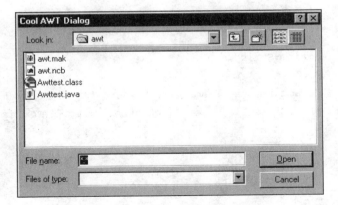

FIGURE 4.6 OUR FIRST AWT DIALOG BOX.

Actually, we're cheating a little here. The `FileDialog` object handles the event loop all by itself. With real code, we'll have to respond to events. (As you'll see, we won't have to write an event loop. That's internal to Java.)

Before you go on with this text, try to adjust some of the FileDialog's characteristics before you `show()` it. Then throw in a `println()` or two after you `show()` it to see what you're getting.

Getting the hang of this? Let's go on to fix up our last six-legged feature. Let's have this application close itself down politely. All that's needed is an explicit command to exit the program.

Any idea where to go to find such a thing? (Hint: we've been there a lot.) Go back to the InfoViewer and find it.

Did you get it? It's right there where it ought to be, in `java.lang.System`. It's the `exit()` method. Give it an exit code (zero for success), and you're in business. The finished program is shown in Listing 4.6.

LISTING 4.6 A COMPLETED AWT-BASED PROGRAM

```
// Awttest.java

import java.awt.*;

public class Awttest
{
    void main( String argv[] )
    {
        Frame f = new Frame();
        FileDialog fd = new FileDialog(f, "Cool AWT Dialog");

        fd.show();

        System.exit(0);
    }
}

// end of Awttest.java
```

By now you should be itching to start those really cool Java applets that you've been wanting to write, right? You've got to restrain yourself, but not for long. Before we close this chapter, we'll take another lightning-fast tour of the AWT-related classes.

Touring the UI API

Listen to the tour guide. "Welcome to Paris! Glad you could come. Here's the Louvre. There's the Eiffel Tower, l'Arc de Triomphe, Notre Dame, and the Rive Gauche. Hope you enjoyed your visit! Bye."

That's the speed of our tour, too. Paris will reward a much deeper look, of course, and so will the Java AWT, but this isn't the place to look. When we get to the Visual J++ Resource Editor, we'll explore the AWT in depth, a few components at a time. For now, I'll just point out a few things.

First, the components you want are in the toolkit, or they aren't. You've got check boxes and radio buttons. You don't have Windows 95–style tabbed dialog boxes. Make up your mind right now to design for the tools you have, not the ones on a specific platform.

Got that? Don't use platform-specific interfaces. The nature of Java is to write for Windows, the Mac, and Unix simultaneously.

Next, make up your mind that you won't let anything stand in your way if you really want a specific feature. For tabbed forms, for example, there's the `CardLayout` class. (Check the class description.) You'll need to work on the tabs a bit, but if tabbed forms are what you want, roll up your sleeves.

Finally, don't roll up your sleeves and start coding anything as generally useful as a tabbed form until you've gone Net surfing. I'll bet you can find free tabbed forms and really slick commercial tabbed form classes. Maybe even really slick, free tabbed form classes. You're reading the comp.lang.java news, aren't you?

OK, it's tour time. Frames are really main Windows. Dialog boxes are inherited by `Frames`, `Windows`, and as we saw, `FileDialogs`. Gadgets include `Buttons`, the three `CheckBox` classes, `Images`, and lots more. Now go into `java.awt` and click on *any* class you like.

Explore. Wander around at your leisure, on foot. But don't spend too much time there. Chapters 8–13 are all part of our tour of the AWT.

Before we launch into the AWT again, we're going to do a little HTML. We'll want our viewers to launch applets within HTML pages, which means we'll need to take a quick look at HTML. Then we'll get to Part II of this book, which is all about Visual J++'s visual tools.

Summary

You've come a long way. You should be starting to understand Java programming and the online resources you can use to expand your knowledge. If you're still shaky, don't worry. Charge bravely forward. We'll be repeating all of these basics throughout the rest of the book.

We started this chapter with a sample program using the API. We found that the `Date` object kept time by counting the milliseconds elapsed since the start of 1970. We used the `currentTimeMillis()` method to find the current time, Java style and then we used it to write a `delay()` method.

Then we turned our attention to the InfoViewer, looking at Volumes 1 and 2 of the API documentation. You learned to drill down from volume to package to class to descriptions of the class, its constructors, and its methods.

Then we took a look at the four packages in Volume 1. The `java.lang` package, which Java imports by default, contains the functions common to many computer languages. The `java.io` package contains all the console, file, and other device input and output classes. Utility classes are collected in `java.util`, and finally, `java.net` holds the Internet-specific classes.

After this, we turned our attention to the AWT, in the java.awt packaged documented in Volume 2. We started by creating a `Frame` (main window) and passing it to a `FileDialog` that we built. We launched the `FileDialog` with a call to the `show()` method. You learned that the secret to finding methods you want is to trace back through the class extension tree.

Finally, we took a very brief look at the rest of the AWT classes. You resolved to design for the cross-platform tools that Java provides. You also (I hope) resolved to write any UI components that you couldn't find but really wanted. But you're not going to do any heavy coding until you surf around a bit for a freeware or commercial class that's already been written.

By now, you've been up to your elbows in Java for long enough. The next chapter will provide a brief break while we look at HTML. We'll review the basics and then make a nice page to host our first Java applet. Before the end of Chapter 5, however, we'll go back to Java to build the applet, so we can see how good it looks launched in our favorite Web browser.

HTML AND APPLETS

We've covered a lot of ground in the last three chapters. In this chapter we'll be looking at HTML. If you're a Webmaster already, skim quickly all the way to the section titled "Applets." If you don't know an HTML tag from a dog tag, fire up your favorite browser and get ready to have some fun.

We'll start with the basics. We'll learn to use our browser to read our own hard disks (which makes for a *really* fast Web connection). Then we'll look at the basic form of an HTML page, including the tags that are used in almost every page.

After you've looked at the basics (again, may I stress that this will be a lot simpler than Java?), we'll mix headings with text.

After we cover headings and text, we'll really start to play with slick stuff. First we'll do three kinds of lists and then, in the "Adding Spice" section, we'll move on to playing with colors and fonts.

Finally, we'll add hyperlinks to some other sites. (You can add a link to any page on the Web or to other locations on your own hard disk. The latter will be very fast.) By then you'll have created a very slick Web page, which lacks only one thing: a Java applet!

First, we'll Java-enable our HTML page to use our own applet, and then we'll program the applet. You'll see that it's very similar to programming a Java application.

The Basics of HTML

If you already know a little HTML, fire up your browser and a good text editor to create the sample HTML file you'll see in the listings. Type it in, read it in your browser, and make sure that it looks like the figures in the text. I won't be offended if you skip all the text up to the "Applets" section near the end of the chapter.

This section is for people who are not familiar with HTML. It won't make you a Webmaster, but it will get you comfortable with HTML pages and you'll know what you're doing when it's time to embed your applets in HTML pages.

Using Your Browser

We've had Visual J++ call **JVIEW.EXE** to run our Java applications. Similarly, you'll need a browser to display your HTML pages. Go ahead and launch your favorite browser, but don't connect to the Web. We'll be using your local disk instead.

The Uniform Resource Locate (URL) is prefixed with a data source indicator. You've probably used http (HyperText Transfer Protocol), ftp (File Transfer Protocol), and possibly others. The *file* prefix denotes your local disk, as in:

```
file:///C|/JAVABK1/html/sample.html
```

The *C|* version identifies the hard disk. The vertical bar is used instead of the colon because the colon already has its part to play in URL syntax.

You don't have to use the URL, however. Use your favorite text editor to create **SAMPLE.HTML** in a working directory. You can create a text file in Visual J++ if you have it running. A much smaller editor will be handy if you don't happen to have Visual J++ already launched. Suit yourself.

Into **SAMPLE.HTML**, type any text. `Hello, Browser!` would be an appropriate line. Now use your browser's File menu to open this file. Got it?

You should now have a plain text file launched in your browser. It's probably the world's most oversized text file browser, but be patient. It will all work out.

To have fun with your HTML, you'll want to have both your browser and your editor launched. Then you use **Alt+Tab** to toggle between the two. The programmer's edit, compile, link and execute, then edit again cycle is much quicker. It's edit and save, **Alt+Tab** and reload the page to view; then **Alt+Tab** to edit again. It's really fast.

One note on this cycle: **Ctrl+R** reloads the current page in Netscape Navigator. **F5** does the same thing in Microsoft Explorer. (See either product's View menu.)

HTML Tags and Comments

Now let's begin with some background on HTML tags. An HTML page is a text file with embedded tags. The tags are surrounded by angle brackets. These are examples: `<P>` (paragraph), `<BR>` (break), `<LI>` (list item).

Many tags accept parameters (e.g., `<FONT SIZE=2>`). The tags aren't case-sensitive, but it's traditional to use capitals.

Many tags come in pairs that start and stop their effect. For example:

```
<CENTER>This will be centered</CENTER>
```

The close for `<tag>` is always `</tag>`. `Heading 1`, for example, would be written this way:

```
<H1>This is Heading 1</H1>
```

You can use extra lines as freely in HTML as you do in Java. This is the same heading as in the last example:

```
<H1>
This is Heading 1
</H1>
```

Some tags don't have a close, but they will be the exception, and I'll point them out. The rule is to use `<tag>` and `</tag>` pairs. Weird stuff happens when you don't close an open tag. The weirdness in Navigator may be different from the weirdness in Explorer. Be careful to always correctly close tags. Webmasters use utility programs that check all tags for correct closing.

A Commented HTML Template

Now you know just about all you need to know about HTML tags, except what a few of them are. Let's begin working on your **SAMPLE.HTML** file. Start with a proper begin and end comment pair, such as:

```
<! SAMPLE.HTML>

Hello, Browser!

<! end of SAMPLE.HTML>
```

The comment tag is: `<! text of comment>`. It doesn't have an end comment tag because the closing angle bracket closes the comment.

Don't go overboard with comments. The comments get downloaded along with the rest of your Web page. Webmasters use utility programs that strip comments from their pages, so they can write richly commented source pages but put uncommented final pages on the Web.

The <HTML> Tag

The `<HTML>` tag tells the browser that what follows is HTML-coded text. An `<HTML>` ... `</HTML>` pair should surround everything but the comments in your HTML page. For example:

```
<! SAMPLE.HTML>
<HTML>
```

```
Hello, Browser!

</HTML>
<! end of SAMPLE.HTML>
```

The <HEAD> Tag

HTML pages have a head section, followed by a body. The head section should not be used for text that gets displayed. We'll use it here just for the page title shortly. For now, insert a <HEAD> ... </HEAD> pair:

```
<! SAMPLE.HTML>
<HTML>
<HEAD>

</HEAD>

Hello, Browser!

</HTML>
<! end of SAMPLE.HTML>
```

The <BODY> Tag

Everything not in the <HEAD> section should be put into the <BODY> section. Add a <BODY> ... </BODY> pair, as shown here:

```
<! SAMPLE.HTML>
<HTML>
<HEAD>

</HEAD>
<BODY>

Hello, Browser!

</BODY>
</HTML>
<! end of SAMPLE.HTML>
```

Be sure to leave your text inside the <BODY> section.

The <TITLE> Tag

To complete your basic HTML page template, add a <TITLE> ...
</TITLE> pair. The text you place inside this pair is the text that the
browser will pick up for its title. This is not a title displayed on the page
itself.

You can use this style:

```
<TITLE>Sample HTML Page</TITLE>
```

Or you can use this style:

```
<TITLE>
Sample HTML Page
</TITLE>
```

In general, white space in HTML, including returns, is treated as it's treated
in Java or C. It's respected as a separator of elements but otherwise stripped
out. (One function of the browser is to wrap text within the width of the
browser's viewing window, which means it always formats text to suit itself.)

The Finished Template

You should now have a finished HTML template. My version is shown in
Listing 5.1.

LISTING 5.1   A USEFUL HTML TEMPLATE

```
<! sample.html>
<HTML>
<HEAD>

<TITLE>
Sample HTML Page
</TITLE>
```

```
</HEAD>
<BODY>

Hello, Browser!

</BODY>
</HTML>
<! end of sample.html>
```

Save this template in some handy directory and use it whenever you start an HTML page. If you haven't done so already, load it into your browser and admire your work.

Did I say *admire*? It's not really very cool yet, is it? In fact, it's pretty bad. Not to worry—the fun starts now.

You should now understand the basics of HTML, and you've put your overhead in place. Next, we'll start to add neat stuff to make cool pages.

Using Text, Headings, and Breaks

The most basic part of HTML is text. We'll start by seeing how that works, and then we'll add some headings and breaks. You should know enough to play around and have some fun by the time you finish this section.

On the subject of fun: it's optional. Unlike the coding, which you won't really learn if you don't try the samples, you could probably just read this chapter up to the "Applets" section, without trying a single example for yourself. On the other hand, you could mess around with this stuff and see what kinds of neat stuff you can create. The more fun you have here, the better you'll learn this stuff.

Text

Begin by adding a paragraph or two to your <BODY> section. I want you to experiment with resizing your browser and see how it wraps your text, so add enough to see the wrapping. Mine is shown in Listing 5.2.

LISTING 5.2 ADDING TEXT TO TEST WRAPPING

```
<! sample.html>
<HTML>
<HEAD>

<TITLE>
Sample HTML Page
</TITLE>

</HEAD>
<BODY>
This is some text. I'm putting it in here to test the line
wrapping. Now is the time for all good women and men to resize
their browsers to see how this text is formatted to fit within the
available page width.
Four score and seven years ago (or maybe less) Tim Berners-Lee
unleashed on our techno-continent an incredible innovation that
would go on to reshape the world we know into another, which we as
yet only dimly perceive.
</BODY>
</HTML>
<! end of sample.html>
```

With that code in place, save your file, toggle to your browser, and tell it to reload the current page. Then shrink your browser window. The result should be something like what you see in Figure 5.1.

Your browser will wrap all text into one continuous paragraph. This isn't quite what you want, but leave it alone for the moment. Let's add some headings.

Six Levels of Headings

Headings go from <H1>, the most important, to <H6>, the least important. In Listing 5.3, you see that I've added three levels of headings above my text.

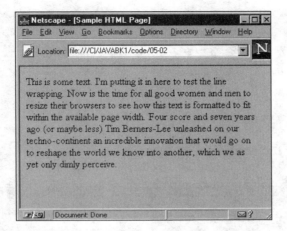

Figure 5.1 TEXT WRAPPED AND RUN TOGETHER.

LISTING **5.3** ADDING HEADINGS

```
<! sample.html>
<HTML>
<HEAD>

<TITLE>
Sample HTML Page
</TITLE>

</HEAD>
<BODY>

<H1>This Is Heading 1</H1>
<H2>This is Heading 2</H2>
<H3>This is Heading 3</H3>
```

This is some text. I'm putting it in here to test the line
wrapping. Now is the time for all good women and men to resize
their browsers to see how this text is formatted to fit within
the available page width.

Four score and seven years ago (or maybe less) Tim Berners-Lee unleashed on our techno-continent an incredible innovation that would go on to reshape the world we know into another, which we as yet only dimly perceive.

```
</BODY>
</HTML>
<! end of sample.html>
```

You can see the result I get in Figure 5.2.

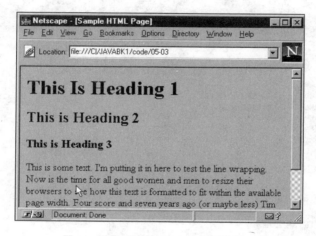

Figure 5.2 THREE HEADINGS DISPLAYED.

How do yours look?

The <Hn> tags accept an "align" parameter with the value `left`, `center`, or `right`. Try modifying those headings so they read like this in the HTML file:

```
<H1 ALIGN=RIGHT > This Is Heading 1 </H1>
<H2 ALIGN=CENTER> This is Heading 2 </H2>
<H3 ALIGN=LEFT  > This is Heading 3 </H3>
```

Figure 5.3 shows the result in my browser.

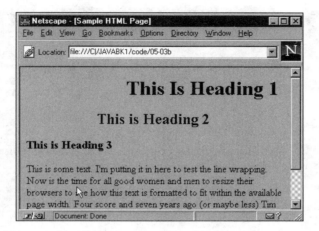

Figure 5.3 VARIOUS HEADING ALIGNMENTS.

Did you notice that I added white space both inside the `<Hn>` tags and before and after the heading text? It has absolutely no effect on the browser output. As in Java, add white space to enhance readability.

Breaks

You just saw that headings imply breaks. A heading won't run together with preceding or following text, or with other headings. That's why I wanted you to do headings before we fixed up the text with breaks.

Now we're ready for breaks in the text. The three breaks we're about to use are the exceptions to the rule. They insert a break, and they don't use an end tag.

The <P> Tag

Between paragraphs, use a paragraph tag. Add the `<P>` tag to your page, as these lines show:

```
...
the available page width.
<P>
```

```
Four score and seven years ago (or maybe less) Tim Berners-Lee
...
```

When you reload the page in your browser, the paragraphs will be neatly separated, as you intended.

The
 Tag

For a line break, and for spacing, you can use the <BR> tag. Try this:

```
One break<BR>
Two breaks<BR><BR>
Three breaks<BR><BR><BR>
Post break
```

What's the difference between <BR> and <P>? Change those <BR> tags to <P> tags and reload the page. What do you get?

You get neatly separated paragraphs. Each paragraph terminates with a

 pair. The first ends the line; the second leaves a blank line. Any number of <P> tags in a row, however, is treated as a single <P> tag.

The <HR> Tag

The <HR> tag places a horizontal rule across your page. It's a very nice effect. Try one.

Putting It All Together

Now I'm going to use everything we've covered so far to make a nice-looking Web page. Take a look at mine, and then do your own. (Do your own on your own. Don't just copy mine.) Figure 5.4 shows the result I got.

The HTML that generates this page is in Listing 5.4. Note how I've used headings in "nonheading" ways, such as for the small copyright notice.

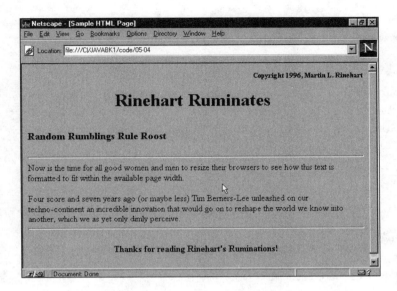

Figure 5.4 THE RINEHART RUMINATES WEB PAGE.

LISTING 5.4 A FINISHED WEB PAGE

```
<! sample.html>
<HTML>
<HEAD>

<TITLE>
Sample HTML Page
</TITLE>

</HEAD>
<BODY>
<H5 ALIGN=RIGHT>Copyright 1996, Martin L. Rinehart</H5>

<H1 ALIGN=CENTER > Rinehart Ruminates </H1>
<BR>
<H3>Random Rumblings Rule Roost</H3>

<HR>
```

```
Now is the time for all good women and men to resize their
browsers to see how this text is formatted to fit within the
available page width.
<P>
Four score and seven years ago (or maybe less) Tim Berners-Lee
unleashed on our techno-continent an incredible innovation that
would go on to reshape the world we know into another, which we
as yet only dimly perceive.

<HR>

<H4 ALIGN=CENTER>Thanks for reading Rinehart's Ruminations!</H4>

</BODY>
</HTML>
<! end of sample.html>
```

Displaying Lists

Of course, there are lots of different Web page elements, and you'll need
to get a good book about Webmastering in general or HTML in particular
if you want to learn them all. I've picked a handful for this chapter that are
easy, fun, and useful. In this section we'll look at lists.

Unordered Lists

The `<UL>` and `</UL>` tags enclose unordered lists. These are lists of bul-
let-point items. The `<LI>` and `</LI>` tags enclose individual list items.
Listing 5.5 shows an example, and Figure 5.5 shows the result in my
browser.

LISTING 5.5 ADDING A BULLET LIST

```
...
<HR>
```

```
<UL>
Good Pizza Toppings<BR>
<LI>Bell peppers</LI>
<LI>Onions</LI>
<LI>Mushrooms</LI>
<BR>
Check the alignment of this text (it's not a list item, but it's
within the Unordered List tags' scope).
</UL>

<HR>

<H4 ALIGN=CENTER>Thanks for reading Rinehart's Ruminations!</H4>
...
```

That <BR> tag after "Pizza Toppings" is interesting. In Netscape
Navigator, you don't need it. You'll get a line break before each bullet
item. But it doesn't hurt and it doesn't cause an extra break. In Microsoft
Explorer, the first List Item will appear next to "Toppings" if you don't
include the explicit <BR>.

The moral of the story: always launch your Web page in as many
browsers as you can find. Browsers have annoying little differences.

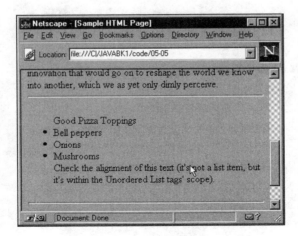

Figure 5.5 A SAMPLE BULLET LIST.

Ordered Lists

Ordered Lists (the tags are <OL> and </OL>) are done the same way unordered lists are, but the browser numbers the items instead of using bullets. Listing 5.6 shows an ordered list added to the HTML, and Figure 5.6 shows the result in the browser.

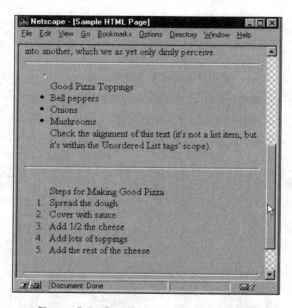

Figure 5.6 COOKING WITH A NUMBERED LIST.

LISTING 5.6   ADDING A NUMBERED LIST

```
...
<HR>

<OL>
Steps for Making Good Pizza<BR>
<LI>Spread the dough</LI>
<LI>Cover with sauce</LI>
<LI>Add 1/2 the cheese</LI>
<LI>Add lots of toppings</LI>
```

```
<LI>Add the rest of the cheese</LI>
</OL>

<HR>

<H4 ALIGN=CENTER>Thanks for reading Rinehart's Ruminations!</H4>
...
```

Descriptive Lists

Descriptive lists are used when you want to have text descriptions set out in a list style. The enclosing tags are `<DL>` and `</DL>` as you would guess. The items are enclosed in `<DD>` and `</DD>` tag pairs, which you probably wouldn't have guessed. Listing 5.7 shows an example and Figure 5.7 shows the result in the browser.

In this list, I've mixed `<H4>` and `<H5>` headings into the list's contents. You can get lots of interesting effects by mixing HTML elements.

LISTING 5.7   ADDING A DESCRIPTIVE LIST

```
...
<HR>

<DL>
<H4>Mastering Pizza Sauce</H4>

<DD><H5>Store-Bought</H5>
Any good pasta sauce will work nicely on your pizza. Use your
favorite variety. </DD>

<DD><H5>Improved Store-Bought</H5>
It's not home-made, but improved store-bought sauce is delicious.
While simmering the sauce, add crushed garlic and finely chopped
onion. Just before your patience runs out, add a generous helping
of basil and oregano.</DD>

<DD><H5>Home-Made</H5>
```

```
Real pizza gourmets make their own sauces. It's more trouble,
but the results are worth it. Begin with fresh, ripe
tomatoes.... </DD>

</DL>

<HR>

<H4 ALIGN=CENTER>Thanks for reading Rinehart's Ruminations!</H4>
...
```

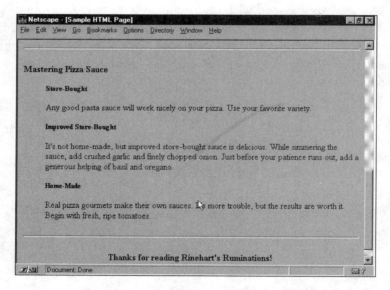

Figure 5.7 DESCRIPTIONS IN A DESCRIPTIVE LIST.

Adding Spice

What would a Web page be without graphics? Boring, unimaginative, colorless?

I don't think so. I think it would be fast to load. I like fast!

I'm not going to cover the <IMG> tag that you'll need to load and position graphics. Without graphics, you can do a lot of very imaginative work that isn't boring just working with fonts and colors.

You can make loud, noisy (did someone say *tasteless*?) Web pages without making anyone wait for a graphic to download. Let's play a few tricks with fonts and colors to spice up our Web page.

Fonts

As you probably guessed, the <FONT> tag takes parameters that let you have some control over the font that appears in the browser, but it's very different from typesetting or even using a good word processor.

The first principle is that you don't know which fonts are available on the client computer. In fact, you don't even know what kind of computer it is. The browser and the local operating system do work together to do their best to respect your design wishes, however.

Let's start by adjusting the font's size.

The <FONT SIZE= n > Tag

You do not get to specify an absolute point size in HTML. The designers thought that specifying a relative size would let the local client hardware and software use some discretion.

The original SIZE values were 1 through 5. SIZE=3 is the default text size. SIZE=1 is the smallest size. SIZE=5 is large, and some browsers support still higher sizes (and because it's only some browsers, you might want to avoid them).

Listing 5.8 shows the HTML I've added to display a range of font sizes, and Figure 5.8 shows the result in the browser.

LISTING 5.8 ADDING A RANGE OF FONT SIZES

```
...
<HR>

<FONT SIZE=1> This is a size 1 font </FONT><BR>
<FONT SIZE=2> This is a size 2 font </FONT><BR>
<FONT SIZE=3> This is a size 3 font </FONT><BR>
```

```
<FONT SIZE=4> This is a size 4 font </FONT><BR>
<FONT SIZE=5> This is a size 5 font </FONT><BR>

<HR>

<H4 ALIGN=CENTER>Thanks for reading Rinehart's Ruminations!</H4>
...
```

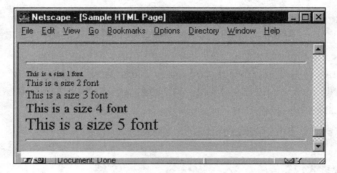

Figure 5.8 FONT SIZES 1–5.

In-Text Variations

What would a modern document be if we couldn't adjust the font characteristics? HTML supports italics, boldface, and more.

To use italics in your text, use an `<I>` ... `</I>` tag pair. Boldface, as you probably guessed, takes a `<B>` ... `</B>` pair. Try these on your own. And make me a promise? Don't overdo either one, OK?

Ready to escape from black text on a gray background? That's our next topic.

Colors

Colors are specified in hexadecimal notation with one hex byte for each of the three RGB (red, green and blue) colors. `00` turns the color completely off, and `FF` specifies maximum intensity. The color specification is prefixed with a # and enclosed in double quotes.

These are some color specifications:

```
"#000000" <! no color, black>
"#ffffff" <! all colors maximum, white>

"#ff0000" <! maximum pure red>
"#00ff00" <! maximum pure green>
"#0000ff" <! maximum pure blue>

"#888888" <! medium gray>
"#008888" <! medium cyan>
```

When you specify colors, bear in mind that your client machine may have as many as 256 colors or as few as 16 in its palette. The browser and operating software are going to find the best match for your specification, but it probably won't be an exact match. If you go for subtle variations, you'll likely end up with no variation at all. (If your Web page is popular enough, some people will even be viewing it in black and white.)

Background Color

You can specify various colors for your page in the `<BODY>` tag. Among the colors you can set are the background color, the default text color, the color for links, and the color for links that have been accessed.

I don't recommend setting the link colors because each client browser includes them as a customizable item. Your users are probably used to the colors they've picked and won't appreciate being confused by different colors. They may even have told their browsers to ignore these specifications.

In general, black text works well, unless you switch to a black background. Try three-quarters white on black, this way:

```
<BODY TEXT = "#CCCCCC" BGCOLOR="#000000">
```

That could be pretty dramatic in a world of white and gray backgrounds, but let's use something a bit more standard, for the moment. This is plain black text on a white background:

```
<BODY BGCOLOR = "#FFFFFF" >
```

Did you try that? It looks like ink on paper, doesn't it?

Font Color

You can easily overdo font color. Used with discretion, color can create dramatic effects and add information to your pages. The <FONT> tag supports a color parameter. The group of lines I've added to use colors are shown in Listing 5.9.

LISTING 5.9 ADDING COLORED TEXT

```
. . .
<HR>

<FONT SIZE=4 COLOR="#FF0000"> This is large, red text </FONT><BR>
<FONT SIZE=4 COLOR="#00FF00"> This is large, green text
</FONT><BR>
<FONT SIZE=4 COLOR="#0000FF"> This is large, blue text </FONT><BR>

<HR>

<H4 ALIGN=CENTER>Thanks for reading Rinehart's Ruminations!</H4>
. . .
```

In a black-and-white book, like this one, we can't illustrate this with a figure, so you'll have to try it yourself. On my machine, the red and blue text is completely readable, but the green is barely legible. Try your pages on a variety of equipment before you go too far with color.

Links

Hypertext wouldn't be "hyper" if you couldn't add links from one page to another, would it? Links are very common, partly because they're very simple to use. To add a link, you simply drop in an anchor tag pair: <A> ... </A>.

The HREF clause of the anchor tag assigns a hypertext cross-reference. You use it this way:

```
<A HREF = "<URL>"> <! fill in a URL>
```

```
<!Example:>

<A HREF = "http://www.sun.com"> <! Sun's home page>
```

The text between the `<A>` and `</A>` anchor markers is the text that is highlighted. When you click that text, off you go!

Just one word on the text to highlight, if you please. Don't write *click here* or words to that effect. Your Web page is being viewed by an intelligent human who knows how to use a Web browser. He or she already clicked several hyperlinks to get to your Web page, after all. Use the name of the site, or words that describe the site, if the name isn't commonly known.

Listing 5.10 shows the hyperlinks I've added at the end of my Web page.

LISTING 5.10 LET'S GO SURFIN' NOW, EVERBODY'S LEARNIN' HOW...

```
...
<HR>

From here you can link to:

<CENTER>

    <A HREF="http://www.microsoft.com">Microsoft's home page</A>

    or

    <A HREF="http://www.netscape.com">Netscape's home page</A>

</CENTER><BR>

<H4 ALIGN=CENTER>Thanks for reading Rinehart's Ruminations!</H4>
...
```

Now that I think of it, I've never actually explained what the `<CENTER>` tag is for, have I?

Of course you can figure it out on your own, but can you figure out exactly how the browser will format those two links?

Give it some thought, and then try it to see if you're right.

There's one more thing. If you're not connected to the Net, clicking those links isn't likely to work. My browser tells me that it can't find the DNS (Domain Name Server) entry for either company. I'm not sure if the browser is being stupid or it is just too polite to tell me that I'm being stupid.

Are you ready to embed an applet in this masterful page? That, of course, is what we've been leading up to all along.

Applets

To you Webmasters and HTML pros who skipped over all the material before this point, welcome back! We've been having some fun developing a Web page that shows some of the basics of HTML and uses some common tags. Listing 5.11 shows the full page as we've developed it so far. You might want to copy it from the book's disk to your own. Look through it to be sure that you're up to speed with the rest of the class.

LISTING 5.11 OUR WEB PAGE SO FAR

```
<! sample.html>
<HTML>
<HEAD>

<TITLE>
Sample HTML Page
</TITLE>

</HEAD>
<BODY BGCOLOR = "#FFFFFF" >
<H5 ALIGN=RIGHT>Copyright 1996, Martin L. Rinehart</H5>

<H1 ALIGN=CENTER > Rinehart Ruminates </H1>
<BR>
<H3>Random Rumblings Rule Roost</H3>

<HR>
```

Now is the time for all good women and men to resize their
browsers to see how this text is formatted to fit within the
available page width.
<P>
Four score and seven years ago (or maybe less) Tim Berners-Lee
unleashed on our techno-continent an incredible innovation that
would go on to reshape the world we know into another, which we
as yet only dimly perceive.

<HR>

<UL>
Good Pizza Toppings
<LI>Bell peppers</LI>
<LI>Onions</LI>
<LI>Mushrooms</LI>

Check the alignment of this text (it's not a list item, but it's
within the Unordered List tags' scope).
</UL>

<HR>

<OL>
Steps for Making Good Pizza
<LI>Spread the dough</LI>
<LI>Cover with sauce</LI>
<LI>Add 1/2 the cheese</LI>
<LI>Add lots of toppings</LI>
<LI>Add the rest of the cheese</LI>
</OL>

<HR>

<DL>
<H4>Mastering Pizza Sauce</H4>

<DD><H5>Store-Bought</H5>

Any good pasta sauce will work nicely on your pizza. Use your
favorite variety. </DD>

<DD><H5>Improved Store-Bought</H5>
It's not home-made, but improved store-bought sauce is delicious.
While simmering the sauce, add crushed garlic and finely chopped
onion. Just before your patience runs out, add a generous helping
of basil and oregano.</DD>

<DD><H5>Home-Made</H5>
Real pizza gourmets make their own sauces. It's more trouble,
but the results are worth it. Begin with fresh, ripe
tomatoes.... </DD>

</DL>

<HR>

<FONT SIZE=1> This is a size 1 font </FONT>
<FONT SIZE=2> This is a size 2 font </FONT>
<FONT SIZE=3> This is a size 3 font </FONT>
<FONT SIZE=4> This is a size 4 font </FONT>
<FONT SIZE=5> This is a size 5 font </FONT>

<HR>

<FONT SIZE=4 COLOR="#FF0000"> This is large, red text </FONT>
<FONT SIZE=4 COLOR="#00FF00"> This is large, green text
</FONT>
<FONT SIZE=4 COLOR="#0000FF"> This is large, blue text </FONT>

<HR>

From here you can link to:

<CENTER>

    <A HREF="http://www.microsoft.com">Microsoft's home page</A>

    or

```
    <A HREF="http://www.netscape.com">Netscape's home page</A>

</CENTER><BR>

<H4 ALIGN=CENTER>Thanks for reading Rinehart's Ruminations!</H4>

</BODY>
</HTML>
<! end of sample.html>
```

At this point you'll want to launch your favorite Web browser and load this page. Glance at the lists near the bottom. Do they make you hungry?

Now we're ready to get to work. We have to do two things. If we were Java-enabled, we'd launch one thread to write the applet and a second thread to add the links in our HTML page. Obviously, either one alone is useless, but this is a book, and most of us can only use one keyboard at a time, so we have to do one thing at a time.

We'll begin by adding the link to our applet to our HTML page.

Linking to the Applet

You link to a Java applet with the <APPLET> ... </APPLET> tag pair. The <APPLET> tag accepts several parameters, of which three are mandatory:

> CODE—The name of the applet
> HEIGHT—The applet's size
> WIDTH—Measured in pixels

For our **SAMPLE.HTML** file, we'll create `Sample.class` (from `Sample.java`) as our first applet. This will launch it in our Web page:

```
<APPLET CODE = "Sample.class" HEIGHT = 150 WIDTH= 300 >
</APPLET>
```

Add this link to your Web page and load it into your browser. Mine tells me that it can't start the applet because it can't find the code. Our next job is to create the applet.

In the section "Adjusting the Applet," we'll get to the other clauses of the <APPLET> tag that let you position the applet more precisely, supply text for Web browsers that aren't Java-enabled, and do other tricks. Right now, though, what we need is an applet.

Programming the Applet

The applet is what the browser is looking for. In Java, an *applet* is an instance of the Applet class. Actually, it's an instance of a class that extends the Applet class. (It's time to put on your case-sensitive Java hat again.)

The first thing your applet code should do is import the java.applet.Applet class. If you're going to use any graphical user interface components, you'll want to import the Abstract Windows Toolkit classes, too. Most applets start like this:

```
import java.applet.Applet;
import java.awt.*;

public class Myclass extends Applet
{
    // code here
}
```

About the only real difference between an application and an applet is that the applet starts with an init() method, while our applications started with a main() method.

Of course, the applet will be running in the browser, so you don't want to use a crude tool like System.out.println(). You want to use the AWT classes. Leaving that aside, Listing 5.12 shows an applet template that you should create and file somewhere as your base for applet programming. If you haven't done so yet, you'll want to relaunch Visual J++ to create the template.

LISTING 5.12 A GENERIC APPLET TEMPLATE

```
// Template.java

import java.applet.Applet;
import java.awt.*;
```

```
public class Template extends Applet
{

    public void init()
    {

    }

    public boolean action( Event evnt, Object obj )
    {

        return true;
    }
}

// end of Template.java
```

What's the `action()` method? In Java, the event loop is built in. When you use the AWT classes, you provide a method called `action()` that handles events. For the moment, we'll always return `true`.

You'll need only one other method of the `Applet` class to create AWT-based applets. That's the `add()` method, which you use to add Java objects to an applet.

Starting with `Template.java`, create `Sample.java`. Listing 5.13 has the complete code for a working Java applet.

LISTING 5.13 YOUR FIRST AWT APPLET

```
// Sample.java

import java.applet.Applet;
import java.awt.*;

public class Sample extends Applet
{
```

```
TextField t1;
Button b1;

public void init()
{
    t1 = new TextField("My First Applet");
    add(t1);
    b1 = new Button("Hello");
    add(b1);
}

public boolean action( Event evnt, Object obj )
{
    if( evnt.target == b1 )
    {
        t1.setText( "Hello, AWT!" );
    }
    return true;
}
}
```

```
// end of Sample.java
```

The data members of our `Sample` class are a `TextField` object and a `Button` object. The `init()` function creates these by calling constructors that accept a string argument. It uses `add()` to attach them to the `Sample` (`Applet`-based) object.

The `action()` method is simple. When the Java event loop detects an event, it calls your `action()` routine. Your routine then handles the event and returns `true`, or, if it can't handle the event, it could return `false`. We're going to return `true` always, which has the effect of ignoring any events that we don't explicitly program.

A more sophisticated `action()` routine would have an outer layer that tests the target data member against each object in your applet. Once it picked the correct object, it would test against each possible event type. Here we're just checking to see if the event applies to the button. If it does, we assume that button was clicked and reset the text in the `TextField` object.

Ready to run? Go ahead and compile and run. Let Visual J++ create a default workspace and put the output in `Sample.class`, which is where our HTML page expects to find it. This time, ask Visual J++ to generate an applet for Internet Explorer instead of an application for **JVIEW.EXE**.

When you're compiled, Visual J++ will launch Explorer with a local HTML page that is created just to test your applet. When it's loaded, you'll be able to click your applet's button. Hello, AWT! My applet is shown in Figure 5.9.

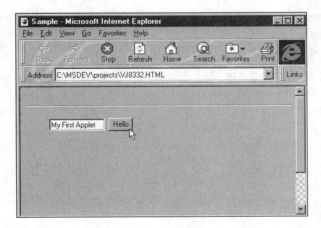

Figure 5.9 SAYING HELLO TO **AWT** APPLET PROGRAMMING.

Just to be sure, use the File/Open dialog box in Explorer to open your own **Sample.html** page. The applet will run again. Applets are run when the page that embeds them is opened. They are closed when the page is closed. When you load your page, you'll be able to click your applet's button and see your message in the text field. Reload the page to do it again.

For now, use Explorer as your companion to Visual J++ for developing applets. You'll certainly want to test your applets in Navigator, too, but don't worry about that yet. Microsoft has done a nice job of tying Explorer to Visual J++ as an applet test vehicle. Wait until you've got real applets to go on the Web before you worry about Navigator.

When you're ready to load your applet on the Web, you'll need to know where to put it. Your friendly local Webmaster or ISP contact will tell you where your HTML and `Java.class` files go. You'll put your files there (or, more, precisely, you'll provide the files for your Webmaster or ISP, and someone will put your files in the designated place) and you'll adjust the addresses in your HTML links to match the final locations.

Adjusting the Applet

Did that applet happen so quickly you almost didn't notice? You wanted a `Button` object in your applet, so all you did was create a `Button`. You didn't even have to tell the Applet where to put it. You wanted to change the text in a `TextField`, so all you did was call the `setText()` method. No repainting instructions, no complications—it just happened.

Welcome to the late 90s! There's really nothing that you have to do that Java doesn't handle with some reasonable default. For example, it lines your objects up from left to right, top to bottom, if you don't give it other instructions. Rest assured, however, that you are the boss. You can override almost everything that Java does when you need to.

For now, let's take a closer look at the way your HTML can adjust the applet. (In Chapters 8–13 we'll be looking at the ways your applets can adjust themselves.)

Sizing the Applet

You've already seen that you supply `HEIGHT` and `WIDTH` parameters in the `<APPLET>` tag. These are given values, in pixels, that size the applet. We wrote the tag this way:

```
<APPLET CODE = "Sample.class" HEIGHT = 150 WIDTH= 300 >
```

You can also write the tag this way:

```
<APPLET CODE = "Sample.class"
        HEIGHT = 150
        WIDTH= 300 >
```

You'll see that the latter form makes sense as you add additional tags.

The Applet's Alignment

You control the applet's positioning first by the location of the `<APPLET>` tag in the HTML page. At that point, you can further control it with the `ALIGN` parameter, this way:

```
<APPLET ALIGN = MIDDLE
        CODE = "Sample.class"
        HEIGHT = 150
        WIDTH= 300 >
```

The other possible alignments are `LEFT`, `RIGHT`, `TOP`, `TEXTTOP`, `MIDDLE`, `ABSMIDDLE`, `BASELINE`, `BOTTOM`, and `ABSBOTTOM`. Go back to the edit-HTML, reload-page-in-browser cycle to test these options.

Space Padding

You can add additional pixels to the left and above your applet with the `HSPACE` and `VSPACE` parameters, as in:

```
<APPLET ALIGN = MIDDLE
        CODE = "Sample.class"
        HEIGHT = 150
        HSPACE = 20
        WIDTH= 300
        VSPACE = 10 >
```

Alternate Text

The first browsers became Java-enabled in 1996 (or the year before, if you count beta versions). Earlier browsers and even some current ones cannot run Java applets. The `ALT` parameter lets you specify text that will be displayed by browsers that can't run your applet.

Keep in mind that some people will turn off the Java capability in even the newest browsers for security or other reasons.

Summary

In this chapter we spent most of our time acquainting readers who didn't speak HTML with the wonderful world of Web page building. This is necessary, of course, because applets run inside Web pages.

We began with the basic superstructure of an HTML page, including `<HTML>`, `<HEAD>`, `<BODY>`, and `<TITLE>` tags. We used `<!comments>` and saw how `<tag>` ends with `</tag>`.

Then we went to work adding text and the headings from `<H1>` through `<H6>`. We also used `<P>`, `<BR>`, and `<HL>` breaks to divide up our pages. We tied this work together building an attractive (though nonsensical) page.

Next, we added lists. We used unordered (bulleted) lists, ordered (numbered) lists, and descriptive lists. We mixed headings and breaks into the lists. We also saw that Navigator and Explorer aren't quite identical, which proves that testing hasn't gone out of style.

Then we added some decorative touches. We varied the font sizes (`SIZE=`) and learned to use italic (`<I>`) and boldface (`<B>`) tags within the text. We learned about the `#rrggbb` color specification, and we learned to use the `BGCOLOR` parameter of the `<BODY>` tag to change the background color. Next, we added `COLOR` parameters to our `<FONT>` tags to change text colors in the page.

As a last step before adding an applet, we learned to add hypertext links. Then we went on to add an applet.

We added the `<APPLET>` tag to our HTML page, and then we wrote an applet. We built a simple applet that changes the text in a `TextField` object in response to the click of a `Button` object. We used `init()` and `action()` methods in a class that extends `java.applet.Applet` to do this.

Congratulations. You've learned a lot about Java and enough HTML to embed Java applets in Web pages. Now we're ready to get on to the fun part of the book. In Part II, we'll spend most of our time using visual programming tools and figuring out clever ways to build cool applets without doing any real hard work.

## PART II

THE VISUAL J++ DEVELOPER STUDIO

## CHAPTER 6

VISUAL J++, A GUIDED TOUR

When you first saw Visual J++ you looked at a complex array of unknown tools. Way back in Chapter 1 we stripped it down to a minimum. We made a simple little Cessna out of a complex jet fighter. Since then we've been adding back pieces, a few at a time. By now you're past the basics and adept with some portions of the product. Why would you want a guided tour?

This isn't the sort of tour that typical tourists take. This is the sort of tour you would take if you visited your old friend Pierre in Paris, and he promised to take you around to some of the interesting, out of the way spots that most tourists miss.

We'll start with the main window and deliberately create the most complex, jet fighter–like arrangement we can. Then we'll look at controlling the docking of dockable windows. Finally, we'll take another look at full-screen view.

In the InfoViewer, we'll explore the three views: info, class, and file, but we'll start by customizing the keyboard to make it a handier tool.

In the text editor, we'll look at some less obvious components, such as the splitters that are tucked away on the scroll bars.

We'll also take a look at the tools we'll be using throughout the rest of this book, the dialog and image editors. Finally, we'll take a short look at the debugger. These last three stops will be brief; we'll cover these tools in depth later on.

Let's start with the main window.

The Main Window

My first tip about the main window is to leave the tips turned on. When you're in a hurry, pressing the **Enter** key shuts the tip window. If you look at the tip for a moment, however, you might catch a pointer that will repay the time you spent many times over. It's surprising how often I find that the tip that I ignored yesterday solves a real problem today.

My next tip is that if you've turned the tips off, you can use the Help menu to turn them back on. Choose **Help/Tip of the Day...** and then check the **Show tips at startup** box.

Now let's get started on some serious mess making.

When you launch Visual J++, you're in the main window. At this point, load Visual J++, switch out of full-screen view if you're in it, and then use **Ctrl+F4** to close any open child windows. If the Workspace Window is open, right-click it and choose **Hide** from the popup menu. Now let's start to work building a really intimidating jet fighter cockpit.

Figure 6.1 shows what we're shooting for.

Is your status bar turned on? That's on the **Tools/Options...** dialog box, in the Workspace tab, shown in Figure 6.2.

Go ahead and turn the status bar on. In fact, turn everything on. Check every box on the Options Workspace tab. Don't forget to scroll the list of docking views to make sure you got them all.

It won't appear to do too much, but it's mischief will begin to show up as we move along.

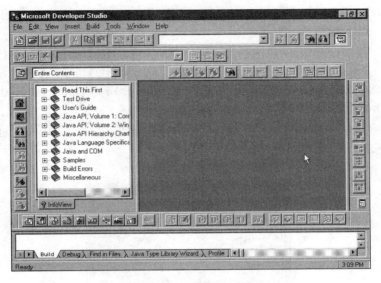

FIGURE 6.1   AN UNWORKABLE COCKPIT.

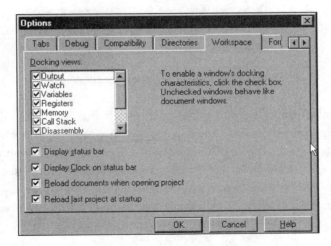

FIGURE 6.2   CONTROLLING THE WORKSPACE.

Toolbars

One of the things I like best about the Visual J++ interface is that I can really customize it to suit myself. I like to work with the mouse in the visual editors and with the keyboard in the text editor. I really dislike having to switch from keyboard to mouse during a single operation.

You have your own style, too. I'm pretty sure that it doesn't match mine and that's fine. Visual J++ will let you work your way and me work my way. Let's begin by turning all the toolbars on. While you do that, take a good look at any that are new to you.

Choose **View/Toolbars...** to launch the Toolbars dialog box shown in Figure 6.3.

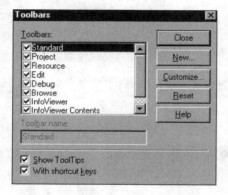

FIGURE 6.3 TURNING TOO MANY TOOLBARS ON.

Check all of them. Some toolbars will attach themselves to edges of your main window. Others will float in their own windows. You want to attach the floaters to the edges of your window. To do that, just grab the title bar of the toolbar's window and drag it to a screen edge. You'll see the outline of the toolbar appear, positioned roughly as the toolbar will appear. If you drag from edge to edge, you'll see the toolbar outline hop as you reach each edge.

After you drop a toolbar at an edge, you can move it to a different edge or reposition it on its edge by dragging. The trick is to find some space that isn't occupied by a button to grab the toolbar.

When you position toolbars (for fun or to actually get some work done) you can save expensive screen real estate by positioning the toolbars to fit as tightly as possible.

You can also customize all your toolbars. Figure 6.4 shows the Toolbars tab of the Customize dialog box (launched from **Tools/Customize...**). You can drag any button onto any toolbar with this dialog box.

FIGURE 6.4 CUSTOMIZING THE TOOLBARS.

The buttons are arranged by category here. Just grab any button you like and drop it onto any toolbar, roughly where you want it. You can also drag buttons from one toolbar to another. To delete an unwanted button, just drag it off its toolbar and drop it anywhere except another toolbar.

A couple points might be helpful. First, if you have two toolbars that *almost* fit across the top (or bottom or side) of your screen, look for the button you'll use least. Use the Customize dialog box's Toolbars tab to get rid of that button. You can recapture a lot of screen just by losing a button or two.

Second, there's no law that says the Debug toolbar, for instance, has to apply to debugging. You could pick your own collection of Things I Do Most Often and use this or any other toolbar to hold those buttons.

By the way, those wide buttons that take text, like the Finder tool on the main toolbar, are discarded when you attach the toolbar to a side of your screen.

Is your screen really cluttered with toolbars? Good.

Docking Windows

A docked window attaches itself to a side of your main window's client area. It then behaves like part of the main window, not like a child window. Other child windows will open in the remaining part of the client area. This can rapidly eat into your precious screen real estate or it can be extremely handy.

Open your Workspace window (which includes the InfoViewer). If you right-click, you'll see that Docking View is checked in the popup menu. (Click it if it's not checked.)

Docking windows are like toolbars in that they can be dragged to dock on any edge of your client area. The trick is to grab the docked edge and drag it around the screen, just as you grabbed a toolbar by an unused area. (Grabbing the docked edge isn't always easy. Persistence pays.)

You can dock at any edge. If there are other docked windows, they can share an edge, or use their own edges. Figure 6.5 shows the Workspace window docked on the left with the Output window docked on the bottom.

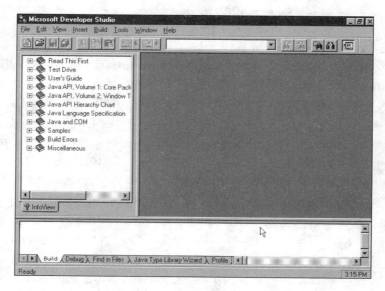

FIGURE 6.5   LEFT- AND BOTTOM-DOCKED CHILD WINDOWS

Figure 6.6 shows another alternative. Here, both windows are docked at the left edge. The trick to doing this is to pay close attention to the outline of the docked window as you drag it around the screen. You'll see this form pop into the right shape when you are near (but not too near) the lower-left corner.

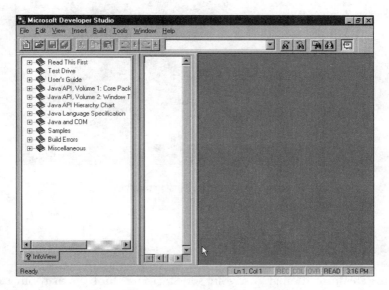

FIGURE 6.6 DOUBLED LEFT-DOCKED WINDOWS.

Docked windows and toolbars have similar precedence in the main window. That means you can do really interesting things, like docking windows outside of the toolbars, as shown in Figure 6.7. Try dragging the docked window outside the scrollbars to get this arrangement. It doesn't always work. The alternative, which should always work, is to drag the toolbar inside the docked window.

Now, as a practical matter, some windows work well vertically and others work horizontally. The Output window's most important service is to show error messages from the compiler and linker. These are wide, so a horizontal docking works well for this window. None of the views of the Workspace window take up much horizontal space, so a vertical arrangement works well with this window.

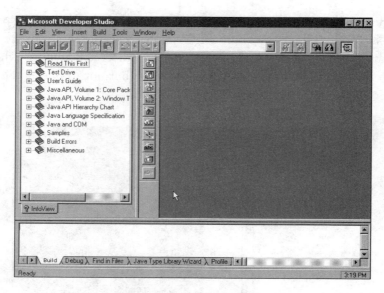

FIGURE 6.7   DOCKING OUTSIDE THE TOOLBARS.

Full-Screen View

With all those toolbars on your screen, there's not much room to work. Flip to full-screen view (**Alt+V**, **U** for full screen) and all the toolbars disappear. The menus disappear, the window title disappears, and the taskbar's gone, too. The result is lots of working space.

Actually, for a long time I thought that the full-screen view didn't show toolbars, but this isn't true. The truth is that full-screen view has its own setup information, which defaults to no toolbars. You can set up the full-screen view just as you set up the main window. (It's really an alternate main window.)

Try turning the Standard toolbar on or choose your own favorite toolbar, but this time, keep just one row of tools across whichever edge you prefer.

These views are so quick to flip around that I work in any way that suits the job at hand. Figure 6.8 shows a very typical setup for me.

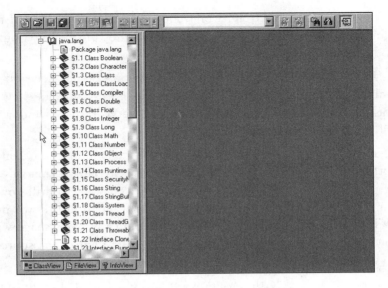

FIGURE 6.8 MY WORKING FULL-SCREEN SETUP.

Adjust the full-screen setup to suit yourself. Then go back to the main window and turn off toolbars and undock windows until you've got a reasonable working arrangement. Or, if you're like me, do all your work in full-screen view.

The only advantage to using the standard main window over the full-screen view is that it includes the menu bar. By now you know most of those menus, don't you?

One final tip: I leave the taskbar switched off in full-screen view and switched on in the main window. That way I can toggle back and forth when the taskbar is helpful.

The Amazing Workspace and InfoViewer

As our programming tools have grown, so, too, has our need for documentation. Online documentation is now commonly many megabytes. There's no indication that this trend won't continue. Microsoft decided that on online table of contents, which they named the InfoViewer, would be a good addition to the Developer Studio.

They were right, of course. One interesting design decision was to combine the online contents with the class view and the file view in the Workspace window. Except for the fact that the Workspace window is now badly misnamed, the design works.

You'll find yourself constantly referring to one or the other of the Workspace views. The information needs here are almost mutually exclusive, so this means of organization works. If you want to drill down into your own code, the class view works. If you want to drill down into the AWT, the InfoViewer works. For me, keeping the Workspace window, showing the AWT, my classes, or whatever to the left of the source code also works.

I do like to toggle this window on and off. Part of the default setup that I don't like is that there is no simple way to tell the Workspace window to get lost. **Alt+0** opens the window, but once it's open, **Alt+0** becomes a NOP.

So let's turn **Alt+0** into a toggle that opens and closes the InfoViewer.

Keyboard Customization

Keyboard customization is a powerful way to make the Developer Studio your own product. Figure 6.9 shows the Keyboard tab of the Customize dialog box (**Tools/Customize...**). I'm using it to assign **Alt+0** to toggle the Workspace window.

When you do this, the keyboard customization dialog box will politely tell you that **Alt+0** is already in use and what it's used for, but it allows you to change it.

Assign **Alt+0** to toggle the Workspace window or assign some other key, if you prefer—it's your Developer Studio. I think you'll be happy with the result.

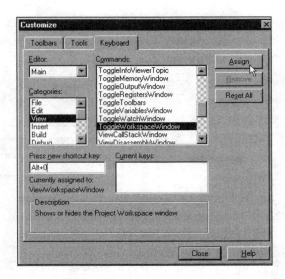

FIGURE 6.9 CHANGING ALT+0 INTO A TOGGLE.

The Info View

We've already made extensive use of the InfoViewer drilling into the two volumes of the Java API. The InfoViewer is all about finding information, so I'll just add one tip.

Inside the *User's Guide*, two line below the Introduction, you'll find a topic "Finding Information." Figure 6.10 shows my InfoViewer drilling down into this topic.

Finding Information is a treasure trove of useful tips and techniques.

Class View

We haven't used the class view extensively yet. It becomes more useful as your applets become larger. By the time your applets have lots of classes and methods, you'll be using the class view constantly. Here's how.

The class view lets you drill down into your own classes. For each class, there's a complete list of your data members and methods. Just as double-clicking an information topic opens the right document in the Infoview Topic window, double-clicking a class member opens the source code.

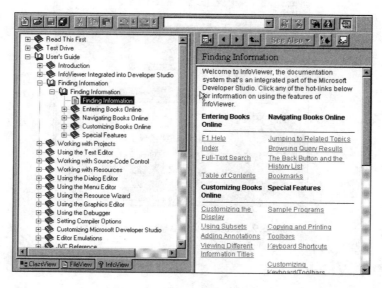

FIGURE 6.10 FINDING OUT ABOUT FINDING OUT.

Try it. Don't open any source files. Open the Workspace window and drill down into any Infoviewer topic. Now click the Class view tab. You should see the `Sample` class we built in the last chapter. (If you've worked on a different applet in the meantime, that's fine, too.)

Open the `Sample` class and double-click the `action()` method. Bingo! Your source code is opened and the cursor is positioned to the start of this method. Nice, no? It's functionally identical to the InfoViewer.

File View

The file view is like the class view in that we could easily dispense with it for a very simple project, but you won't be able to live without it as your projects get more complex.

Over time, your applets and applications will spread across lots of files for source code and for resources. This tool will make it easy to stay organized.

Can you guess what happens when you double-click a file in the file view? I thought so.

Text Editor

I'm sure you've figured out a lot of the text editor already. I'm going to collect some random observations here, some of which may be helpful.

Horizontal Scrolling

First, in writing for books and magazines I've been restricted to various output widths. A width of 60 characters is typical, although some magazines go as low as 52. I always code this way now. Using 6 point type, 60 column code can be printed in portrait mode in three columns on a standard 8.5 by 11 page. Each column shows about 100 lines. This is very useful for looking at a lot of code on a few pages.

It also means that you can turn the horizontal scrollbar off in the editor (**Tools/Options...**, Editor tab). This adds vertical real estate, which is in short supply on the screen.

I'm not sure if this is a design feature or a six-legged thing, but when you turn the horizontal scroll bar off in the editor, it's turned off in the output window as well. To read those long error messages, drop the cursor on the message and use your arrow keys to scroll.

Window Splitters

Figure 6.11 shows the editor window split, with independently scrolling top and bottom portions. The splitter bar can be dragged to suit your needs.

The splitter bar parks conveniently above the top arrow of the vertical scrollbar. This makes it very handy, but it's also very easy to overlook if you don't know it's there. Drag it out and see for yourself. (When your cursor is over it, the cursor changes to the standard window pane adjustment shape.)

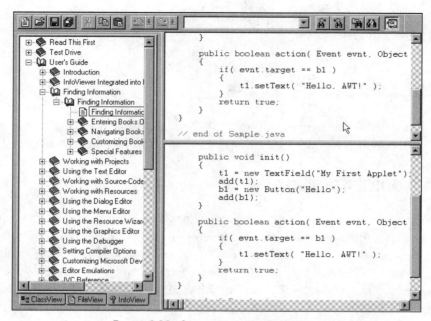

FIGURE 6.11 SPLITTING THE EDITOR WINDOW.

There's a splitter available on the horizontal scrollbar, too. I'm not sure why you'd want it, but then again, I keep that scrollbar turned off. I'm not likely to use an editor split left and right.

You can split the window horizontally and vertically simultaneously if you want, too. That just confuses me, but it's there.

The Finder Tool

The text entry field (which includes a drop-down history list) on the General toolbar is a very convenient substitute for the text editor's find command (**Alt+F3**). The Find Next and Find Prev buttons next to the text field work in a nice circle. **Alt+F3** gives you more power, but this tool is often easier to use.

If you look at the Toolbars tab of the Customize dialog box (**Tools/Customize...**) you'll see that this finder tool is considered an Edit button. I presume that it's placed on the General toolbar so that people like me can leave the Edit toolbar turned off.

Dialog Editor

So far on this tour we've been exploring the territory where you've already been working. Now we're going to wander into the unknown, beginning with a brief visit to the Dialog editor.

The next three sections will be very brief, but don't worry. We'll explore each of these tools more thoroughly when we start working with them. This is just a quick introduction so you'll know what to expect.

To get to the Dialog editor, use **Insert/Resource** and choose **Dialog**. As you go by, notice that there are lots of other resources and that each one has its own editor. We'll look at a class of these in the next section on the Image editor. For now, let's focus on dialog boxes.

Figure 6.12 shows a default dialog box.

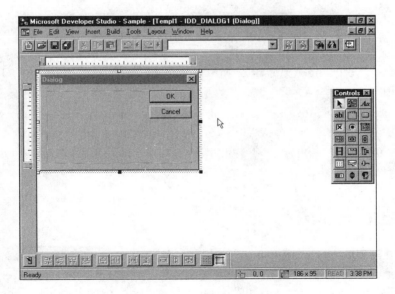

FIGURE 6.12 BEGINNING WORK ON A DIALOG BOX.

If you are familiar with Visual Basic, Delphi, or any of a wide variety of other Windows-based products, this will look familiar.

You select the widgets and gadgets you want in your dialog box from a tool palette. You "drag and drop," shifting components from the toolbar to the dialog box. (Technically, it's click, point, and drag, not really drag and drop, but everybody calls it drag and drop.)

With your components in place, you can right-click and select **Properties** from the popup menu. Figure 6.13 shows the Dialog Properties dialog box. You can see that its tabs include General, Styles, More Styles, and Extended Styles. You've got lots of style choices!

FIGURE 6.13   SETTING DIALOG BOX PROPERTIES.

Here, I've changed the title. All your changes are reflected in the Dialog editor, of course.

As we get into the individual dialog box components, we'll be paying close attention to the way all the style choices map to the Java Virtual Machine. The Developer Studio, of course, has a pronounced affinity for Windows.

Image Editor

Figure 6.14 shows the Bitmap editor. The image editing technology is shared by the bitmap, icon, and cursor editing tools. (The other resource tools, such as accelerators and string tables, are mostly data files to be filled with text.) If you are familiar with Microsoft Paint or any art editor, you'll recognize this technology.

Here you select a tool from the tool palette. The line tool draws lines, the filled-rectangle tool creates solid rectangles, and so on. You choose a color from the color palette, and then you draw by dragging your line, rectangle, or other shape onto the bitmap.

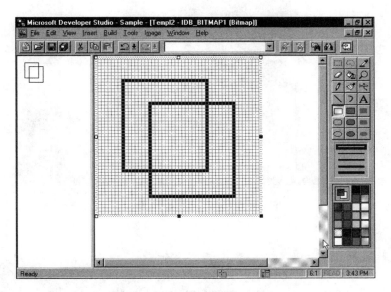

FIGURE 6.14   CREATING A BITMAP.

There are brushes that let you paint directly, a pencil for coloring pixels individually, and an eraser (my most heavily used tool).

The only trick to using the Image editor is to develop the habit of always choosing the tool and then the color (or vice-versa). Otherwise, you consistently find yourself drawing in the wrong color.

Figure 6.15 shows the cursor editor. You can see that the Image editor is there, too.

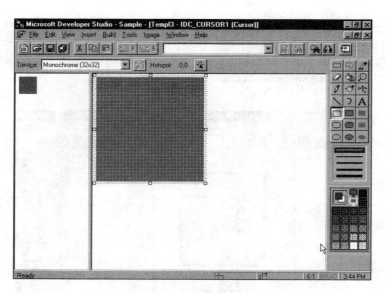

FIGURE 6.15   CREATING A CURSOR.

Debugger

The debugger is tightly integrated into the Developer Studio. Debug is just another option on the Build menu. When you run your program under the debugger, you have all the facilities you expect from a modern debugger. You can single-step, trace into routines, run to breakpoints, set watches, view data, and use all the techniques you know from most modern debuggers.

As you see in Figure 6.16, the debugger launches the Debug toolbar automatically and uses your source code as the basic control window.

Here I've shown two variables in the source and in the watch window. The first has been initialized, but the second hasn't been so it is showing random bits. You can drive the debugger from its toolbar with the mouse or from the keyboard using the same functionality.

Conveniently, you can edit the source in the source window as soon as you find your trouble spot. Then choose **Debug** from the Build menu again, and you get the same polite, "Shall I recompile this for you?" dialog box the **Shift+F5** gives you when you are running outside the debugger.

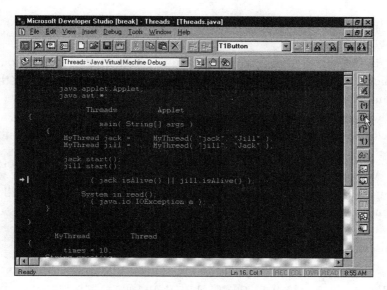

FIGURE 6.16 DEBUGGING AN APPLICATION.

We'll make more extensive use of the debugger in Chapter 15 when we use multi-threaded code.

Summary

That wraps up our tour of Visual J++'s main work areas.

We started with the main window, making it a complex mess. As we did this, we explored toolbars. We selected them, moved them around, and talked about customizing them.

We looked at docking windows, using them as added parts to the main window. We docked them all over, even outside the toolbars.

Then we went to the full-screen view, which I use almost all the time. We used what we learned to set up a sensible, working arrangement. I hope yours isn't identical to mine.

Then we went on the Workspace window and the InfoViewer. You'd already become a serious InfoViewer user in Chapter 4, when we explored the Java API. This time, we customized the keyboard so that **Alt+0** (or some other key that you picked) toggled the Workspace window on and off at our convenience.

In the next section we visited the text editor where I pointed out some topics that some people miss. I showed you how to get by without the horizontal scrollbar (and told you why you might want to). Then we played with the window splitter that hides just past the arrow in the scrollbar. Finally, we saw how the Finder tool on the General toolbar can substitute for the editor's Find dialog box.

We closed the chapter with three short previews of areas that we'll be using extensively in the remaining chapters. The Dialog editor will be our main tool in Chapters 8–13. The Image editor, a painting tool, is used to make bitmaps, icons and cursors. Finally, we saw the debugger, a set of tools integrated with the rest of the Developer Studio.

By now, you should be starting to think that Visual J++ isn't nearly as confusing as it was when you got started. In the next chapter, we'll be writing lots of code with it, or more exactly, we'll begin having Visual J++ write lots of code for us.

CHAPTER **7**

THE FRIENDLY WIZARDS

Visual J++ has Wizards that write code for you. The Java Applet Wizard writes the skeleton of a Java program that can be run, if you choose, as an application or as an applet. The Resource Wizard converts resources created with one of the resource editors (e.g., a dialog box) into Java Abstract Windows Toolkit (AWT) code. The Java Type Library Wizard, which we'll touch on only briefly, helps you use ActiveX components in your Java programs.

In this chapter we're going to explore the first two Wizards in depth. Before we begin, however, we're going to take a closer look at Java applications and applets. In Chapter 5 we used the applet's init() method in place of the application's main() method. That served its purpose, but it didn't tell the whole story.

After you've learned all about the applet's interface to its calling program, we'll go on to using the Java Applet Wizard to create code for us. We'll look at each of its options and, except for multi-threading which we'll postpone until Chapter 15, we'll explore their precise effects on the code the Wizard generates.

Our goal is to make you completely confident that you are writing the code, and the Wizard is your high-speed assistant. I don't want you to think that you are working for the Wizards. They're working for you.

When we've completed our deep look at the Applet Wizard's code, we'll go on to explore the Resource Wizard's operation, which is very simple, and its code, which is not simple. We'll be going into this Wizard's code in depth as we explore individual components in Chapters 8–13 so this look will be just a brief one.

Finally, I'll add remarks about the Java Type Library Wizard.

Applets and Applications

In Chapter 5, we built an applet by hand using the `init()` method as if it was an alternative to the application's `main()` method. That works, but it's not the whole story. In this section we'll look at the entire interface between the browser and the applet. That will clarify the relationship between applet and application, too.

First, to the operating system your Web browser is the `main()` program. It calls the browser and the browser, in turn, calls the applet. The browser can call four applet methods: `init()`, `start()`, `stop()`, and `destroy()`.

The `start()`, `stop()`, and `destroy()` methods are provided by the `Applet` class, so you can omit them if you like, or you can override them with your own code. We'll cover each one in turn.

The `init()` Method

The `init()` method is called when the browser processes the `<APPLET>` tag. It should do any initialization. It can serve as a complete substitute for the `main()` method of an application if you have a simple applet.

The `start()` and `stop()` Methods

As their names imply, `start()` and `stop()` control processing. The `start()` method is called after the browser calls `init()` (possibly after it completes loading the HTML page and associated files) and the `stop()` method is called before the browser calls `destroy()`.

The `start()` and `stop()` methods control the event loop. After `stop()` is called, your applet is effectively sleeping. A common browser implementation doesn't take advantage of these calls, but you should plan on them being fully used during the life of your applet. One use of these calls would be to start the applet when it is visible and to stop the applet when it is scrolled off the screen.

With the techniques we'll use, hanging all our application code off the event loop, your applets will be fully prepared for a complete implementation of `start()` and `stop()`.

The `destroy()` Method

The `destroy()` method is called before the HTML page is unloaded (when another page is loaded, or when the current page is reloaded). As always, Java handles all routine memory cleanup for you. In general you can omit a `destroy()` method.

There are applications, however, where you may have cleanup work. For example, you may want a chance to say something like `You did not complete this order. Cancel it?`

Overriding the `destroy()` method gives you the opportunity to ensure that everything is properly completed.

An Application Running an Applet

To run an applet, your application has to behave like a browser. That means that it should call the applet's `init()`, `start()`, `stop()`, and `destroy()` methods in turn. Here's class `Foo`'s `main()` method:

```
// Foo.main() written to drive an applet

    public void main( String args[] )
    {

        Foo f = new Foo();

        f.init();
        f.start();
        f.stop();
        f.destroy();

    }
```

This omits details, of course. You'll see the details of creating a main window and centering the applet in the window, for example, in the listings in this chapter.

You can include a `main()` method in an applet, but the browser doesn't know it exists and will not call it. If you have a `main()` such as the one in the last example, it will be a harmless bit of uncalled code when you run your class code as an applet.

Now you see how it's possible for the Applet Wizard to write code that can be both an applet and an application. You write the program with the applet's methods and then provide a `main()` that does the same calling job that a browser will do.

With that background, let's run the Applet Wizard and take a look at the code it generates.

The Applet Wizard

The job of the Applet Wizard is to write a skeleton program that will serve as both an application and applet (assuming you request it). I recommend that you do request both, even if your intention is simply to write an applet. Debugging is simplified if you have an application.

You can strip the application code from the applet as a last step before you make it available on the Web, but the savings are so small that you might not even bother with this step.

Running the Applet Wizard

To run the Applet Wizard, begin by choosing **File/New (Ctrl+N)** and choose **Project Workspace** from the New dialog box. That will launch the New Project Workspace dialog box, shown in Figure 7.1.

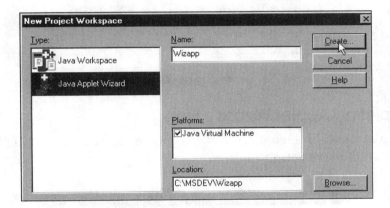

FIGURE 7.1 STARTING THE APPLET WIZARD.

Provide a name and adjust the location to suit yourself. The name will be the source and class names, as in all Java programming.

This will launch the Applet Wizard.

Completing Applet Wizard's Step 1

Step 1 is shown in Figure 7.2. I recommend that you always generate for both applet and application. For now, let's get a completely commented listing.

Once you get handy with this tool, you can press **Finish** as soon as you complete step 1. For now, though, let's go one step at a time. Pressing **Next** takes you to step 2.

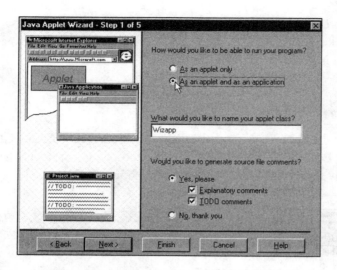

FIGURE 7.2 SPECIFYING CODE GENERATION BASICS.

Completing Applet Wizard's Step 2

Step 2, shown in Figure 7.3, lets you choose to get a sample HTML file and to adjust the default applet size.

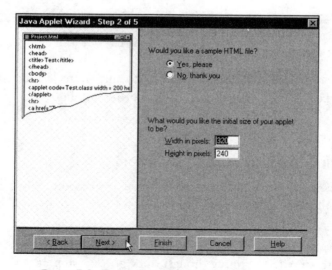

FIGURE 7.3 CHOOSING HTML AND THE DEFAULT SIZE.

Accept the HTML file. As you'll see, it's tiny and it's useful.

Completing Applet Wizard's Step 3

As you can see in Figure 7.4, step 3 lets you select multithreading sample animation images if you do want multithreading and some common event-handling methods.

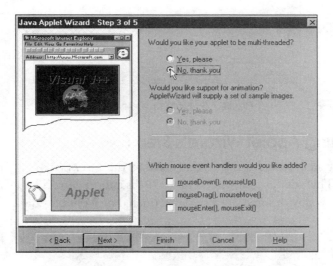

FIGURE 7.4 CHOOSING MULTITHREADING AND EVENTS.

We'll cover multithreading in Chapter 15. For now, leave it out of the generated code. We'll come back to the event handlers later in this chapter. Leave them out, too, for now.

Completing Applet Wizard's Step 4

Parameters can be passed to an application if it is run from a command prompt (as in a DOS session). You can also pass parameters from within the <APPLET> tag in an HTML page. This would be useful if you wanted to run the same applet from multiple HTML pages but with slight variations that depended on the page.

This is a powerful feature, but for now I'm leaving it entirely out, as Figure 7.5 shows.

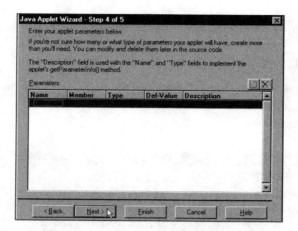

FIGURE 7.5 NOT USING PARAMETERS.

Completing Applet Wizard's Step 5

The last step provides the text string that the getAppInfo() method will return. This window, shown in Figure 7.6, is a text editor. The Wizard politely provides you with some suggested text (including a plug for the Wizard).

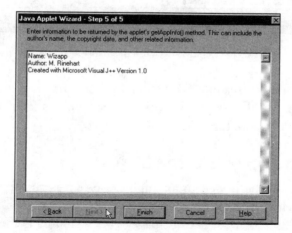

FIGURE 7.6 SUGGESTED TEXT IN A TEXT EDITOR WINDOW.

Edit the text to suit yourself, and then press **Finish**. This will launch the summary page you see in Figure 7.7.

FIGURE 7.7   THE APPLET WIZARD SUMMARIZES THINGS.

Pressing **Cancel** here gives you a final chance to stop the process before everything is written. Clicking **OK** launches the code generation process, which takes only a second or two.

The Wizard's Code

Now that you've run the Applet Wizard, you'll have four files written to the location you specified. If you named the project **Sample**, the files would be **Sample.java**, **SampleFrame.java**, **Sample.html**, and **Sample.mak**.

The first two are Java source programs. **Sample.java** holds all the applet code. Sample extends `java.applet.Applet`. **SampleFrame.java** holds the application code. In the AWT, a `Frame` object is a main window. Your `SampleFrame` class extends the `Frame` class.

We'll take a brief look at the HTML and the make files after we've looked at the Java code.

Reading the Fully Commented Code

Microsoft's full comments go a long way toward explaining exactly what the code is up to. (One could hope for a bit more white space, but let's not be picky.) In the listings that follow, I've added my own comments with my initials, this way:

```
// The Applet Wizard wrote this comment.
//mlr// I added this note.
```

The Applet Code

LISTING 7.1 FULLY COMMENTED APPLET CODE

```
//*************************************************************
// Wizapp.java:    Applet
//mlr// attn: Microsoft - date and time would be nice, no?
//
//*************************************************************
import java.applet.*;
import java.awt.*;
import WizappFrame;


//============================================================
// Main Class for applet Wizapp
//
//============================================================
public class Wizapp extends Applet
{
    // STANDALONE APPLICATION SUPPORT:
    // m_fStandAlone will be set to true if applet is run standalone
    //-------------------------------------
    boolean m_fStandAlone = false;

    // STANDALONE APPLICATION SUPPORT
```

```
//     The main() method acts as the applet's entry point when
//     it is run
// as a standalone application. It is ignored if the applet is
// run from
// within an HTML page.
//----------------------------------
public static void main(String args[])
{
    // Create Toplevel Window to contain applet Wizapp
    //----------------------------------
    WizappFrame frame = new WizappFrame("Wizapp");
      //mlr// this code comes in the next listing


    // Must show Frame before we size it so insets() will return
    // valid values
    //----------------------------------
    frame.show();
    frame.resize(frame.insets().left + frame.insets().right  + 320,
            frame.insets().top  + frame.insets().bottom + 240);
      //mlr//insets: the border size. This leaves the client
      //mlr//area set to the size you specified.
      //mlr//See Java API, Vol. 2, awt, Container.
      //mlr//Frame extends Window. Window extends Container.


    // The following code starts the applet running within the
    // frame window.
    // It also calls GetParameters() to retrieve parameter
    // values from the
    // command line, and sets m_fStandAlone to true to prevent
    // init() from
    // trying to get them from the HTML page.
    //----------------------------------
    Wizapp applet_Wizapp = new Wizapp();

    frame.add("Center", applet_Wizapp);
      //mlr//add() is also inherited from Container
    applet_Wizapp.m_fStandAlone = true;
    applet_Wizapp.init();
```

```
        applet_Wizapp.start();
}

// Wizapp Class Constructor
//-------------------------------------
public Wizapp()
{
    // TODO: Add constructor code here
}


// APPLET INFO SUPPORT:
//      The getAppletInfo() method returns a string describing
//      the applet's
// author, copyright date, or miscellaneous information.
 //-------------------------------------
public String getAppletInfo()
{
    return "Name: Wizapp\r\n" +
           "Author: Martin L. Rinehart\r\n" +
           "Created with Microsoft Visual J++ Version 1.0";
 } //mlr// "AB"+"CD" yields "ABCD"


// The init() method is called by the AWT when an applet is
// first loaded or
// reloaded.  Override this method to perform whatever
// initialization your
// applet needs, such as initializing data structures, loading
// images or
// fonts, creating frame windows, setting the layout manager,
// or adding UI
// components.
 //-------------------------------------
public void init()
{
        // If you use a ResourceWizard-generated "control creator"
        // class to
        // arrange controls in your applet, you may want to call
        // its
```

```
      // CreateControls() method from within this method. Remove
      // the following
      // call to resize() before adding the call to
      // CreateControls();
      // CreateControls() does its own resizing.
      //---------------------------------
   resize(320, 240);

      // TODO: Place additional initialization code here
}


// Place additional applet clean up code here.  destroy() is
// called when
// when you applet is terminating and being unloaded.
//-----------------------------------
public void destroy()
{
    // TODO: Place applet cleanup code here
}


// Wizapp Paint Handler
//-----------------------------------
public void paint(Graphics g)
{
}


//       The start() method is called when the page containing
//       the applet
// first appears on the screen. The AppletWizard's initial
// implementation
// of this method starts execution of the applet's thread.
//-----------------------------------
 //mlr//start() could be called repeatedly by the browser
public void start()
{
    // TODO: Place additional applet start code here
}
```

```
//          The stop() method is called when the page containing
//          the applet is
// no longer on the screen. The AppletWizard's initial
// implementation of
// this method stops execution of the applet's thread.
//-----------------------------------
public void stop()
{
}

    // TODO: Place additional applet code here

.end_code
```

The Application Code

The xxxFrame.java file holds the code needed to run the program as an application.

LISTING 7.2   FULLY-COMMENTED APPLICATION CODE

```
//**********************************************************
// WizappFrame.java:
//
//**********************************************************
import java.awt.*;

//==========================================================
// STANDALONE APPLICATION SUPPORT
//     This frame class acts as a top-level window in which the
//     applet appears
// when it's run as a standalone application.
//==========================================================
class WizappFrame extends Frame
{
    // WizappFrame constructor
    //-----------------------------------
    public WizappFrame(String str)
    //mlr// str param is the window's title
```

```
    {
        // TODO: Add additional construction code here
           super (str); //mlr// calls parent's constructor

    }


    // The handleEvent() method receives all events generated
    // within the frame
    // window. You can use this method to respond to window events.
    // To respond
    // to events generated by menus, buttons, etc. or other
    // controls in the
    // frame window but not managed by the applet, override the
    // window's
    // action() method.
    //-----------------------------------
    public boolean handleEvent(Event evt)
      { //mlr//that's Component.handleEvent() - Container extends
        //Component
        //mlr//we'll be getting deeply into events very soon
        switch (evt.id)
        {
            // Application shutdown (e.g. user chooses Close from the
            // system menu).
            //--------------------------------
            case Event.WINDOW_DESTROY:
                // TODO: Place additional clean up code here
                dispose();
                System.exit(0);
                return true;

            default:
                return super.handleEvent(evt);

        }
      }
    }
```

Using Just TODO Comments

Now that you've read the code, including those profuse comments, I suggest that you decline everything except the TODO comments in the future. I generated **Wizap2** to illustrate this. Except for the name, **Wizap2** is the same as the **Wizapp** in Listing 7.1, but it includes only the TODO comments, which provide a useful way to quickly locate spots to hook your own code.

The Applet Code

The **Wizap2.java** applet code is given in Listing 7.3.

LISTING 7.3 WORKING APPLET CODE

```
import java.applet.*;
import java.awt.*;
import Wizap2Frame;

public class Wizap2 extends Applet
{
    // STANDALONE APPLICATION SUPPORT:
    //      m_fStandAlone will be set to true if applet is run
    //      standalone
    //------------------------------------
    boolean m_fStandAlone = false;

    public static void main(String args[])
    {
        Wizap2Frame frame = new Wizap2Frame("Wizap2");

        // Must show Frame before we size it so insets() will return
        // valid values
        //----------------------------------
        frame.show();
        frame.resize(frame.insets().left + frame.insets().right +
            320, frame.insets().top + frame.insets().bottom +
            240);

        Wizap2 applet_Wizap2 = new Wizap2();
```

```java
    frame.add("Center", applet_Wizap2);
    applet_Wizap2.m_fStandAlone = true;
    applet_Wizap2.init();
    applet_Wizap2.start();
}

public Wizap2()
{
    // TODO: Add constructor code here
}

public String getAppletInfo()
{
    return "Marty's Marvelous App\r\n" +
           "\r\n" +
           "Sample text, Step 5 in JavaWiz\r\n" +
           "";
}

public void init()
{
    // If you use a ResourceWizard-generated "control creator"
    // class to
    // arrange controls in your applet, you may want to call
    // its
    // CreateControls() method from within this method. Remove
    // the following
    // call to resize() before adding the call to
    // CreateControls();
    // CreateControls() does its own resizing.
    //----------------------------------
    resize(320, 240);

    // TODO: Place additional initialization code here
}

public void destroy()
{
```

```
        // TODO: Place applet cleanup code here
   }

   public void paint(Graphics g)
   {
   }

   public void start()
   {
        // TODO: Place additional applet start code here
   }

   public void stop()
   {
   }

   // TODO: Place additional applet code here

}
```

The Application Code

As you see here, the **Wizap2Frame.java** (application) code is really very simple:

LISTING 7.4 WORKING APPLICATION CODE

```java
import java.awt.*;

class Wizap2Frame extends Frame
{
   public Wizap2Frame(String str)
   {
        // TODO: Add additional construction code here
        super (str);
   }

   public boolean handleEvent(Event evt)
   {
```

```
    switch (evt.id)
    {
        case Event.WINDOW_DESTROY:
            // TODO: Place additional clean up code here
            dispose();
            System.exit(0);
            return true;

        default:
            return super.handleEvent(evt);
    }
  }
}
```

The HTML Page

When you accept the HTML page (Listing 7.5), you get a very simple page. It's got two horizontal rules surrounding your applet. Below the second rule, a handy cross reference allows you to pop up your **.java** source code in the browser. (Did you ever think of a Web browser as a debugging tool?)

LISTING 7.5 AN HTML STUB PAGE

```
<html>
<head>
<title>Wizapp</title>
</head>
<body>
<hr>
<applet
    code=Wizapp.class
    width=320
    height=240 >
</applet>
<hr>
```

```
<a href="Wizapp.java">The source.</a>
</body>
</html>
```

The MAKE File

The final file is generated by the Developer Studio for compiling and linking your application. I've included it here for those who already know the MAKE programming language.

MAKE is a Unix utility designed for constructing program executables. Its basic job is to see which sources have changed since the executable was last constructed. It then gives operating system commands that recompile and link as required, based on the files that have changed.

Microsoft's version of MAKE is called NMAKE (Listing 7.6). If you've never used MAKE, I'll just note that comments begin with the # character. You'll probably want to respect the second line of this file.

LISTING 7.6 THE NMAKE PROGRAM

```
# Microsoft Developer Studio Generated NMAKE File, Format Version
4.20

# ** DO NOT EDIT **

# TARGTYPE "Java Virtual Machine Java Workspace" 0x0809

!IF "$(CFG)" == ""
CFG=Wizapp - Java Virtual Machine Debug
!MESSAGE No configuration specified.  Defaulting to Wizapp - Java
Virtual\
 Machine Debug.
!ENDIF

!IF "$(CFG)" != "Wizapp - Java Virtual Machine Release" &&
"$(CFG)" !=\
 "Wizapp - Java Virtual Machine Debug"
!MESSAGE Invalid configuration "$(CFG)" specified.
```

```
!MESSAGE You can specify a configuration when running NMAKE on this makefile
!MESSAGE by defining the macro CFG on the command line.  For example:
!MESSAGE
!MESSAGE NMAKE /f "Wizapp.mak" CFG="Wizapp - Java Virtual Machine Debug"
!MESSAGE
!MESSAGE Possible choices for configuration are:
!MESSAGE
!MESSAGE "Wizapp - Java Virtual Machine Release" (based on\
 "Java Virtual Machine Java Workspace")
!MESSAGE "Wizapp - Java Virtual Machine Debug" (based on\
 "Java Virtual Machine Java Workspace")
!MESSAGE
!ERROR An invalid configuration is specified.
!ENDIF

!IF "$(OS)" == "Windows_NT"
NULL=
!ELSE
NULL=nul
!ENDIF
################################################################
Begin Project
JAVA=jvc.exe

!IF  "$(CFG)" == "Wizapp - Java Virtual Machine Release"

# PROP BASE Use_MFC 0
# PROP BASE Use_Debug_Libraries 0
# PROP BASE Output_Dir ""
# PROP BASE Intermediate_Dir ""
# PROP BASE Target_Dir ""
# PROP Use_MFC 0
# PROP Use_Debug_Libraries 0
# PROP Output_Dir ""
# PROP Intermediate_Dir ""
# PROP Target_Dir ""
OUTDIR=.
```

```
INTDIR=.

ALL : "$(OUTDIR)\Wizapp.class" "$(OUTDIR)\WizappFrame.class"

CLEAN :
   -@erase "$(INTDIR)\Wizapp.class"
   -@erase "$(INTDIR)\WizappFrame.class"

# ADD BASE JAVA /O
# ADD JAVA /O

!ELSEIF  "$(CFG)" == "Wizapp - Java Virtual Machine Debug"

# PROP BASE Use_MFC 0
# PROP BASE Use_Debug_Libraries 1
# PROP BASE Output_Dir ""
# PROP BASE Intermediate_Dir ""
# PROP BASE Target_Dir ""
# PROP Use_MFC 0
# PROP Use_Debug_Libraries 1
# PROP Output_Dir ""
# PROP Intermediate_Dir ""
# PROP Target_Dir ""
OUTDIR=.
INTDIR=.

ALL : "$(OUTDIR)\Wizapp.class" "$(OUTDIR)\WizappFrame.class"

CLEAN :
   -@erase "$(INTDIR)\Wizapp.class"
   -@erase "$(INTDIR)\WizappFrame.class"

# ADD BASE JAVA /g
# ADD JAVA /g

!ENDIF

############################################################
```

```
# Begin Target

# Name "Wizapp - Java Virtual Machine Release"
# Name "Wizapp - Java Virtual Machine Debug"

!IF   "$(CFG)" == "Wizapp - Java Virtual Machine Release"

!ELSEIF   "$(CFG)" == "Wizapp - Java Virtual Machine Debug"

!ENDIF

################################################################
Begin Source File

SOURCE=.\Wizapp.java

!IF   "$(CFG)" == "Wizapp - Java Virtual Machine Release"

"$(INTDIR)\Wizapp.class" : $(SOURCE) "$(INTDIR)"

!ELSEIF   "$(CFG)" == "Wizapp - Java Virtual Machine Debug"

"$(INTDIR)\Wizapp.class" : $(SOURCE) "$(INTDIR)"

!ENDIF

# End Source File
################################################################
Begin Source File

SOURCE=.\WizappFrame.java

!IF   "$(CFG)" == "Wizapp - Java Virtual Machine Release"

"$(INTDIR)\WizappFrame.class" : $(SOURCE) "$(INTDIR)"

!ELSEIF   "$(CFG)" == "Wizapp - Java Virtual Machine Debug"

"$(INTDIR)\WizappFrame.class" : $(SOURCE) "$(INTDIR)"

!ENDIF
```

```
# End Source File
############################################################
Begin Source File

SOURCE=.\Wizapp.html

!IF  "$(CFG)" == "Wizapp - Java Virtual Machine Release"

!ELSEIF  "$(CFG)" == "Wizapp - Java Virtual Machine Debug"

!ENDIF

# End Source File
# End Target
# End Project
############################################################
```

Controlling the Code

In the generated code, you've seen lots of places where, for example, the name of the program is used. Java's a big fan of using your program name. In this section I'll note where some of your other choices control the code.

The Size of the Program

The size you specify is used in the applet code file's definition of the `main()` routine to create a `Frame` that is the appropriate size. Note that your frame's client area is the size you specify.

It's also used in this file in the definition of the `init()` method for the applet.

The Event Handlers

If you check any of the event handlers, you'll get code like this:

```
public boolean mouseDown(Event evt, int x, int y)
{
```

```
        // TODO: Place applet mouseDown code here
        return true;
    }

    public boolean mouseUp(Event evt, int x, int y)
    {
        // TODO: Place applet mouseUp code here
        return true;
    }
```

These are inserted in the applet source after the definition of the `stop()` method. As you see, it's still up to you to write the code that makes `mouseDown()`, for example, actually do something.

The Description String

The text editor's contents are written into the `getAppletInfo()` method. This immediately follows the class's constructor in the applet code file.

The Resource Wizard

The Resource Wizard is a powerful tool. In fact, it's a collection of powerful tools. It understands resources such as menus and dialog boxes. It understands dialog components such as buttons and list boxes. For each resource, it understands how to write Java code using the AWT. This means that it writes code to run these resources in Windows, Macintosh, and Unix environments, to name a few.

The operation of the Resource Wizard is even simpler than the operation of the Applet Wizard, but there's one important consideration that you must always bear in mind. The Developer Studio is common to several Microsoft products, including Visual C++. Microsoft's products, of course, write code that takes advantage of Microsoft's operating systems. Java is both broader and more limited by the fact that it is *not* a Windows-based product.

Our AWT is a cross-platform tool. The Developer Studio is a Windows tool. You'll find that there are surprisingly few limitations here, but you must keep focused on the fact that your Java code will run on Macs and Sparcs as well as on Windows. (Does this sound simple and obvious? Try to remember it as you run a Windows product under Windows on a Windows-based PC!)

Running the Resource Wizard

The Resource Wizard is not invoked from the File/New menu, as the Applet Wizard is. Rather, you find it under the Tools menu. Once you launch it, its operation is a simple, two-step process.

Figure 7.8 shows the first step. (If you don't have a resource file, don't worry. We'll start building them in the next chapter. You don't need to follow these steps online.)

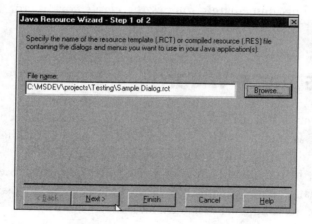

FIGURE 7.8 CHOOSING THE RESOURCE FILE IN STEP 1.

Figure 7.9 shows the second step. The resource editors, including the dialog editor, supply Windows-style names to your resources. Here you have an opportunity to change them to something more Java-flavored.

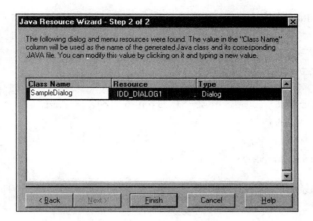

FIGURE 7.9 PROVIDING JAVA-STYLE NAMES IN STEP 2.

Once you've chosen your file and supplied names, click **Finish** and the Wizard goes to work. In less time than it takes to read this sentence, the Resource Wizard creates the Java code you need. Figure 7.10 shows the completion report that the Wizard provides.

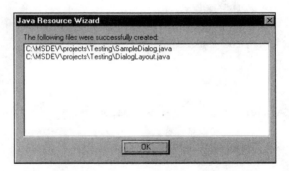

FIGURE 7.10 THE WIZARD'S JOB IS COMPLETE.

The Resource Wizard's Code

I created a simple dialog box with just a pair of checkboxes in addition to the default pair of buttons (OK and Cancel). Listing 7.7 shows the source code the Resource Wizard created. Don't worry about the parts you don't understand yet. We'll be working on this code in the next six chapters.

LISTING 7.7 THE DIALOG CODE

```
//mlr//Minor reformatting was done to reduce the line width
//----------------------------
// SampleDialog.java:
// Implementation of "control creator" class SampleDialog
//----------------------------
import java.awt.*;
import DialogLayout;

public class SampleDialog
{
    Container    m_Parent        = null;
    boolean      m_fInitialized = false;
    DialogLayout m_Layout;

    // Control definitions
     //--------------------------
    Button          IDOK;
    Button          IDCANCEL;
    Checkbox        IDC_CHECK1;
    Checkbox        IDC_CHECK2;

    // Constructor
     //--------------------------
    public SampleDialog (Container parent)
    {
        m_Parent = parent;
    }

    // Initialization.
     //--------------------------
    public boolean CreateControls()
    {
        // CreateControls should be called only once
         //--------------------------
        if (m_fInitialized || m_Parent == null)
```

```
   return false;

// m_Parent must be extended from the Container class
  //-------------------------
if (!(m_Parent instanceof Container))
   return false;

  // Since a given font may not be supported across
  // all platforms, it is safe to modify only the size
  // of the font, not the typeface.
  //-------------------------
Font OldFnt = m_Parent.getFont();
if (OldFnt != null)
{
     Font NewFnt = new Font(OldFnt.getName(),
                               OldFnt.getStyle(), 8);

   m_Parent.setFont(NewFnt);
}

  // All position and sizes are in dialog logical
  // units, so we use a DialogLayout as our layout
  // manager.
  //-------------------------
m_Layout = new DialogLayout(m_Parent, 186, 95);
m_Parent.setLayout(m_Layout);
m_Parent.addNotify();

Dimension size   = m_Layout.getDialogSize();
Insets     insets = m_Parent.insets();

  m_Parent.resize(
       insets.left + size.width  + insets.right,
       insets.top  + size.height + insets.bottom);

// Control creation
  //-------------------------
IDOK = new Button ("OK");
```

```
        m_Parent.add(IDOK);
        m_Layout.setShape(IDOK, 129, 7, 50, 14);

        IDCANCEL = new Button ("Cancel");
        m_Parent.add(IDCANCEL);
        m_Layout.setShape(IDCANCEL, 129, 24, 50, 14);

        IDC_CHECK1 = new Checkbox ("Check1");
        m_Parent.add(IDC_CHECK1);
        m_Layout.setShape(IDC_CHECK1, 42, 25, 41, 10);

        IDC_CHECK2 = new Checkbox ("Check2");
        m_Parent.add(IDC_CHECK2);
        m_Layout.setShape(IDC_CHECK2, 42, 42, 41, 10);

        m_fInitialized = true;
        return true;
    }
}
```

In addition to the code application-specific code shown in Listing 7.7, the Resource Wizard generates a second file named **DialogLayout.java**. This defines the `DialogLayout` class, which is Microsoft's preferred `LayoutManager`. We'll get to `LayoutManager` operations in more detail in the coming chapters. For now, the job of the `LayoutManager` is to arrange your components on screen at whatever size the user chooses.

Be aware that the Resource Wizard is going to create a fresh copy of **DialogLayout.java** each time you run it. It's small enough that you might not mind a separate copy in every project folder, but you don't, for example, want to include it in your backup procedures.

The Java Type Library Wizard

Microsoft's Component Object Model (COM) and its distributed object model, DCOM, support Type Libraries, which contain information about components. The Java Type Library Wizard helps you use this information to use `ActiveX` components with your Java programs.

I'm sure that most of you know there is a war going on for control of the Internet. It's a war between Microsoft's and Netscape's browsers and server programs. And it's a war between Microsoft's ActiveX technology and everyone else's OMG CORBA–based technology (Object Management Group, Common Object Request Broker Architecture), notably OpenDoc.

Most of the major players in the industry (IBM, Apple, Netscape, Sun) have aligned themselves with OpenDoc, against Microsoft. Most observers feel that Microsoft vs. everybody else is a fairly even fight.

Java will benefit greatly from a robust component aftermarket, just as Microsoft's Visual Basic (and, to a lesser extent, others such as IBM's Visual Age products) has benefited from being extended with components that do almost anything you can imagine.

With lots of components, even complex programming jobs become a matter of a little Net surfing to find what you need, a little coding to integrate, and you're ready to ship your applet or application.

We're not there, yet. As I write this, ActiveX controls are a Windows-specific tool. Combining ActiveX and Java gives you the worst of both worlds: you sacrifice Windows capabilities for Java's cross-platform power, and then you lose Java's cross-platform power by adding Windows-specific components.

A CORBA-based component technology, such as the OpenDoc initiative, may become available. Proponents say it will happen and that it will be truly cross-platform, as Java is. If you took Microsoft's side in this fight, you might point out that OpenDoc has support on the Macintosh, OS/2, and Unix, but none on Windows. Windows-based computers comprise, after all, about three-fourths of all the computers in the world, today.

OpenDoc will be available on Windows, we're promised. Similarly, ActiveX will be available on Unix and for the Macintosh, we're promised. By the time you read this, either or both of these promises may be realized, of course, but they aren't as I write this. After the supporting programs (e.g., code to run ActiveX on the Macintosh) become available, it will be some time before they are widely distributed so that you can count on the ones you need being available.

I've lived through lots of computer programming revolutions. The relational revolution took 15 years from drawing board to widespread acceptance. Object-oriented programming took almost as long. The "overnight" success of the Web has already taken about 5 years and its long-term impact is only beginning to be felt.

If Microsoft wins the war, it will be unlike anything Microsoft has done before. DCOM won't become a widespread success unless Microsoft throws its technology wide open. In fact, they'll have to copy Sun's brilliantly executed Java strategy, licensing everything to all comers at a modest price that encourages competition, not monopoly.

On the other hand, the anti-DCOM forces have never shown much ability to work together to counter a determined Microsoft. If IBM's DSOM or another OMG-based technology is to win, the players are going to have to beat Microsoft head on. They've never been able to do this yet.

What should you do? I recommend staying out of the war. Sooner or later we'll get true cross-platform capabilities based on ActiveX, OpenDoc, or something altogether different.

If I were going to place a bet, I'd bet that Java components will be written in Java, and they'll look very much like Visual Basic controls (nee VBX, then renamed OCX and now ActiveX) have looked. True distributed objects may happen, but they won't happen overnight. In the meantime, prewritten Java classes will flourish.

Who needs a war? We've got work to do and we've got a good language to do it in.

Summary

We began this chapter with a deeper look at the relationship between the browser and the applet. The browser calls an applet's `init()` routine once. It calls `start()` and `stop()` as needed (at a minimum, it calls `start()` once when the HTML page is loaded and `stop()` when the page is unloaded). It calls `destroy()` before changing to another HTML page.

We saw that you can create an application that runs an applet if the application calls these four methods in its `main()` routine. An application that works this way can also be used as an applet. Its `main()` routine will be ignored by a browser, but it will be harmless.

Using this background, we went on to run the Applet Wizard, which creates code that serves as both applet and application, using this technique. We took a careful look at the Java code this Wizard produces. We also took a quick look at the sample HTML page and the **.MAK** file that the Wizard builds.

We then looked at a run of the Resource Wizard. This is a very powerful tool, and its use is trivially simple. In the following chapters we'll use this tool as we work with the individual components it can create in Java code.

Finally, we considered the Java Type Library Wizard, a tool for integrating Microsoft COM objects (ActiveX controls) with your Java programs. I didn't recommend using either ActiveX or the competing CORBA-based components because at this point neither matches the cross-platform capabilities of Java.

In the next chapter, we're going to dive into Java programming, using the Java event model.

8

EVENTS AND BUTTONS

If you've slogged through the hard work this far, the good news is that you're at the top of the hill. Now we can get started on the way down. This is where it starts to come together, and we can have some fun, but first, we're going to need to learn more about events, which is our first topic.

It seems that all event-driven models share one trait: you have to know everything before you can do anything. In Visual J++, you have to master the IDE to do your work, and you have know the Java language. You've got both of these basics under your belt. Now you've got to learn about Java's event model. Then you'll have to master the Dialog editor and learn to integrate Applet Wizard code with Resource Wizard code. When we get to that, you'll have to study the LayoutManager interface, and then....

Well, you get the point. We could easily spend four more chapters on theory before you get to write some working code. If you're like me, you'd rather write code and learn the theory from actually practicing it. That's the way we'll work, but you'll have to accept the consequences: I'm going to do some things and just tell you to do it my way and not worry about why.

If you're like me, you'll very much want to know why. Have patience. This chapter and next five will explain all the mysteries. We won't cover all of Java or Visual J++, but you'll learn enough so that you'll be able to open Volume I or II of the API reference to find out what you need to know.

We'll start with one more section on theory, and then we'll start coding. It's the Java event model, including the `Event` and `Component` classes, that we'll be looking at.

Once you've got this theory in hand (or, as it works for me, sort of in hand but "I gotta write some code" or I'm never sure that I know it), we'll build some dialog boxes, populate them with buttons, and add event handlers that make the buttons come alive.

Handling Events

If you've done any Windows programming you'll probably be amazed by how simple Java makes event handling. If you like working very hard to do very little, you can always go back to writing C and interfacing directly with the Windows API.

On the other hand, if you are focused on getting results, you'll love the way Java simplifies things. But simplifying things is often a complicated thing to do and that's what this section explains.

First, the Abstract Windows Toolkit (AWT) handles the basic event loop. It starts the loop when needed, and terminates it when done. When it gets an event, it returns it to your `Component`'s `handleEvent()` method.

A `Component` is an *abstract* superclass. We'll cover the `abstract` keyword in Chapter 9. For now, you can't instantiate an object from an `abstract` class. You must extend the `abstract` class with a nonabstract class. The Button class, for example, extends the `Component` class. You can create `Button` objects, of course.

Each `Component`-based object has a `handleEvent()` method. If you don't override the `Component.handleEvent()` method, it will automatically call an appropriate handler. For example, `mouseDown()` is called when a mouse key is pressed with the mouse cursor in a `Component`.

(Actually, the Java event loop will combine a MOUSE_DOWN and a MOUSE_UP event inside a Button into a single call to the button's action() method. That simplifies your coding, but it complicates our discussion. For the moment, we'll just talk about mouseDown() handlers.)

If you're content to let a button respond to either a left or right mouse click, the only code you need to provide is a mouseDown() routine that calls whatever code you want to execute when the button is clicked.

The event loop is far more thorough than you'll want to be most of the time. For example, it would notify the button that it got focus, that the mouse entered the button, that the mouse was moved in the button, and so on. If you don't care about these activities, you don't write handlers for them. The event loop will tell the Button object about all of these events, but the Button object will, in essence, say, "I don't care."

Two things happen when the event loop finds an event that your Button or other object doesn't explicitly handle. First, if your Component-based object doesn't provide, for example, a mouseMove(), a mouseMove() method is found in the Component class. (Again, Button *extends* Component.) The inherited event handlers are all boolean methods that return false, which is event handler–speak for, "I didn't use this event."

The event handler doesn't give up when a Button (or whatever) returns false.

If a Button ignores a mouse event, the event loop will look "underneath" the button to find other components that might want to know. You've probably got a Frame or Window object under the Button object's screen real estate. This would be told, in turn, about the mouse's movement. If you haven't programmed a mouseMove() method for an underlying component, they will all say, "I don't care," (i.e., return false) when the event loop notifies them.

Eventually, the event loop will get a return message that says, "I handled the event," (true), or it will decide that nobody cares. In either case, it goes on to the next event.

All of this means that the only thing you have to code are event handlers for events that are relevant to your application or applet. If you have a status bar that displays messages appropriate to the component under the mouse cursor, for example, you'll need to respond to mouseEnter() (display the status bar message) and mouseExit() (blank the status bar message) events. If you don't have a status bar, you can simply ignore these events.

The Component Object

A Frame extends a Window by adding main window characteristics, such as the ability to have a menu (MenuBar object). A Window is a Container—an AWT component that contains other components. In turn, a Container object is a Component, which is any AWT object than can respond to events. The built-in Java event loop talks to Component objects, passing them Event objects as the user manipulates the Java program.

The Component class is abstract. You cannot instantiate a Component object. You build UI objects from classes that extend the Component class. Because there are no Component objects, there are no object data members of this class. There are, however, a long list of component methods.

Component Event-Handling Methods

Many of the component methods are event-related functions. All are boolean methods. A true value is returned if the component handles an event; false is returned otherwise. All these functions are designed to be overridden by your own code.

Because there is no Component object, all the event-handling functions of the Component class return false. This means two things.

First, you don't need to write an event handler unless your component wants to take action for an event. A Button, for example, normally ignores mouseEnter() and mouseExit() method calls. More exactly, the Button lets the default methods return false, telling the event loop that it did not handle these events.

Second, it also means that you are free to handle events in any way that suits your needs. You may wish to update a status bar message when the mouse is over a button. You could do that this way:

```
// Button code that updates a status bar message:

mouseEnter()
{
    setSBMsg( "Pushing this button will ..." );
}

mouseExit()
{
    setSBMsg( "" );
}
```

There is no built-in status bar object in Java, by the way. You'll need to create your own if you want one. You might start by extending the `TextArea` class.

You are free to handle events in less obvious ways. For example, an `Image` object displays a graphic. It's normally just displayed. You could, however, have it respond to a mouse click by providing a `mouseDown()` method. (Toolbars aren't native to Java. You could build one from Image objects that respond to `mouseDown()`.)

Component.handleEvent()

The `handleEvent()` method handles events, logically enough. It's job is to call the appropriate handler for each type of event. Think of it like this:

```
class Component extends Object
{
    ...
    public boolean handleEvent( Event evnt )
    {
        boolean handled_it = false;

        switch ( evnt.id )
        {
            case Event.MOUSE_DOWN:
                handled_it = mouseDown( evnt ... ); break;
```

```
      case Event.MOUSE_UP:
         handled_it = mouseUp( evnt ... ); break;


      ...

   }

   return handled_it


}

}
```

You can override handleEvent() if you like, but you won't need to very often. Remember that if you provide a mouseDown() method, it will be called by handleEvent(), and the Event object will be passed along. Your code can check the Event object for details (Which button was pressed? Is the **Ctrl** key down?), or it can ignore the Event object and just respond to a generic MOUSE_DOWN or other event type.

The Event Object

When the built-in event loop detects an event, it packages all the relevant information about that event into an Event object and passes that object to the component or components that should know about the event. The Event object lists what happened (e.g., keypress, mouse move), where the mouse was when it happened, what the status of the keyboard shifts was, and so on. We'll look first at the Event object's data members and then at the Event class's data members. Finally, we'll look at the Event's methods.

The Event Object's Data Members

The data members are completely documented in Volume 2 of the Java API online reference. Here, I'll mention some of the more important ones that you'll work with.

The id of the Event tells you what type of event occurred. (See "The Event Class's Data Members" for a categorical listing of id values.) You could use it this way:

```
// user pressed a mouse button?
    if ( evnt.id == evnt.MOUSE_DOWN ) ...
```

The key data member identifies the key that was pressed in keystroke events.

The modifiers integer combines the shift (**Shift**, **Ctrl**, **Alt** and meta) status of the keyboard.

The target is the `Object` over which the event occurred. Of course, everything in Java is an `Object`. You can use the `instanceof` operator to if you want to know more. For example:

```
// mouse over a Button?
    if ( evnt.target instanceof Button ) ...
```

The when data member is the Java-style time stamp of the event. It's the number of milliseconds elapsed since January 1, 1970 at the time of the event.

Finally, the `x` and `y` members are integers that give the position of the mouse when the event occurred.

The Event Class's Data Members

All the Event class's data members (as opposed to the individual Event object's data members) are *final static* values.

The keyword `static` qualifies data members and methods as belonging to the class, not to individual objects. The keyword `final` tells the compiler that a component cannot be changed, which lets the compiler generate more efficient code. A `final` method cannot be overridden. A `final` variable's value cannot be changed. This means that a `final` variable is a constant.

If you combine these two keywords, you can attach constants to a class as data members. This lets the compiler generate the best possible code because it knows that the value is a constant. It also means that you don't have to worry about name conflicts with constants in other classes.

The final static data declaration has one more implication: these data members will look funny to newcomers to the Java language. Consider this class declaration:

```
class Myclass
{
    int int1
    public int int2
    final static int int3
    ...
}
```

When you want to use the value of int3, you prefix it with the class name, or with an object name, as always:

```
Myclass m = new Myclass();

... = m.int3        // or:
... = Myclass.int3
```

Both forms are equivalent, and both evaluate to the constant value assigned to int3. C programmers do the same thing with #define statements, which have a very different feel but are functionally identical. C++ programmers call a constant const, which also achieves the same effect. (This is a very rare instance in which C++ is more direct than Java.)

You might declare that class more readably using a technique like this:

```
class Myclass
{
    // class constants:
        final static int int3

    // object data members:
        int int1
        public int int2
    ...
}
```

The events that the AWT handles are enumerated by `final static` `ints` attached to the `Event` class. You'll find them all detailed in Volume 2 of the Java API online documentation. They're listed alphabetically in that reference. I've organized them here by categories so you can see what types of events you can work with.

The event categories I define are:

- Mouse
- Scrollbar
- Window
- Keyboard
- List
- Focus
- Action

The mouse events are:

- `MOUSE_ENTER`—The mouse cursor entered a component
- `MOUSE_EXIT`—The mouse cursor exited a component
- `MOUSE_MOVE`—The mouse moved without a button pressed
- `MOUSE_DRAG`—The user moved the mouse with a button pressed
- `MOUSE_DOWN`—The user pressed a mouse button
- `MOUSE_UP`—The user released a mouse button

Scrollbar events are:

- `SCROLL_ABSOLUTE`—The scrollbar thumb was moved
- `SCROLL_LINE_UP`—The user clicked a scrollbar's up arrow
- `SCROLL_LINE_DOWN`—The user clicked a scrollbar's down arrow
- `SCROLL_PAGE_UP`—The user clicked a scrollbar's page up area
- `SCROLL_PAGE_DOWN`—The user clicked a scrollbar's page down area

Window events are:

- WINDOW_EXPOSE—A window has become exposed
- WINDOW_MOVED—A window was moved
- WINDOW_ICONIFY—A window should be made into an icon
- WINDOW_DEICONIFY—A window will be restored from an icon
- WINDOW_DESTROY—A window will be destroyed

Keyboard events are:

- KEY_ACTION—The user pressed an action key
- KEY_ACTION_RELEASE—The user released the action key
- KEY_PRESS—The user pressed a non-action key
- KEY_RELEASE—The user released a non-action key

List events are:

- LIST_SELECT—The user selected a list choice
- LIST_DESELECT—The user deselected a list choice

Focus events are:

- GOT_FOCUS—The component got focus
- LOST_FOCUS—The component lost focus

Action events are:

- ACTION_EVENT—The user triggers an action
- LOAD_FILE—A file is loaded
- SAVE_FILE—A file is saved

In addition to these events, the following named constants signify that the corresponding key has been pressed:

- UP, DOWN, LEFT, RIGHT
- PGUP, PGDN, HOME, END
- F1, F2, ..., F12

The keyboard's shift status and **Alt**, **Ctrl**, and meta keys are signaled as down or pressed by:

- SHIFT_MASK—**Shift** key is pressed
- ALT_MASK—**Alt** key is pressed
- CTRL_MASK—**Ctrl** key is pressed
- META_MASK—The meta key is pressed

These masks are positive integers, each with a single bit set, so they can be ORd together into the Event object's modifiers field. That field can be examined with bitwise ANDs and ORs to check these values. There are Event methods for the most common shift status. You'll need to go straight to the modifiers field for combinations (e.g., **Ctrl+Shift**):

```
// was a shift key pressed?
if ( (evnt.modifiers || evnt.SHIFT_MASK) > 0 ) ...
```

The Event Class's Methods

Except for using the toString() method for full generality, and using the paramString() method for debugging, you may never use an Event method.

If you care about the keyboard's shifts, you may find it convenient to use one or more of controlDown(), metaDown(), and shiftDown(). These are booleans that return true if the corresponding **Shift** was pressed when the event occurred.

Using Component Classes

Classes that inherit from an AWT class work beautifully with the AWT event model. At first you may think it seems odd to create a class that will have exactly one object instantiated, but that's often the best and simplest way to write Java programs. Consider this example:

```
class OKButton extends Button
{
    public boolean mouseDown( Event e ... )
    {
        ... // code here executed on click over OK button

        return true;
    }
}
```

This class will ignore all events except for mouse button presses over the OK button. (Presumably, you will instantiate exactly one of these buttons for a form.) This class's `mouseDown()` method will be called when the user clicks the **OK** button. It will return `true` ("I handled it") to the event loop when the button is clicked, and `false` otherwise.

And this is all the code you need!

The event loop is built into Java. The switch that calls your `mouseDown()` routine is built into the `Component` class. When you instantiate a button, you'll call the constructor for the `Button` class. The generic button class provides the tools to assign a button label, size and position the button and so on. You only program the specific behavior triggered by the particular button and put that behavior in the appropriately named method in a class pertinent to a particular button.

Ready to try some action programming? Let's get to it!

Programming Frames and Buttons with Events

Let's start with an application/applet combination generated by the Applet Wizard. Begin with **File/New** (or **Ctrl+N**) and choose **Project Workspace**. Then choose **Applet Wizard** and use a name that includes an initial capital letter, so it will be a standard Java class and source file name (mine's **Chp08**). Make these entries in the Applet Wizard:

1. Choose both applet and application; get just TODO comments.
2. OK as is.
3. Don't choose multithreading; do choose mouseUp/Down events; (Finish possible here).
4. OK as is.
5. Edit if you want; Finish.

You should now have a project workspace open with your new **Chp08java** (if you're not writing a book, pick a better name!) ready to run.

Launching a Frame

Open your **Chp08.java**. Press **Ctrl+F5** to build and run the applet. This will launch a nearly null applet in Internet Explorer. Close the **Explorer** and choose **Build/Settings**. Select the **Debug** tab, and make the change shown in Figure 8.1.

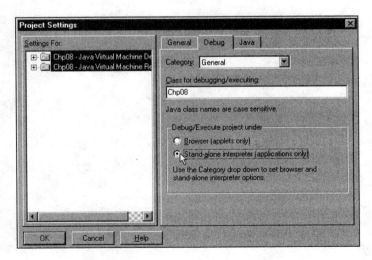

FIGURE 8.1 CHOOSING TO DEBUG AS AN APPLICATION.

This will switch from Internet Explorer to **JVIEW.EXE** for debugging. **JVIEW** is much smaller, so it is faster, which you'll appreciate as you debug applets. Press **Ctrl+F5** again and you should get a nice `Frame` launched in **JVIEW.EXE**, as shown in Figure 8.2.

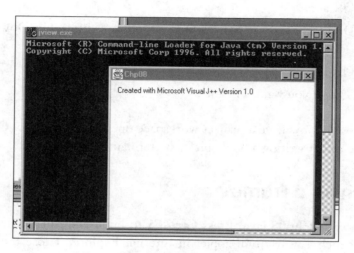

FIGURE 8.2 OUR `Frame` IS LAUNCHED.

My code, through this step, is shown in Listing 8.1. Be sure that your code is similar; we'll be building on this program base for the rest of this chapter.

LISTING 8.1 APPLICATION FOR LAUNCHING A FRAME

```
import java.applet.*;
import java.awt.*;
import Chp08Frame;

public class Chp08 extends Applet
{
    // STANDALONE APPLICATION SUPPORT:
    //      m_fStandAlone will be set to true if applet is run
standalone
    //-------------------------------------
```

```
boolean m_fStandAlone = false;

public static void main(String args[])
{
    Chp08Frame frame = new Chp08Frame("Chp08");

    // Must show Frame before we size it so insets() will return
    // valid values
    //-----------------------------------
    frame.show();
      frame.hide();
    frame.resize(frame.insets().left + frame.insets().right  +
          320, frame.insets().top  +
          frame.insets().bottom + 240);

    Chp08 applet_Chp08 = new Chp08();

    frame.add("Center", applet_Chp08);
    applet_Chp08.m_fStandAlone = true;
    applet_Chp08.init();
    applet_Chp08.start();
      frame.show();
}

public Chp08()
{
    // TODO: Add constructor code here
}

public String getAppletInfo()
{
    return "Name: Chp08\r\n" +
          "Author: Martin L. Rinehart\r\n" +
          "Created with Microsoft Visual J++ Version 1.0";
}

public void init()
{
```

```
        // If you use a ResourceWizard-generated "control creator"
        // class to
        // arrange controls in your applet, you may want to call
        // its
        // CreateControls() method from within this method. Remove
        // the following
        // call to resize() before adding the call to
        // CreateControls();
        // CreateControls() does its own resizing.
        //----------------------------------
    resize(320, 240);

        // TODO: Place additional initialization code here
    }

    public void destroy()
    {
        // TODO: Place applet cleanup code here
    }

    public void paint(Graphics g)
    {
        g.drawString(
          "Created with Microsoft Visual J++ Version 1.0", 10, 20);
    }

    public void start()
    {
        // TODO: Place additional applet start code here
    }

    public void stop()
    {
    }

    public boolean mouseDown(Event evt, int x, int y)
    {
        // TODO: Place applet mouseDown code here
        return true;
```

```
    }

    public boolean mouseUp(Event evt, int x, int y)
    {
        // TODO: Place applet mouseUp code here
        return true;
    }

    // TODO: Place additional applet code here

}
```

Adding a Button

To understand what the `Button`'s doing, we're going to need to take a look at events in real time. Fortunately, that's easy because the Applet Wizard was kind enough to write skeleton `mouseDown()` and `mouseUp()` methods for our applet. Bear in mind that these are for the applet—they report mouse events within the client area of our `Frame`.

Reporting Mouse Events In the Frame

Add a `System.out.println()` call to each of these methods, reporting this way:

```
    public boolean mouseDown(Event evt, int x, int y)
    {
        // TODO: Place applet mouseDown code here
        System.out.println( "Mouse Down " ); //      <- ADD!
        return true;
    }

    public boolean mouseUp(Event evt, int x, int y)
    {
        // TODO: Place applet mouseUp code here
        System.out.println( "            and Up " ); // <-!
        return true;
    }
```

Compile and test this. You'll see that the standard output is directed to the **JVIEW.EXE** window. As you click the mouse, you'll see the appropriate reports on the mouse's button status.

Adding an OKButton Class

Now let's add that button. Begin by adding an OKButton class to the end of the source file. Mine looks like this:

```
class OKButton extends Button
{
    public boolean action( Event e, Object o )
    {
        System.out.println("Button click");
        return true;
    }
}
```

When we get this running, you'll see what the action() method does. The event loop will see that mouse button press in a Button, and it will wait for a corresponding button release. When it gets both press and release, it calls action(). It does all sorts of processing for you. When this is running, try things like pressing the mouse down inside a button, sliding outside, and releasing the mouse.

If you're uncomfortable about creating a whole class to create a single object, be assured that this isn't just the easiest way to write this code. It's also the most efficient. We'll look more closely at how this works in Chapter 11.

Adding an OKButton Object

For now, let's create a button and add it to our form. Exactly as the Wizard's TODO comment suggests, add this new initialization code. While you're there, comment out the line in the paint() method.

```
    // TODO: Place additional initialization code here
    OKButton okb = new OKButton(); // <- NEW!
```

```
        okb.setLabel( "    OK    " );  // <- NEW!
        add( okb );                    // <- NEW!
}

public void destroy()
{
    // TODO: Place applet cleanup code here
}

public void paint(Graphics g)
    {   // COMMENT OUT NEXT LINE!
        // g.drawString(" ...
    }
```

Got those changes? Run them, and see what happens. Figure 8.3 shows me running the new program.

FIGURE 8.3 CLICKING IN A **Frame.**

The setLabel() method sets a button's label, as you would expect. The button's default size is taken from the length of the label string, which is why I've used some blank padding. The add() method puts the button into the LayoutManager. We'll begin talking about LayoutManagers in Chapter 10. For now, try resizing your Frame when your application is running. You'll see that the button stays centered near the top of the client area.

Got that? `LayoutManagers` are complicated and immensely useful. For now, we're using the default.

Experimenting With the OKButton

After you've resized enough to see what happens to your button, add a `mouseDown()` method to the `OKButton` class. Copy the one from your applet and then change the output line to report something like "Button down." (You want to know which routine is reporting.) When you compile and run, you'll see that `mouseDown()` is never called inside the button.

The `action()` method replaces `mouseDown()` and `mouseUp()` events when the mouse cursor is inside a button. The built-in event loop handles this combination. Then it calls `action()` with both the event and the object in which the event occurred. If you've written a one-object extending class, you won't need to look at the `Object`. It's the `this` in your method.

Test some strange mouse sequences. Press the mouse button inside the `Button` object. Slide the mouse cursor off the button and release the mouse button. What happens? What would you want to happen?

I'll think you'll agree that Java is going a long way to take the pain out of writing event-driven interface code.

Adding a Second Button

The Dialog editor default is a dialog box with OK and Cancel buttons. Let's add a Cancel button to our program. While we're at it, let's make it actually exit the frame, as if this were a dialog box.

Begin by creating a `CancelButton` class. Mine's shown here:

```
class CancelButton extends Button
{
    public boolean action( Event e, Object o )
    {
        System.exit(0); // Return errorlevel code
        return true;
```

```
        }
}
```

The return true will never be reached, but the compiler requires it. I always put the return true in an event handler. Actually, I insert the entire event handler skeleton (make a little file that has a nice, generic skeleton, and insert it whenever you need one) before I add any action code.

The only other thing you need to do is to create and add an instance of the CancelButton class. The last three lines of the following fragment show what I've added.

```
// TODO: Place additional initialization code here
OKButton okb = new OKButton();
okb.setLabel( "     OK     " );
add( okb );

CancelButton cb = new CancelButton();
cb.setLabel( " Cancel " );
add( cb );
```

Ready? When you run this improved version, you'll see that you start with a pair of buttons, as Figure 8.4 shows.

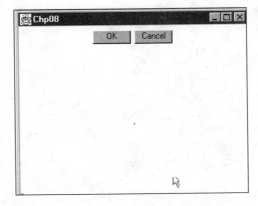

FIGURE **8.4 FlowLayout** SHOWS TWO BUTTONS.

Try making your window narrower. Figure 8.5 shows how the FlowLayout manager handles these components.

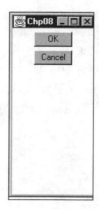

FIGURE 8.5   FlowLayout REARRANGES BUTTONS.

Of course, when you click **Cancel**, you're canceled!

Listing 8.2 shows the full program to this point.

LISTING 8.2   AN OK AND CANCEL APPLICATION

```
import java.applet.*;
import java.awt.*;
import Chp08Frame;

public class Chp08 extends Applet
{
    // STANDALONE APPLICATION SUPPORT:
    //      m_fStandAlone will be set to true if applet is run
    //      standalone
    //------------------------------------
    boolean m_fStandAlone = false;

    public static void main(String args[])
    {
        Chp08Frame frame = new Chp08Frame("Chp08");
```

```
// Must show Frame before we size it so insets() will return
// valid values
//---------------------------------
frame.show();
   frame.hide();
frame.resize(frame.insets().left + frame.insets().right  +
     320, frame.insets().top  +
     frame.insets().bottom + 240);

Chp08 applet_Chp08 = new Chp08();

frame.add("Center", applet_Chp08);
applet_Chp08.m_fStandAlone = true;
applet_Chp08.init();
applet_Chp08.start();
   frame.show();
}


public Chp08()
{
   // TODO: Add constructor code here
}


public String getAppletInfo()
{
   return "Name: Chp08\r\n" +
        "Author: Martin L. Rinehart\r\n" +
        "Created with Microsoft Visual J++ Version 1.0";
}


public void init()
{
    // If you use a ResourceWizard-generated "control creator"
    // class to
    // arrange controls in your applet, you may want to call
    // its
    // CreateControls() method from within this method. Remove
    // the following
```

```
        // call to resize() before adding the call to
        // CreateControls();
        // CreateControls() does its own resizing.
        //----------------------------------
    resize(320, 240);

    // TODO: Place additional initialization code here
    OKButton okb = new OKButton();
    okb.setLabel( "    OK    " );
    add( okb );

    CancelButton cb = new CancelButton();
    cb.setLabel( " Cancel " );
    add( cb );
}

public void destroy()
{
    // TODO: Place applet cleanup code here
}

public void paint(Graphics g)
{
    // g.drawString(
        "Created with Microsoft Visual J++ Version 1.0",
        10, 20);
}

public void start()
{
    // TODO: Place additional applet start code here
}

public void stop()
{
}
```

```java
public boolean mouseDown(Event evt, int x, int y)
{
    // TODO: Place applet mouseDown code here
    System.out.println( "Mouse Down " );
    return true;
}

public boolean mouseUp(Event evt, int x, int y)
{
    // TODO: Place applet mouseUp code here
    System.out.println( "            and Up " );
    return true;
}

// TODO: Place additional applet code here

}

class OKButton extends Button
{
    public boolean action( Event e, Object o )
    {
        System.out.println("Button click");
        return true;
    }
}

class CancelButton extends Button
{
    public boolean action( Event e, Object o )
    {
        System.exit(0); // Return errorlevel code
        return true;
    }
}
```

Summary

We began this chapter with a long look at Java's event model. The underlying concepts are probably new to you. There's a lot to understand, but the effect of all of it is to make your programming amazingly simple.

We started with a look at the `Component` class. This is an abstract class (you can extend it, but you can't instantiate a `Component` object). It provides the methods that any GUI component will need to respond to events.

You learned that the event loop is built into the Java Abstract Windows Toolkit (AWT). It calls a `handleEvent()` routine in the component where the event occurred. The `handleEvent()` method, in turn, calls methods such as `mouseDown()`. The only event-handling code that you have to write is, for example, a `mouseDown()` routine that takes the appropriate action.

In some cases you'll find it easier to override a Java `Component`'s built-in `eventHandler()`, but that isn't common. In general, you'll want to extend a class such as `Button` to create a class that instantiates a single button. In that one-object class, you simply write routines such as a `mouseDown()` handler.

After looking at the `Component` class, we turned to a class that was full of data members, the `Event` class. Most of those members were `final static` data, or class-specific constants. They enumerated, among other things, all the values of the `Event`'s `id` member, which tells `handleEvent()` that an event such as `MOUSE_DOWN` has occurred.

With that background, we turned our attention back to programming. In the forthcoming chapters, we'll have a lot more programming and less theory. Here, we used Applet Wizard code to launch a `Frame` in an application (running under **JVIEW.EXE**, not the much larger Web browser).

After we launched our `Frame`, we added `mouseDown()` and `mouseUp()` methods that used standard output (to **JVIEW.EXE**'s window) to report these events. Each handler was a simple call to `System.out.println()` added to the Wizard-generated code.

Then we added an `OKButton` class with an `action()` method. The `action()` method is called when the event loop detects a `MOUSE_DOWN` followed by a `MOUSE_UP` within a `Button` object. We used it to report the button clicks.

Three lines of code were enough to create this button in the applet's `init()` method. One used the `new` operator to create an `OKButton`. The next set the "OK" label, and the third added it, courtesy of the layout manager, to the `Frame`.

Finally, we went on to add a second button class and object, a `CancelButton`. You saw that the layout manager handled arranging these buttons as you resized the form and it took no loop programming, or event switch programming, to create these buttons.

In Chapter 9 we'll take a closer look at the `Window` and `Frame` classes, and we'll add a `MenuBar` object with attached `Menu` objects. We'll use the Resource Editor to simplify the coding.

CHAPTER 9

FRAMES, WINDOWS, AND MENUS

In the last chapter you found that adding a lot of knowledge about events let you add a minimal amount of code to program for events. In this chapter we'll find much the same thing. Once you understand the `Frame` and `Menu` classes (actually, a family of menu-related classes) you'll be able to complete a menu system inside a main window with almost no code at all.

We'll start with a look at the `Frame` and `Window` classes. Both are extensions of the abstract `Container` class, which we'll also examine. Then we'll write some code that looks inside the `handleEvent()` method in a `Frame`.

From there we'll go on to the `Menu` and its related classes. A `MenuBar` serves as our main menu. It's populated with `MenuItem` objects. Commonly, the `MenuItems` in a `MenuBar` are actually drop-down `Menu` objects. These, in turn, are populated with additional `MenuItem` objects, which can also be further `Menu` objects.

These sets of menus, beginning with a `MenuBar`, are simple to draw using the Menu editor, one of the resource editors that we'll be using for visual programming.

Once you've created a picture of your menu system, the Resource Wizard will write the necessary code. It writes quite a bit of code because Java menus are built in Java code. (Windows programmers are used to creating a compiled resource, which is not a source-code item.) It takes only a few lines of Java to link the Resource Wizard's menu code to the Applet Wizard's application code.

Once you've created a menu system, you have to tap into the event loop in the `Frame`, to respond to menu selections. This is the last topic we'll look at. When you do this, you've completed a main window with a menu system.

We'll begin by looking at the windowing hierarchy.

Frames, Windows, and Containers

We've already used the abstract `Component` class. It's the one that every object that responds to events extends. The `Container` is another abstract class. It extends the `Component` class, adding the logic needed when a window component contains other window components.

The Window class extends the `Container` class to build functioning (nonabstract) `Window` objects. In turn, the `Frame` class extends the `Window` class to create `Frame` objects, which are main program windows. A program (applet or application) can begin with a `Frame` that includes a menu system. Its child windows and dialog boxes will probably be built with `Window` objects.

We'll start looking at these classes from the top down, beginning with `Frame`. In these discussions, I'll summarize the capabilities of each class so that you'll know what to expect. As you code, you'll want to refer to the details in the online Java API reference, Volume 2, for the `java.awt` package.

The Frame Class

The `Frame` class is the main window. You'll want to begin most applets and applications with a `Frame`. Conveniently, the Applet Wizard writes the basic `Frame`-related code for you. Even if you don't need a menu system, the `Frame` object handles other details, such as establishing the cursor type.

The Frame's Fields

The data members, or fields, of the `Frame` class are all `final static` (constant) `int` fields. They are used by the `setCursor()` method. The available choices are:

- `DEFAULT_CURSOR`
- `HAND_CURSOR`
- `CROSSHAIR_CURSOR`
- `MOVE_CURSOR`
- `TEXT_CURSOR`
- `WAIT_CURSOR`
- `xx_RESIZE_CURSOR`

The `xx` in `xx_RESIZE_CURSOR` is a compass direction that identifies the edge or corner of a window where the resizing is taking place. Clockwise from the top, the choices are `N`, `NE`, `E`, `SE`, `S`, `SW`, `W`, and `NW`.

The Frame's Constructors

You can create an untitled frame, passing no parameters, or you can add the title, passing a single `String` object, this way:

```
Frame main = new Frame( "My Cool App" );
```

By the way, that use of white space inside parentheses is a habit I adopted several years (and languages) ago. I use it to help improve readability. I leave a space inside the first level of parentheses, omit the space at the next level, leave a space at the third level, and so on. (Beyond three levels, I try to recode with less nesting.) Consider these examples:

```
x = foo( arg1 )
y = bar( arg1, foo(arg2) )
z = toodeep( arg1, bar(arg2, foo( arg3 )) )
```

This style makes it easier to visually match the opening and closing parenthesis pairs. It makes no difference to the compiler, of course.

The Frame's Methods

The important methods of the `Frame` class are mostly `getX()` and `setX()` methods. `X` can be `CursorType`, `MenuBar`, or `Title`. The `isResizable()` and `setResizable()` methods perform the same function for the boolean resizable characteristic.

When you look at methods in the online API documentation, ignore the `getNotify()` and `setNotify()` methods, as well as all the methods that contain either `toolkit` or `peer`. These are vital for the pioneers who implement Java, but they aren't necessary for those of us who use the language.

The `Frame` is a simple class, as you can see, but don't stop here. `Frame` extends `Window`, which extends `Container`, which extends `Component`. You've got to understand the hierarchy or you'll miss key points. For example, the `Window` (which means the `Frame`, too) is invisible when you create it. You have to call its `show()` method when you want to see it.

The Window Class

Used by itself, a `Window` is a modal dialog window. `Frame` extends `Window`, overriding the modal characteristic. Your program must have a `Frame` to create a standalone Window.

The `Window` class has no fields.

The Window Class's Constructor

You create a `Window` by passing it the `Frame` parent, this way:

```
Frame f = new Frame("Main App");

Window modal_dialog = new Window( f );
```

The Window Class's Methods

There are four important methods in this class:

- show()
- pack()
- toBack()
- toFront()

When you create a Window (including a Frame) it is not visible. You have to use the show() method to see the Window. The Window's show() method overrides the Component's show() method. The Window inherits hide() from the Component.

The pack() method uses the LayoutManager to arrange the components it contains—the Window is a Container object. We'll look more closely at the LayoutManager, beginning in Chapter 10.

Finally, toBack() and toFront(), as you would guess, move Window objects in an on-screen stack.

The Abstract Container Class

A Container is an AWT component that contains a group of other AWT components. It lets you add and remove individual components, and it includes that LayoutManager that will position the components when they are drawn on the screen.

The Container Is an Abstract Class

You'll use the constructor for a Window, Frame, or other class that extends Container because you cannot instantiate an object from an abstract class. An abstract class is used when you'll want to inherit common data members or methods from a class, but by itself, the extended class doesn't provide complete objects.

We've already seen that Container-derived objects and all other visible AWT components extend the abstract Component class that provides event-handling abilities. To make a class abstract, you simply add the `abstract` modifier to its declaration:

```
public abstract class Abclass
```

```
// or:
public abstract class Abclass extends Otherclass
```

The `abstract` class can provide whatever data members and methods you like. Well-designed, of course, the abstract class will add a specific functionality, as the `Component` and `Container` classes do.

You use the `abstract` modifier when you want the compiler to reject any attempt to instantiate an object of the `abstract` class. This error will be trapped by the compiler:

```
Container c = new Container(); // ERROR!
```

The Container Class's Methods

The `Container` class provides methods that add and remove components from a `Container`. The most important is `add()`, which we've already used to add a `Button` to a `Frame`.

The `insets()` method returns an `Insets` object. `Insets.left` is the number of pixels used by the border of the container on the left. The `Insets` object also has `Insets.top`, `Insets.right`, and `Insets.bottom` fields that hold the same values for the other edges. You'll use these to find or set the size of a `Container`'s client area.

We'll begin covering `LayoutManager`'s class methods in Chapter 10. The `getLayout()` and `setLayout()` methods let you check and change the `LayoutManager` associated with your `Container`.

We'll learn more about `preferredSize()` when we cover `LayoutManager` concepts in Chapter 10. In Chapter 12, we'll get to `Graphics` objects, which you'll need to make sense of the `paintComponents()` method.

And that brings us from theory to practice.

Tracking Events in a Frame

Normally, I'll introduce you to a class, and then we'll start using it in code. But we've already been using `Frame` objects because you can't do much with Java without a `Frame`. So here we'll dive into another aspect. We'll look at the `handleEvent()` traffic that takes place inside an `Applet` and a `Frame`.

Begin by making a new project workspace and using the Applet Wizard to create another application/applet combination skeleton. Don't include explanatory comments or multithreading code, and this time, don't include any of the event-handling methods.

When the Wizard has made your project workspace and your two source files, use the Build/Settings Debug page to switch from using the browser to viewing standalone, with **JVIEW.EXE**.

Now let's take a look at events that happen in the Applet.

Events in the Applet

I've added a simple `handleEvent()` routine, where the TODO comment suggests Applet code:

```
// TODO: Place additional applet code here

public boolean handleEvent( Event e )
{
    System.out.println( "Applet: " +
        e.toString() );
    return super.handleEvent( e );
}
```

The line that calls `System.out.println()` uses the + operator to concatenate strings. `Events` have a `toString()` method that gives you a lot of data from the `Event` object. When we add the report from the `Frame`, you'll see why you need to include `Applet:` here.

The following line returns super.handleEvent(). Here `super`, a Java keyword, refers to the `Applet`. In general, `this` is the current object.

It's normally applied by default. Referring to `this.member` is what you do when you simply write `member`. Similarly, `this.method()` is the same as `method()`.

Referring to `super` specifies the member or method that belongs to the class `this` extends. Returning `super.handleEvent()` lets you trap events, take a look at them, and then have the other code do its work.

Figure 9.1 shows my `Frame` launched and busily reporting in **JVIEW.EXE**'s window. Events 501–506 are mouse events. Compile and run your own version to see what you get. If you move the mouse (or click or drag) you'll get `50?` events. If you press a key, you'll get `40?` events. Try resizing the `Frame`, dragging it by its titlebar, and whatever else you can think of.

FIGURE 9.1   THE **Frame** LAUNCHED AND REPORTING IN **JVIEW.EXE**.

The point I want to make here is that these are the events reported to the `Applet` class object. Next, we'll look into the events in the `Frame` object.

If you have trouble getting your results to match mine, the full file is shown in Listing 9.1.

LISTING 9.1   THE FULL <NAME>.JAVA FILE

```java
import java.applet.*;
import java.awt.*;
import Chp09Frame;

public class Chp09 extends Applet
{
    // STANDALONE APPLICATION SUPPORT:
    //      m_fStandAlone will be set to true if applet is run
    //      standalone
    //-------------------------------------------------------------
    boolean m_fStandAlone = false;

    public static void main(String args[])
    {
        Chp09Frame frame = new Chp09Frame("Chp09");

        // Must show Frame before we size it so insets() will return
        // valid values
        //-------------------------------------------------------------
        frame.show();
          frame.hide();
        frame.resize(frame.insets().left + frame.insets().right  +
                320, frame.insets().top  +
                frame.insets().bottom + 240);

        Chp09 applet_Chp09 = new Chp09();

        frame.add("Center", applet_Chp09);
        applet_Chp09.m_fStandAlone = true;
        applet_Chp09.init();
        applet_Chp09.start();
          frame.show();
    }

    public Chp09()
    {
        // TODO: Add constructor code here
```

```
    }

    public String getAppletInfo()
    {
        return "Name: Chp09\r\n" +
                "Author: Martin L. Rinehart\r\n" +
                "Created with Microsoft Visual J++ Version 1.0";
    }

    public void init()
    {
        // If you use a ResourceWizard-generated "control creator"
        // class to
        // arrange controls in your applet, you may want to call
        // its
        // CreateControls() method from within this method. Remove
        // the following
        // call to resize() before adding the call to
        // CreateControls();
        // CreateControls() does its own resizing.
        //--------------------------------------------------------
    resize(320, 240);

        // TODO: Place additional initialization code here
    }

    public void destroy()
    {
        // TODO: Place applet cleanup code here
    }

    public void paint(Graphics g)
    {
       g.drawString(
          "Created with Microsoft Visual J++ Version 1.0", 10, 20);
    }

    public void start()
    {
```

```
        // TODO: Place additional applet start code here
    }

    public void stop()
    {
    }

    // TODO: Place additional applet code here

    public boolean handleEvent( Event e )
    {
        System.out.println( "Applet: " +
            e.toString() );
        return super.handleEvent( e );
    }

}
```

Events in the Frame

Next edit your <name>Frame.java source file and add the call to
System.out.println() that you see here:

```
    public boolean handleEvent(Event evt)
    {
        // ADD THIS CALL:
        System.out.println( "Frame: " +
            evt.toString() );

        switch (evt.id)
```

If you're having trouble, Listing 9.2 shows the full file.

LISTING 9.2   THE FULL <NAME>FRAME.JAVA FILE

```
import java.awt.*;

class Chp09Frame extends Frame
{
```

```
public Chp09Frame(String str)
{
    // TODO: Add additional construction code here
    super (str);
}

public boolean handleEvent(Event evt)
{
    // ADD THIS CALL:
        System.out.println( "Frame: " +
            evt.toString() );

    switch (evt.id)
    {
        case Event.WINDOW_DESTROY:
            // TODO: Place additional clean up code here
            dispose();
            System.exit(0);
            return true;

        default:
            return super.handleEvent(evt);
    }
}
}
```

When you run the program with this report, you'll see that you are getting most events reported in the Applet also reported in the Frame. When we add a MenuBar, you'll see that the two handleEvent() routines can report very different happenings.

The Pane Class

Except for this quick mention, we're not going to cover the Pane class. You can study Pane objects, if you like, by using the Java API online documentation.

A `Pane` is the simplest `Container`. You can use `Pane` objects to divide a `Window` into separate panes, if you like. You can include `Pane` objects as a component contained in other `Pane` objects.

Even if you ignore the `Pane` class for now, as I'm doing, you'll be using a `Pane` inadvertently: the `Applet` class extends `Pane`, so an `Applet` is a `Pane`. (Insert your own puns here.) The `Applet` class is documented in Volume 2, but it's in the `java.applet` package, not `java.awt` where we've been looking at the other components.

Menu-Related Classes

Let's begin with a brief overview, and then we'll take a quick look at each of the individual classes.

The `MenuBar` class defines the menu that you see attached to the main window. Each item on this menu (File, Edit, etc.) is a `MenuItem` object.

A `MenuItem` can trigger an action, such as the Save item in the File menu. It can also be another drop-down menu. Typical `MenuItem` objects on the `MenuBar` are `Menu` objects.

The Menu class extends the `MenuItem` class. A `Menu` is a drop-down menu. Java also supports tear-off menus. It collects another group of `MenuItem` objects. These `MenuItem` objects can also be simple items or additional `Menu` objects.

Another class that extends the `MenuItem` is the `CheckboxMenuItem`. As you would guess, that's a `MenuItem` that you can check (or clear the checkmark) with a mouse click. I'll let you go on to use `CheckboxMenuItem` objects on your own. They're completely straightforward once you understand Java menus.

The last class in this set is the `MenuComponent`. It's an abstract class that is extended by all the other menu classes. If for some reason you want your program to be at odds with all the other programs the user knows, you can use the `getFont()` and `setFont()` methods of this class to do your mischief, but don't blame the result on me—I'm going to ignore this class.

The MenuBar Class

The MenuBar class has no fields, and its only constructor takes no arguments. The only method you're likely to need is the add() method. After you've built your menus, you attach them to the MenuBar this way:

```
// mfile is a file Menu
// medit is an edit Menu, etc.

// mb is your MenuBar

mb.add( mfile );
mb.add( medit );
...
mb.add( mhelp );
```

The only other method you're likely to use with a MenuBar is the Frame's setMenuBar() method, which is simple enough:

```
Frame f = new Frame( "Cool App" );

MenuBar mb = new MenuBar();
// attach Menu objects here, then:

f.setMenuBar( mb );
```

Can you think of a simpler way to do any of this? I can't.

When your program wants to get very sophisticated, changing menus dynamically in response to user actions, you'll find the necessary additional methods available in the MenuBar class. We'll deal with the simpler case in which you paint your menu structure, and it's fixed for each application.

The MenuItem Class

There are no fields in the MenuItem class, and the only constructor takes a String argument, which is the item's label. These are two examples:

```
MenuItem msave = new MenuItem( "&Save" );

MenuItem msepar = new MenuItem( "-" );
```

The ampersand (&) in the `String` goes before the letter that will be underlined, showing the user which letter to press to immediately invoke the item. The special string `"-"` identifies the `MenuItem` as a separator: a line used to group the other items visually.

You can use the methods `disable()` and `enable()` to control items that temporarily become inappropriate, such as a `Save` option when no file is open. The `enable()` method doesn't require an argument, but it allows a boolean. This code flips the enabled status:

```
// mi is a MenuItem

mi.enable( !mi.isEnabled() ); // flip status
```

The Menu Class

The `Menu` class extends `MenuItem`. A `Menu` is a drop-down menu attached to the `MenuBar`, or a popup menu triggered from another menu. This class has no fields, and its simpler constructor takes a label `String`, just as a `MenuItem` does. You can create a File pull-down menu this way:

```
Menu mfile = new Menu( "&File" );
```

The menu methods are straightforward. You can check the online documentation, or you can ignore them. The Resource Wizard knows all it needs to know to create the menus you paint.

The only thing about menus that the Menu editor and the Resource Wizard doesn't understand is that Java supports tear-off menus. Check the online documentation if you want to give these a try. If you can resist the temptation to hand-code tear-offs, you'll find that the Menu editor and Resource Wizard is a powerful combination.

Using the Menu Editor

If you've used any of the common GUI-based menu painters, you can probably use the Menu editor already. In this section we'll use the Menu editor to create this tree of menus:

```
MenuBar
    &File
        &New
        &Open
            &Text File
            &Presents
        -separator-
        &Save
        Save &As
        -separator-
        e&Xit
    &Edit
        Cu&t
        &Copy
        &Paste
    &Help
        &About
```

If you can, go ahead and create this menu tree and then skip ahead to the section titled "Using Menu Wizard Code." This section is for those who haven't used a tool such as this one.

Launching the Menu Editor

To launch the menu editor, choose **Insert/Resource**. That launches the Insert Resource dialog box. As Figure 9.2 shows, choose **Menu** from this dialog box.

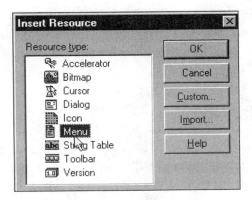

FIGURE 9.2 CHOOSING A MENU RESOURCE.

That choice launches the Menu editor. It's a remarkably simple tool, but the face it presents doesn't really give the first-time user a clue. It's shown in Figure 9.3.

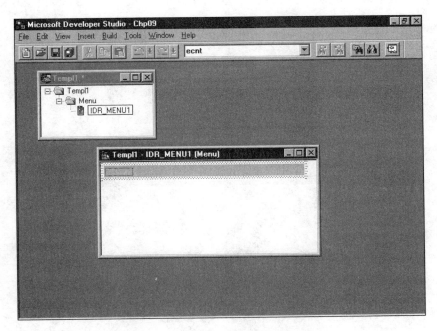

FIGURE 9.3 THE MENU EDITOR'S BLANK STARE.

If you want to get the view shown in Figure 9.3, you'll have to exit full-screen mode and turn off everything except the windows shown. As you'll see, this doesn't really help you, but it might make things clearer the first time around.

Filling the MenuBar

The next step in using this tool is to type something. In this case, start with &File. Again, the ampersand tells the menu machinery that you want the *F* to be underscored so that, for example, an **Alt+F** keypress launches the File menu.

When you start typing, the Menu Item Properties dialog box is launched, and your keystrokes fill in both the menu item's label in the menu and the Caption field in the dialog box. As you see in Figure 9.4, new rectangles appear on the Menu editor window where the next item on the menubar will appear, and where the first item in the File menu will appear.

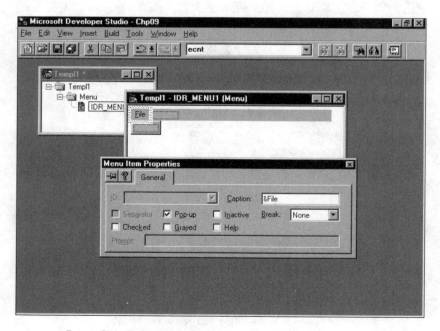

FIGURE 9.4 THE MENU EDITOR SHOWS THE NEXT ITEM FOR THE MENU.

The default status of a `MenuItem` on the menubar is `Pop-up`, which is why the menu grows in both directions. When you press **Enter** (there's no need to use the other components in the Menu Item Properties dialog box), you'll return to the Menu editor screen, where a dotted line rectangle shows the location of the first item in the File pull-down menu.

The default entry sequence is a depth-first traversal, which I like, but for the moment I'd like to work across the menubar. Click the rectangle to the right of the File `MenuItem` or use the **Tab** key to get focus on this new item. Enter `&Edit` as its caption. Repeat this to add `&Help`.

Experiment with the **Ins** and **Del** keys. **Ins** creates a new `MenuItem` to the left of the highlighted item. **Del** deletes the highlighted item. Now let's go on to a drop-down menu.

A Simple Drop-Down Menu

I've got a more complex menu planned for the File drop-down menu, so let's do a simple one under the Edit item. Click on **Edit** or from the keyboard, tab to Edit and then press the down arrow. Enter `Cu&t` and press **Enter**.

Then type `&Copy`, press **Enter**; type `&Paste` and press **Enter**. You should be able to do it faster than you can read this little paragraph.

If you make a mistake, edit the label in the Caption field of the dialog box or use **Ins** and **Del** to get rid of a bad mistake and add a new item. If you get items out of order, dragging with the mouse will move items.

Don't worry about the empty item at the bottom of the menu. That's where you would go to append additional items. It will disappear when the code is generated.

A Complex MenuBar

Now let's create a more complex drop-down, with separators and a nested menu. This is the structure:

```
&File
        &New
        &Open
                &Text File
                &Presents
        -separator-
        &Save
        Save &As
        -separator-
        e&Xit
```

I'll give you two hints and then let you work it out on your own. First, after you type a menu prompt, check the Pop-up box in the Menu Item dialog box. That box was already checked when you entered `MenuBar` items. It defaults to not checked in other menus.

For separators, instead of typing a label, press **Enter**. That will open the Menu Item dialog box. Then check the Separator box without entering a caption.

Figure 9.5 shows my version of this structure in the Menu editor.

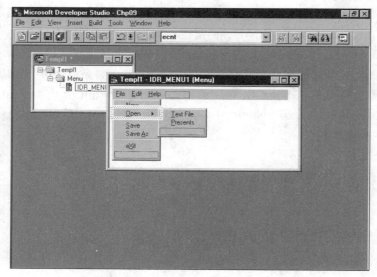

FIGURE 9.5 NESTED PULL-DOWNS IN THE MENU EDITOR.

Once yours looks like this, we're ready to go on.

More on the Menu Editor

First, save your work in the same workspace project folder we used earlier in this chapter. If you're only going to use a single menu resource file (the typical case), you can use a name like **Menu.rct**. The Resource Wizard will be looking for the .rct extension, so keeping it will make things simpler.

The resource editor has other capabilities. For example, the Prompt text field specifies the prompt that will be shown in the status bar. Of course, Java doesn't have a status-bar component.

Again, the Developer Studio is a multiproduct tool that fully supports Microsoft's Windows operating system and programming tools, such as MFC. You can't take advantage of every one of its features in Java. On the other hand, Visual C++ doesn't generate code that runs on OS/2 or Solaris, does it?

Using Menu Wizard Code

Once your menu painting is ready to go, the Windows programmer used to launch a resource compiler, which generated a binary **.RES**, unique to the Windows environments. Java likes only Java source. Fortunately, Visual J++'s Resource Wizard understands this.

Generating the Code

To get the necessary code, launch the Resource Wizard (**Tools/Java Resource Wizard**). In step 1, I use the Browse option to find my **.rct** file. In step 2, I provide a more Java-like name. In this case, I'm using **Chp09Menu**.

Once you press **Finish** in the Resource Wizard, your code is written faster than the Wizard can paint the screen the tells you it's done. Mine wrote the menu code shown here in Listing 9.3.

LISTING 9.3 WIZARD-GENERATED MENU CODE

```
//-------------------------------------------------------------
// Chp09Menu.java:
//      Implementation for menu creation class Chp09Menu
//
//-------------------------------------------------------------
import java.awt.*;

public class Chp09Menu
{
    Frame    m_Frame       = null;
    boolean m_fInitialized = false;

    // MenuBar definitions
    //-------------------------------------------------------------
    MenuBar mb;

    // Menu and Menu item definitions
    //-------------------------------------------------------------
    Menu m1;    // &File
    MenuItem ID_FILE_NEW;    // &New
    Menu m3;    // &Open
    MenuItem ID_FILE_OPEN_TEXTFILE;    // &Text File
    MenuItem ID_FILE_OPEN_PRESENTS;    // &Presents
    MenuItem m6;    // Separator
    MenuItem ID_FILE_SAVE;    // &Save
    MenuItem ID_FILE_SAVEAS;    // Save &As
    MenuItem m9;    // Separator
    MenuItem ID_FILE_EXIT;    // e&Xit
    Menu m11;    // &Edit
    MenuItem ID_EDIT_CUT;    // Cu&t
    MenuItem ID_EDIT_COPY;    // &Copy
    MenuItem ID_EDIT_PASTE;    // &Paste
    Menu m15;    // &Help

    // Constructor
```

```
//-------------------------------------------------------------
public Chp09Menu (Frame frame)
{
   m_Frame = frame;
}

// Initialization.
//-------------------------------------------------------------
public boolean CreateMenu()
{
   // Can only init controls once
   //---------------------------------------------------------
   if (m_fInitialized || m_Frame == null)
      return false;

   // Create menubar and attach to the frame
   //---------------------------------------------------------
   mb = new MenuBar();
   m_Frame.setMenuBar(mb);

   // Create menu and menu items and assign to menubar
   //---------------------------------------------------------
   m1 = new Menu("&File");
   mb.add(m1);
      ID_FILE_NEW = new MenuItem("&New");
      m1.add(ID_FILE_NEW);
      m3 = new Menu("&Open");
      m1.add(m3);
         ID_FILE_OPEN_TEXTFILE = new MenuItem("&Text File");
         m3.add(ID_FILE_OPEN_TEXTFILE);
         ID_FILE_OPEN_PRESENTS = new MenuItem("&Presents");
         m3.add(ID_FILE_OPEN_PRESENTS);
      m6 = new MenuItem("-");
      m1.add(m6);
      ID_FILE_SAVE = new MenuItem("&Save");
      m1.add(ID_FILE_SAVE);
      ID_FILE_SAVEAS = new MenuItem("Save &As");
```

```
        m1.add(ID_FILE_SAVEAS);
        m9 = new MenuItem("-");
        m1.add(m9);
        ID_FILE_EXIT = new MenuItem("e&Xit");
        m1.add(ID_FILE_EXIT);
    m11 = new Menu("&Edit");
    mb.add(m11);
        ID_EDIT_CUT = new MenuItem("Cu&t");
        m11.add(ID_EDIT_CUT);
        ID_EDIT_COPY = new MenuItem("&Copy");
        m11.add(ID_EDIT_COPY);
        ID_EDIT_PASTE = new MenuItem("&Paste");
        m11.add(ID_EDIT_PASTE);
    m15 = new Menu("&Help");
    mb.add(m15);

    m_fInitialized = true;
    return true;
    }
}
```

Use **Insert/Files Into Project** to put the generated code in your project
workspace. (Note to Microsoft: wouldn't it be nice to have the Wizard do
this?) Now we're ready to go, except for one detail.

Attaching the Menus

If you rebuild, you won't have any menus. You have to create and attach
these menus to your Frame if you want to see them. This is very little work.

Listing 9.4 shows the three statements needed to create and attach
your menus. Note that the capitalization of CreateMenu() makes it look
like a constructor, but it isn't. (Check Listing 9.3. I don't recommend editing the Wizard's code.)

LISTING 9.4 CREATING AND ATTACHING THE MENUS

```
applet_Chp09.start();

Chp09Menu m = new Chp09Menu( frame );      // NEW!
m.CreateMenu();                            // NEW!
frame.setMenuBar( m.mb );                  // NEW!

frame.show();
```

The new `Chp09Menu` object you create here is not a `MenuBar`. It includes a `MenuBar` as a data member, which is the parameter that `setMenuBar ( m.mb )` uses.

Make those additions to your **<name>.java** file, compile, and run, and you'll have menus! Figure 9.6 shows my new menus pulled down to Open/Presents.

FIGURE 9.6 NEW MENUS PULLED DOWN TO OPEN/PRESENTS.

If you look closely at Figure 9.6, or check in your own **JVIEW.EXE** window, you'll see an event where `id = 1001`. Look carefully. You'll see that this event is reported by the `Frame` but not by the `Applet`. And that brings us to our last menu subject.

Responding to Menu Events

We've done everything except the one thing that all this leads to: respond-
ing to the user's menu selections. In your application you can now click
File/Save or **Open/Presents** or whatever and your `Frame` is notified that
the user wants something to happen.

It does nothing with that information.

The `Frame` is notified via an `Event` whose `id` is `1001`, which is an
`Event.ACTION_EVENT`. Whenever the user says, "Please, do something,"
the `Event` is posted to a `Component`'s `handleEvent()` method, which in
turn calls the `Component`'s `action()` method. The `action()` method is
called with an `Event` and another parameter. In this case the second parameter is the `String` that labels the selected `MenuItem`.

Begin by commenting out the `handleEvent()` routine we added to
report on events in the `Applet` (it's in **<name>.java**). Also comment out
the event report we added to `handleEvent()` in the `Frame` (in
<name>Frame.java).

As a reminder to those of you who are not C programmers, you can comment out a block of lines by placing `/*` at the start and `*/` at the end of the
code you want to eliminate. C programmers do this rather than deleting lines
because it's easy to bring the code back if you later decide it has some use.

Then add the `action()` method shown here in Listing 9.5. Add it at
the end of the class in **<name>Frame.java**. (In my version of the online
User Guide, Microsoft forgot that their Wizard generated a
<name>Frame.java and included a lot of steps you don't have to take.
This way is much easier.)

LISTING 9.5   REPORTING THE WHAT PARAMETER

```
public boolean action(Event e, Object o)
{
    System.out.println( o );

    return true;
}
```

When you compile and run with that code, you'll see a nice report of the label of each `MenuItem` that you select from the menus. Note that items which are themselves menus don't send an action `Event` to the `Frame`. They wait for you to select an action from a submenu. In **File/Open/Text File**, for example, only `&Text File` is reported.

As our last step, let's expand the code in the `action()` method so that you'll have the structure needed to call real action methods. Listing 9.6 shows code that will do the job.

LISTING 9.6 SELECTING AN APPROPRIATE ACTION

```
public boolean action(Event e, Object o)
{
    if ( o.equals("&New") )
        System.out.println( "New File" );

    else if ( o.equals("&Save") )
        System.out.println( "Save File" );

    else if ( o.equals("Save &As") )
        System.out.println( "Save File As" );

    else
        System.out.println( "Not handled: " +
            o );

    return true;
}
```

Of course, your applications will have to do some real work, not just call `println()`, but this shows how it's done.

Summary

This was the second chapter in which you learned a lot and coded just a little. That's the point of Java and Visual J++. You use the friendly Wizards to do the grunt work, and you sit back and enjoy the fruits of their labor.

In this chapter we studied the hierarchy ending with the Frame, or main window, class. The Frame class extends the Window class, which creates modal dialog window objects. Window, in turn, extends the Container class. This is an abstract class, like the Component class, which it extends.

You can't instantiate a Component or a Container. These classes exist to provide broadly applicable functionality to the classes that extend them. Component-based classes can handle GUI events and Container-based classes can collect multiple components.

After we studied this hierarchy, we added handleEvent() methods (overriding the Component's handleEvent() method) to our Applet and our Frame. These let us look in on the event traffic inside these objects.

Then we studied the menu-related classes. The MenuBar attaches the main menu to a Frame. The MenuItem adds individual items to menus. Menu objects are an extended MenuItem, used to attach pull-down menus to the MenuBar and other Menu objects.

After this, we went on to use the Menu editor. To some of you, this was old news. The others discovered that in spite of its somewhat uncommunicative initial look, the Menu editor makes constructing modern menu structures an almost trivial job.

Finally, we had the Resource Wizard write the code that corresponded to the structure we created in the Menu editor. After including the generated code in our project workspace, we added just three lines to our applet code to bring the menus to life in our application. As a last step, we wrote an action() method in the Frame class (the Applet doesn't get menu Event reports) that let us respond to the selected actions.

In the next chapter, we examine how to get more information from the user. We'll read words, numbers, and blocks of text into our application, using more GUI components.

## CHAPTER 10

ENTERING DATA

The first thing most applets need is a little data. In this chapter we'll use `TextFields` and `TextAreas` to get data from the user. First we'll spend a little time looking at the Developer Studio and the ways we can customize it.

The first new API class we'll consider is the `Label` class. As its name suggests, you'll use it to put labels in your dialog boxes and other windows.

After labels we'll move on to `TextField` objects, the basic data entry tool used for names, numbers, and other data. You may be disappointed to find out that you'll face some serious programming to take in, for example, a date.

The `TextArea` class will be our next subject. This is the multiline version of the `TextField` class. You use it to display or enter and edit blocks of text. You'll be pleasantly surprised at how much work the Abstract Windows Toolkit (AWT) takes care of in `TextArea` objects.

All of this work will be done with the `FlowLayout` class managing the placement of our objects on the screen. In the last section of this chapter we'll look at the `LayoutManager` interface and the `FlowLayout` and `BorderLayout` classes, which implement the `LayoutManager` interface.

Before we get started, let's take a look at our studios.

Customizing Your Studio

One of the best things about Visual J++ and the Developer Studio is the ability they give us to tailor a personal version of the studio. Here I'll show you some of the tricks I use to get my studio to suit my work style. Go ahead and try everything my way but don't stop there.

The essential point is that you can make your own studio. Don't settle for copying my studio.

The Best Toolbars

Back in Chapter 6, we looked at customizing the toolbars. Here's a quick review. Turn on any toolbar you want to work on, and then choose the **Toolbars** tab from **Tools/Customize**. You can drag buttons from one toolbar to another while this dialog box is active. You can drag buttons from one place to another on the toolbar to make the arrangement suit your needs.

If you don't want a button on the toolbar, drag it off the toolbar and drop it over any nontoolbar space. If you want to add a new button, select it from the dialog box and drag it to the toolbar.

Now, here's the secret to developing the perfect Standard toolbar. Every time you launch Visual J++, look seriously at this toolbar. Pick a button that you seldom (or never) use and get rid of it. Then pick a replacement from all the other buttons and put it on the Standard toolbar.

Keep doing this until you can't find a replacement button that you'd use more often than any existing button. That's your perfect toolbar.

The Find Control

One of the startup tips suggests that you can resize the editor control. That's the drop-down list box on my toolbar. You can see it in Figure 10.1.

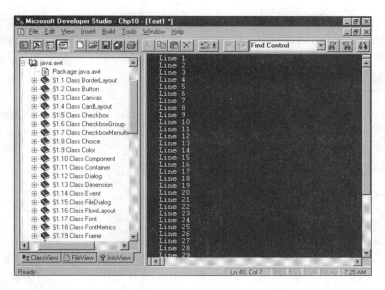

FIGURE 10.1   MY STANDARD TOOLBAR AND STUDIO.

The startup tip calls the find control *the edit control*, and doesn't quite explain how to vary its size. It's not hard. Launch the Customize dialog box (**Tools/Customize**), and select the **Toolbars** tab. Delete the existing find control (drag it off the toolbar and drop it in the client area). Then drag a new find control from the dialog box (it's in the Edit group) into position on the toolbar. Immediately after you drop the control, its outline is highlighted and you can grab and drag the right edge to resize it.

Shrinking this tool a bit will let you add a button (or two or three) to the toolbar.

View Controls

In Figure 10.1 you can see that I've got some unusual buttons on the left side of my toolbar. The first is the full-screen toggle button. I do most of my programming in full-screen mode, but I like to get the menus and status bar back when I use the resource editors.

The next button toggles the Output window. With each compile, the Output window quite properly appears. After it shows me the dumb mistakes I've made, I toggle it off after I fix the source code. (I also have **Alt+O** attached to this command for keyboard use).

The next two buttons toggle the InfoViewer Topic window and the Project Workspace window (InfoViewer contents). Go to the View list in the Toolbars Customize dialog box and pick these, or any others that you'll use frequently. Drop them at the left end.

You'll see that there's a good reason to put these buttons on the left instead of the right.

Full-Screen View

The scarcest resource in my studio is text lines in the editor. I can never see as much source code as I want. (Murphy's law derives theorem 72: you always need to see at least one more line of code than fits on your screen.) Figure 10.1 shows that I can see 29 lines of source in the standard view. Figure 10.2 shows my full-screen view. As you can see, aggressively pursuing added source lines gets about a third more lines than the standard setup.

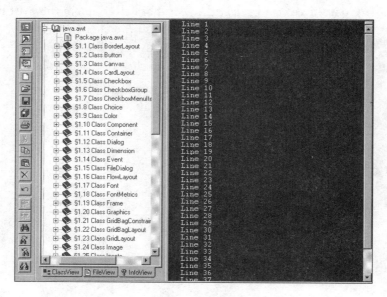

FIGURE 10.2 VIEWING 37 LINES.

If you haven't tried it yet, go to full-screen view and drag your Standard toolbar to the left or right edge. The find control (or any others that accept data entry) is discarded when you go vertical. If you size it correctly, you'll be able to nicely fit all the other buttons in a vertical toolbar.

The only difficulty here is that the horizontal docking windows or toolbars run the full width of the screen, blocking out the top or bottom buttons on your toolbar. If your Output window is docked horizontally, toggle it on and you'll see what I mean. The bottom buttons on the toolbar disappear. (The bottom buttons are the ones on the right in a horizontal layout.) Figure 10.3 shows my Output window blocking several buttons.

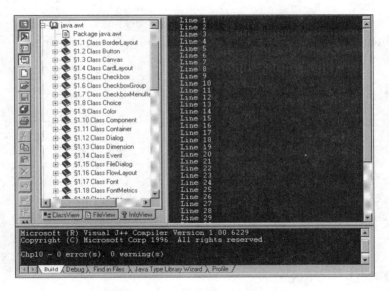

FIGURE 10.3 THE OUTPUT WINDOW HIDES BUTTONS.

Figure 10.3 also shows that even a small Output window costs 8 lines of source code in the text editor. Unfortunately, the error messages (the reason you really need the Output window) are very wide, and they don't wrap. A vertical Output window doesn't work.

I've already mentioned that I don't use wide text lines in my source code. I learned this from formatting code to fit in books and magazine listings, but decided I liked it in general when I found that I could print narrow code in three columns, getting over 300 lines of code on a single printed page (using 7 point type).

Toggling the Project Workspace window off (from either the keyboard or the toolbar) gives me all the source code width I need, so I don't need the horizontal scrollbar. (**Tools/Options/Editor** tab lets you control the scrollbars.) The setting for this scrollbar is stored separately for standard and full-screen views. I leave it on in the standard view, where I'm not fighting for maximum vertical space.

A final word: it's your studio. You'll be spending a lot of time here, so it pays to give it some thought.

Remember when we went looking for the Cessna in Chapter 1? You've come a long way since then! Now we're working on customizing the jet fighter. Get comfortable in your cockpit, and we'll start coding.

Using Label Objects

Before we start putting `Label` objects into our windows, let me mention the way we're positioning them.

A `LayoutManager` determines where components are placed. The last section of this chapter will dive into the subject of the `LayoutManager` interface. Before we get there I'll warn you that the default manager for an `Applet` is different from the default for a `Frame`. We'll start with the `FlowLayout`, the Applet's default.

Create a Project

Begin by creating a new project workspace. Mine's named **Chp10**.

Use the Applet Wizard to create a combined applet and application. Don't use multithreading, don't include the explanatory comments, and don't add any event handlers if you want to match my code exactly.

After the Wizard writes it, open your **<name>.java** file, and we'll start by adding text labels. Before you enter new code, let's tour the `Label` class. It's very simple.

The Label Class

Labels in your programs are the fixed text that the user can't edit. (Bear in mind that your program can change labels. It's the user who can't change them.)

The class has three `final static` (constant) `int` fields: `LEFT`, `CENTER`, and `RIGHT`. These are constants that you can supply to the constructor. This is a sample constructor call:

```
Label l1 = new Label( "Name: ", Label.RIGHT )
```

You can omit the alignment parameter and just provide a `String` in the constructor. You can even omit the `String` and create a `Label` with a null `String`.

The interesting methods are `getText()` and `setText()`. The former returns and the latter assigns the text that the label will display.

By the way, if you look up the `Label` in your online documentation, you'll see that the methods end with Footnotes. This doesn't refer to a method but adds a note. In this class it doesn't matter, but the same footnotes appear in the `TextField` and `TextArea` classes we'll cover next. They're important for `TextFields`.

Add a Label

This is a simple class, right? Let's add a `Label` to our application's `Frame`. Add the two new lines shown here:

```
// TODO: Place additional initialization code here

Label l1 = new Label( "My First Label" ); // NEW
add( l1 );                                 // NEW
```

Compile and run, and your result should look like the one you see in Figure 10.4.

FIGURE 10.4 Using A `Label`.

Before we go on to actual data entry, let's add an OK pushbutton so we can conveniently exit from the program.

Add this code to the initialization section:

```
// TODO: Place additional initialization code here

Label l1 = new Label( "My First Label" );
add( l1 );

  OKButton okb = new OKButton(); // NEW
  okb.setLabel( "   OK   " );    // NEW
  add( okb );                    // NEW
```

Then create the `OKButton` class at the end of the file:

```
  // TODO: Place additional applet code here

}   // lines below this one are NEW

class OKButton extends Button
{
   public boolean action( Event e, Object o )
   {
      System.exit(0);
      return true;
```

```
        }
    }
```

When you compile and run this code, you'll get a result like the one you see in Figure 10.5.

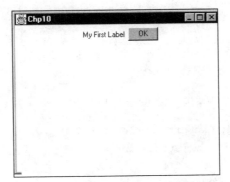

FIGURE 10.5 IT WORKS, SORT OF.

You probably would have put that button elsewhere, but we'll get to that later. For now, you've got a `Label` and a `Button` that closes the form. Listing 10.1 shows the full program.

LISTING 10.1 THE LABEL AND BUTTON PROGRAM

```java
import java.applet.*;
import java.awt.*;
import Chp10Frame;

public class Chp10 extends Applet
{
    // STANDALONE APPLICATION SUPPORT:
    //      m_fStandAlone will be set to true if applet is run
    //      standalone
    //-----------------------------------------------------------
    boolean m_fStandAlone = false;

    public static void main(String args[])
```

```
    {
        Chp10Frame frame = new Chp10Frame("Chp10");

        // Must show Frame before we size it so insets() will return
        // valid values
        //-----------------------------------------------------------
        frame.show();
          frame.hide();
        frame.resize(frame.insets().left + frame.insets().right  +
              320, frame.insets().top  +
              frame.insets().bottom + 240);

        Chp10 applet_Chp10 = new Chp10();

        frame.add("Center", applet_Chp10);
        applet_Chp10.m_fStandAlone = true;
        applet_Chp10.init();
        applet_Chp10.start();
          frame.show();
    }

public Chp10()
{
    // TODO: Add constructor code here
}

public String getAppletInfo()
{
    return "Name: Chp10\r\n" +
           "Author: Martin L. Rinehart\r\n" +
           "Created with Microsoft Visual J++ Version 1.0";
}

public void init()
{
    // If you use a ResourceWizard-generated "control creator"
    // class to
    // arrange controls in your applet, you may want to call
    // its
```

```
    // CreateControls() method from within this method. Remove
    // the following
    // call to resize() before adding the call to
    // CreateControls();
    // CreateControls() does its own resizing.
    //--------------------------------------------------------
resize(320, 240);

// TODO: Place additional initialization code here

Label l1 = new Label( "My First Label" );
add( l1 );

OKButton okb = new OKButton();
okb.setLabel( "   OK   " );
add( okb );

}

public void destroy()
{
    // TODO: Place applet cleanup code here
}

public void paint(Graphics g)
{
    // g.drawString(
        "Created with Microsoft Visual J++ Version 1.0",
        10, 20);
}

public void start()
{
    // TODO: Place additional applet start code here
}

public void stop()
{
}
```

```
       // TODO: Place additional applet code here

}

class OKButton extends Button
{
    public boolean action( Event e, Object o )
    {
        System.exit(0);
        return true;
    }
}
```

Now we can go on to entering data.

Using TextField Objects

A `TextField` object displays and optionally allows entering and editing data. Don't be misled by the name, however. You use a `TextField` whenever you want a name, number, or other item—use it for anything more complex than a check box or radio button can handle.

The `TextField` object looks like one that the user will manipulate. (You can make it uneditable, but a `Label` is a better choice for most uneditable displays.)

The TextField Class

The `TextField` class is simple, perhaps too simple. We'll begin with what it includes. There are no fields, but there is a nice assortment of constructors. These are examples:

```
TextField t;

t = new TextField();
    // null text, default width
```

```
t = new TextField( "characters" );
    // data assigned, sized to fit "characters"

t = new TextField( 20 );
    // empty field, 20 characters wide

t = new TextField( "Smith", 20 );
    // "Smith" in a field 20 characters wide
```

The `TextField` and `TextArray` classes are measured in characters, not pixels. (The sizes are based on average character width. Except with mono-spaced fonts, the size is an approximation.)

Both the `TextField` and `TextArea` extend the `TextComponent` class. This provides these self-descriptive methods: `getText()` and `setText()`; `isEditable()` and `setEditable()`.

The `TextField` class adds `getEchoChar()` and `setEchoChar()`. Normally, any key the user types is echoed to the `TextField`. If you set an echo character, it will appear when the user types (use this to echo asterisks when the user enters a password).

The `TextField` also inherits the `action()` and other event routines of the `Component` class. Each keypress triggers an `Event` that you can handle any way you like. Suppose you want to accept an American or Canadian telephone number, formatted this way:

```
(###) ###-####
```

In each # location, you'll accept a decimal digit. After each digit you'll advance the cursor to the next # location. You can do other validation, too.

There is enough power in the `TextField` to program this. The bad news is that you're going to have to do some extensive programming. You will, that is, if you can't find a preprogrammed object online. Every time I do a Web search for "Java classes" I get a bigger set of choices. A little Web surfing should net you a nice supply of programs that will save you from this tedious work.

Now we come to the footnote. There's a substantial difference between Java 1.0 and Java 1.1 noted in the footnote to each `Label`,

`TextField`, and `TextArea`. Java 1.0 didn't send these components the events that Java 1.1 adds.

Sun has made a determined effort to freeze the API specifications so that we don't face problems like this. They've been very successful, but they haven't yet achieved perfection. I think Java 1.1 is correct and that you can mostly ignore the 1.0 problem. If you need 1.0 compatibility, you'll have to look at events in the `Frame` or other component under your `TextField` and `TextArea` objects.

Coding with TextField Objects

Now let's add some `Label` objects with appropriate `TextField` objects. Try some like this:

```
// TODO: Place additional initialization code here

Label l1 = new Label( "My First Label" );
add( l1 );

  Label l2 = new Label( "Null: " ); // NEW FROM HERE
add( l2 );

TextField t1 = new TextField();
add( t1 );

Label l3 = new Label( "Fit" );
add( l3 );

TextField t2 = new TextField( "Fit" );
add( t2 );

TextField t3 = new TextField( "Wide", 30 );
  add( t3 );                              // NEW TO HERE

OKButton okb = new OKButton();
okb.setLabel( "   OK   " );
add( okb );
}
```

When you run this program, you should get a result like the one you see in Figure 10.6.

FIGURE 10.6 **TextFields** AND **Labels** ADDED.

Go ahead and add data in your own form.

Of course, the data that you add is discarded as soon as you click the **OK** button. You'll want to expand the `action()` routine of your `OKButton` class to actually use this data.

Listing 10.2 shows the full program.

LISTING 10.2 MORE LABELS AND **TextFields**

```
import java.applet.*;
import java.awt.*;
import Chp10Frame;

public class Chp10 extends Applet
{
    // STANDALONE APPLICATION SUPPORT:
    //      m_fStandAlone will be set to true if applet is run
    //      standalone
    //-------------------------------------------------------------
    boolean m_fStandAlone = false;
```

```
public static void main(String args[])
{
    Chp10Frame frame = new Chp10Frame("Chp10");

    // Must show Frame before we size it so insets() will return
    // valid values
    //-----------------------------------------------------------
    frame.show();
      frame.hide();
    frame.resize(frame.insets().left + frame.insets().right  +
          320, frame.insets().top  +
          frame.insets().bottom + 240);

    Chp10 applet_Chp10 = new Chp10();

    frame.add("Center", applet_Chp10);
    applet_Chp10.m_fStandAlone = true;
    applet_Chp10.init();
    applet_Chp10.start();
      frame.show();
}

public Chp10()
{
    // TODO: Add constructor code here
}

 public String getAppletInfo()
{
    return "Name: Chp10\r\n" +
          "Author: Martin L. Rinehart\r\n" +
          "Created with Microsoft Visual J++ Version 1.0";
}

public void init()
{
    // If you use a ResourceWizard-generated "control creator"
    // class to
```

```
    // arrange controls in your applet, you may want to call
    // its
    // CreateControls() method from within this method. Remove
    // the following
    // call to resize() before adding the call to
    // CreateControls();
    // CreateControls() does its own resizing.
    //-------------------------------------------------------
resize(320, 240);

// TODO: Place additional initialization code here

Label l1 = new Label( "My First Label" );
add( l1 );

Label l2 = new Label( "Null: " );
add( l2 );

TextField t1 = new TextField();
add( t1 );

Label l3 = new Label( "Fit" );
add( l3 );

TextField t2 = new TextField( "Fit" );
add( t2 );

TextField t3 = new TextField( "Wide", 30 );
add( t3 );

OKButton okb = new OKButton();
okb.setLabel( "    OK    " );
add( okb );
}

public void destroy()
{
    // TODO: Place applet cleanup code here
}
```

```
    public void paint(Graphics g)
    {
        // g.drawString(
            "Created with Microsoft Visual J++ Version 1.0",
            10, 20);
    }

    public void start()
    {
        // TODO: Place additional applet start code here
    }

    public void stop()
    {
    }

    // TODO: Place additional applet code here

}

class OKButton extends Button
{
    public boolean action( Event e, Object o )
    {
        System.exit(0);
        return true;
    }
}
```

Are you getting ready to position everything exactly where you want it on that form? We'll get there, but first we'll add one more Component, a TextArea.

Using TextArea Objects

Like the TextField, the TextArea inherits basic functionality from the TextComponent class. It's used when you want more than a single line. If you are using Visual J++'s dialog editor, dropping an edit box onto it will generate a `TextArea` if you check the multiline box (**Properties, Styles** tab). Otherwise, the edit box generates a `TextField`.

The TextArea Class

The `TextArea` class has no fields. Its constructors parallel those for the `TextField`, but where the `TextField` had a single width integer, the `TextArea` takes two integers: rows and columns. Again, the size is given in characters, not in pixels. I think it's a design mistake, but for whatever reason, the number of rows precedes the number of columns. (Almost everything in Java that takes coordinates uses X, Y style, that is, horizontal measure first.)

These are sample constructors:

```
TextArea t;
String str = " ... " ; // String with embedded \n chars

t = new TextArea();
    // all defaults

t = new TextArea( 5, 30 );
    // 5 rows by 30 characters per row

t = new TextArea( str );
    // default size, w/ String

t = new TextArea( str, 5, 30 );
    // fully specified
```

Scrolling in a `TextArea` is automatic. Scrollbars appear and are activated when the amount of text exceeds the size available. (There is no word wrapping, but you can get ready-to-run editors from the Web. Or you can write your own, working with the `KEY_DOWN` Event objects.)

To handle word wrapping, you could use the `getRows()` and `getColumns()` functions. The `appendText()` and `insertText()`

methods do the jobs their names suggest. You also have the `getText()`, `putText()`, and other methods inherited from the `TextComponent` class.

Let's put a `TextArea` into our growing program.

Coding a TextArea

A `TextArea` is a simple addition to our program. Add these new lines in the initialization area we've been using:

```
    TextField t2 = new TextField( "Fit" );
    add( t2 );

/*NEW*/ TextArea a1 = new TextArea( "Line 1", 5, 30 );
/*NEW*/ a1.appendText( " -- more on Line 1" );
/*NEW*/ a1.appendText( "\nLine 2" );
/*NEW*/ a1.appendText( "\n\nLine 4" );
/*NEW*/ add( a1 );

    TextField t3 = new TextField( "Wide", 30 );
    add( t3 );
```

I've used the `appendText()` method to show you how lines depend on new-line characters. For those of you who don't know C, the escape sequence \n specifies a new-line character. If you're used to specifying carriage return/linefeed pairs, stop! DOS uses a CR/LF pair, but neither the Mac nor Unix use this form of new-line. If you specify \n, you let the platform-specific implementations of Java take care of it for you.

Figure 10.7 shows what I get when I launch this program.

Run your own version. Try entering a long line of text, and then go on to additional lines. You'll see the scrollbars come to life, as they should.

Next, we'll go on to making the components fit together more intelligently.

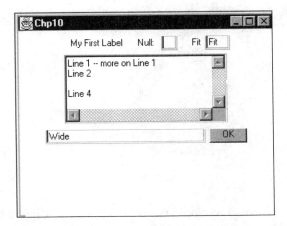

FIGURE 10.7 THE FINAL `FlowLayout`.

The LayoutManager Interface

The purpose of the `LayoutManager` interface is to lay out your components on a form in a sensible fashion.

If you use Visual J++'s dialog editor to lay out your form, and then use the Resource Wizard to generate the code, it will be done on a "what you painted is what you get" basis. The Wizard's code puts things exactly where you draw them.

Actually, the Resource Wizard uses a `LayoutManager` that Microsoft supplies, which is called `DialogLayout`. `DialogLayout` doesn't put things slavishly into position by pixel. It arranges things so that they'll look like what you drew, but it does adjust positions for the size of the font in use. (This is a nice adjustment. Presumably you'll work closer to your laptop's screen; if you work farther back when you're at your 17-inch desktop monitor, you'll probably be using a larger font.)

Why does Java introduce this `LayoutManager` complication? Actually, it's to simplify your programming. Look at the code you've added to the test program. There aren't any coordinates attached to those screen components. We just `add()` them and the `LayoutManager` takes over from there.

A `LayoutManager`-based class is one that implements the `LayoutManager` interface. In Chapter 3 we went over the syntax for an

interface. It looks like a class, but there isn't any code supplied for the
methods:

```
interface bar
{
    boolean bar1( int );

    String bar2( char[] );

    ...
}
```

And we saw how a class implements an interface. It just announces that it
implements the interface and then it does it:

```
class foo implements bar
{
    // this class must define all the functions
    // declared in the bar interface

    boolean bar1( int i )
    {
        ... // code here
        return true; // or false
    }

    String bar2( char[] chars )
    {
        String s = new String();
        ... // code here
        return s;
    }
    ...

}
```

When you use a Container (a Frame is a Container—Frame extends
Window which extends Container) you have an attached
LayoutManager object. The default for an Applet is a FlowLayout.

If you've been looking at the online AWT documentation, you've seen that I've been ignoring methods with names like `preferredSize()`, which are available in most components. Here's where we start to make sense of these.

The FlowLayout Class

The `FlowLayout` is the simplest `LayoutManager`. It arranges components from right to left in the `Container`. When it runs out of space, it starts a new row, working from the top down. It's very handy for quick work, and it's useful for some polished work, too. (On your own, explore using the `FlowLayout` to, for example, organize `Button` objects in a `Panel` you attach with the `BorderLayout` manager.)

`FlowLayout` has three `final static` (constant) `int` fields: `LEFT`, `CENTER`, and `RIGHT`. These are the constructors:

```
FlowLayout f;

f = new FlowLayout();
    // defaults to FlowLayout( FlowLayout.CENTER, 5, 5 );

f = new FlowLayout( FlowLayout.LEFT );
    // or FlowLayout.CENTER or FlowLayout.RIGHT

f = new FlowLayout( align, hgap, vgap );
    // align is one of:
    //        FlowLayout.LEFT
    //        FlowLayout.CENTER
    //        FlowLayout.RIGHT
    // hgap is integer, horizontal gap
    // vgap is integer, vertical gap
```

The gap parameters are given in pixels. This is the space that `FlowLayout` puts between components. The default is 5 pixels.

You'll seldom call a `LayoutManager` method directly. The `Container` class calls the `LayoutManager` class when it adds and deletes components and to do the actual layout work.

The BorderLayout Class

Let's begin by summarizing the other `LayoutManager`-based classes that you could use. The `GridLayout`, as its name suggests, lays components out in rows and columns. We'll look at it in Chapter 11.

The `CardLayout` class puts components on multiple cards. You'd use a `CardLayout` for a tabbed-form-style class. I'll leave the `CardLayout` up to you.

The `GridBagLayout`, which we'll put to work in Chapter 12, is a very sophisticated `LayoutManager`. You accompany what would otherwise be a `GridLayout` with a `GridBagConstraints` object. The constraints say things like: make this cell three times bigger than the previous cell; make this component at least this big but no bigger than that; and so on.

A `GridBagLayout` is quite a bit of trouble to code, but it has the distinct advantage of preserving your intent when one user launches your program using a full 21-inch screen and another gives you about a third of a laptop's window.

The `BorderLayout` sacrifices some of the power of the `GridBagLayout`, but it is considerably easier to use. Its basic conceptual model is of five screen areas. The diagram on the next page shows these areas.

When you add components to a `BorderLayout`, you specify the area with a text string, this way:

```
// "this" is a Container-based object

TextArea a = new TextArea( str, 10, 30 );
add( "Center", a );
```

The first parameter of this `add()` method is one of the strings `"North"`, `"South"`, `"East"`, `"West"`, or `"Center"`. The second parameter is the component to add.

```
-------------------------------------------------
|                                               |
|                    North                      |
|                                               |
    ---------------------------------------
|   |   |                           |   |   |
|   |   |                           |   |   |
|   |   |                           |   |   |
|   |   |                           |   |   |
|   |   |                           |   |   |
|   |   |                           |   |   |
|   |   |                           |   |   |
|   |   |                           |   |   |
| West  |          Center          | East  |
|   |   |                           |   |   |
|   |   |                           |   |   |
|   |   |                           |   |   |
|   |   |                           |   |   |
|   |   |                           |   |   |
|   |   |                           |   |   |
|   |   |                           |   |   |
    ---------------------------------------
|                                               |
|                    South                      |
|                                               |
-------------------------------------------------
```

The BorderLayout takes space for the North and South regions first. It takes whatever vertical space it needs to fit the components in those regions. Then it grabs as much horizontal space as it needs for West and East. Whatever space remains is the Center. If an area isn't used, it gets no space. Having a West but not an East, for example, is not only possible, it's frequently just what you want.

Looking at the BorderLayout Class

There are two constructors. You can specify the horizontal and vertical gaps between areas in the second form. They are:

```
BorderLayout bl;

bl = new BorderLayout();

bl = new BorderLayout( int hgap, int vgap );
```

As with the `FlowLayout`, you won't directly call the methods of the `BorderLayout` class. Your parent `Container` will call these methods. You'll use the two-parameter form of the `add()` method (with `"Left"`, `"Right"`, etc. as your region specifier).

Now let's put a `BorderLayout` to work, organizing a collection of `Label`, `TextField`, and `TextArea` objects.

Programming with a BorderLayout

Let's use the `BorderLayout` class to build a form. We'll center a label on the top. Then we'll put a label to the left of a `TextArea`. Underneath that we'll have a centered OK button.

Let's start with the following code. Delete the other code you added under the TODO comment shown here, and then add this:

```
// TODO: Place additional initialization code here

setLayout( new BorderLayout() );

Label l1 = new Label( "Centered North", Label.CENTER );
add( "North", l1 );

Label l2 = new Label( "West" );
add( "West", l2 );

TextArea a1 = new TextArea( "Center (no East)" );
add( "Center", a1 );
```

```
OKButton okb = new OKButton();
okb.setLabel( "   OK   " );
add( "South", okb );
```

The call to setLayout() is all that we need to install the BorderLayout in place of the default FlowLayout. Then we use a position parameter (North or Center or whatever) in the add() method calls, after we create the individual components.

Now I get the result shown in Figure 10.8.

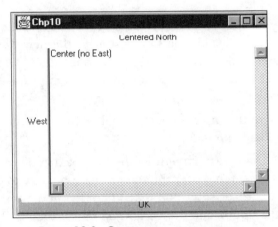

FIGURE 10.8 OUR FIRST **BorderLayout.**

That's not exactly what I had in mind. First, I'd like a little space between the components. That's just a matter of using the alternate constructor and adding a few pixels of padding, this way:

```
setLayout( new BorderLayout(3, 6) );
```

Next, your button has been stretched to fit the entire South region. In fact, all your components were stretched to fit, but that either didn't matter (for the Label objects), or it was precisely what the doctor ordered (for the TextArea). The Button doesn't look right, though.

To fix it, we'll create a Panel object. The components in the Panel will be handled by the FlowLayout by default. We'll put the button into the Panel, and then we'll put the `Panel` into the `South` region of the `BorderLayout`. You can put a `Panel` object in any region of the `BorderLayout`. And you can use any `LayoutManager` you like within the `Panel`.

This is easier to code than it is to describe. You do it this way:

```
Panel p1 = new Panel();
    OKButton okb = new OKButton();
    okb.setLabel( "    OK    " );
    p1.add( okb );
add( "South", p1 );
```

Make sure you look carefully at those two `add()` calls. The first one, `p1.add( okb );`, adds the OK button to the new `Panel`. It uses the `Panel`'s default `FlowLayout`. The second one, `add( "South", p1 );`, adds the panel to the `South` of the `BorderLayout` for the `this` object, which is our `Applet`.

When I run that now, I get the result shown in Figure 10.9, which is exactly what I had in mind.

Go ahead and experiment with the `BorderLayout`. Try to add another `Label` centered over the `TextArea`. One way to do this is to create another `Panel`. Use `setLayout()` to give it a `BorderLayout`. Put the label in the `North` and the `TextArea` in its `Center`. Then `add()` this `Panel` to the `Center` of the `Applet`. The code would use this technique:

```
// laying out a Panel in a BorderLayout region

Panel p5 = new Panel();
p5.setLayout( new BorderLayout() ); // pick a manager

    Whatever w1 = new Whatever();
    p5.add( "North", w1 );

    ... // add more things into p5

add( "Center", p5 ); // put the Panel in place
```

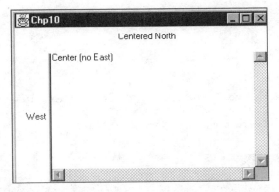

FIGURE 10.9 A SUCCESSFUL `BorderLayout`.

Try resizing over a wide range. You'll see that `BorderLayout` lets you resize but still keeps the program's design intact. The `DialogLayout` that you'd get from the Resource Wizard really doesn't permit successful resizing. And as you've seen, this takes some learning, but it doesn't take very much programming to use successfully.

My full program is shown in Listing 10.3.

LISTING 10.3 THE COMPLETED `BorderLayout` PROGRAM

```
import java.applet.*;
import java.awt.*;
import Chp10Frame;

public class Chp10 extends Applet
{
    // STANDALONE APPLICATION SUPPORT:
    //      m_fStandAlone will be set to true if applet is run
    //      standalone
    //-----------------------------------------------------------
    boolean m_fStandAlone = false;

    public static void main(String args[])
    {
        Chp10Frame frame = new Chp10Frame("Chp10");
```

```
    // Must show Frame before we size it so insets() will return
    // valid values
    //----------------------------------------------------------
    frame.show();
       frame.hide();
    frame.resize(frame.insets().left + frame.insets().right   +
            320, frame.insets().top   +
            frame.insets().bottom + 240);

    Chp10 applet_Chp10 = new Chp10();

    frame.add("Center", applet_Chp10);
    applet_Chp10.m_fStandAlone = true;
    applet_Chp10.init();
    applet_Chp10.start();
       frame.show();
}

public Chp10()
{
    // TODO: Add constructor code here
}

public String getAppletInfo()
{
    return "Name: Chp10\r\n" +
            "Author: Martin L. Rinehart\r\n" +
            "Created with Microsoft Visual J++ Version 1.0";
}

public void init()
{
    // If you use a ResourceWizard-generated "control creator"
    // class to
    // arrange controls in your applet, you may want to call
    // its
    // CreateControls() method from within this method. Remove
    // the following
```

```
        // call to resize() before adding the call to
        // CreateControls();
        // CreateControls() does its own resizing.
        //-------------------------------------------------------
    resize(320, 240);

    // TODO: Place additional initialization code here

    setLayout( new BorderLayout(3, 6) );

    Label l1 = new Label( "Centered North", Label.CENTER );
    add( "North", l1 );

    Label l2 = new Label( "West" );
    add( "West", l2 );

    TextArea a1 = new TextArea( "Center (no East)" );
    add( "Center", a1 );

    Panel p1 = new Panel();
        OKButton okb = new OKButton();
        okb.setLabel( "   OK   " );
        p1.add( okb );
    add( "South", p1 );
}

public void destroy()
{
    // TODO: Place applet cleanup code here
}

public void paint(Graphics g)
{
    // g.drawString(
        "Created with Microsoft Visual J++ Version 1.0",
        10, 20);
}

public void start()
```

```
    {
        // TODO: Place additional applet start code here
    }

    public void stop()
    {
    }

    // TODO: Place additional applet code here

}

class OKButton extends Button
{
    public boolean action( Event e, Object o )
    {
        System.exit(0);
        return true;
    }
}
```

Summary

Congratulations for getting here. You're beginning to do real Java programming. This would be a good time to stop and think through the whole LayoutManager design. It's a complex concept, but it simplifies coding. You should be able to think of things you've done without an equivalent concept that would benefit from some LayoutManager help.

In this chapter, we started by doing some customizing on our studios. I showed you how I tuned mine to get maximum vertical space for source code editing. And you got my advice on customizing your own in your own way.

Then we went on to use our studios to add Label objects to our forms. The Label class is very simple.

We went on to `TextField` objects, which handle all text and other entries. They're simple to use, but you may need to do some Web surfing to find good entry filters for dates, phone numbers, and the like.

`TextFields` share their `TextComponent` class heritage with `TextArea` objects. These are simple to install and handle scrollbars automatically.

Finally, we went on to examine the `LayoutManager` interface and the `FlowLayout` and `BorderLayout` classes that implement this interface. These `LayoutManager`-implementing objects make it possible to write programs that users can size to suit their own requirements, while still looking the way you designed them.

In Chapter 11, we'll go on to using groups of controls, including check boxes and radio buttons, and we'll add the `GridLayout` to our mental equipment.

GROUPING CONTROLS

Ready to have some fun? I'm going to illustrate this chapter with a program that launches a game. We'll start with Tic Tac Toe. Then we'll move on to a more challenging game. It's a version of Tic Tac Toe called *Five-in-a-Row*. You could call Tic Tac Toe *Three in a Row* and you'd get the idea. Five-in-a-Row is more interesting to play, because the playing field isn't just a 5-by-5 grid. I'll use a 12-by-12 grid, which is large enough for fascinating play.

If you're learning Visual J++ in your office, you'd better be prepared to explain the business purpose behind the game we'll be programming.

We'll start by using the `GridLayout` to handle a group of buttons. You'll see that a 3 by 3 grid gives us an instant Tic Tac Toe board. Making the layout size a class constant lets us use the same `GridLayout` for our 12-by-12 game board.

Then we'll go on to using `Panel` objects in a `BorderLayout`. We did this quickly in Chapter 10. This will remind you of how it's done.

Next, we'll add a `Checkbox`. You'll learn to use this for both input and output.

Then we'll finish up by replacing the `Checkbox` with a `Checkbox-Group`. The `CheckboxGroup` collects multiple `Checkbox` objects in a unit, turning them from check boxes into radio buttons. Again, we'll use the radio buttons both to get input and to provide feedback.

In this chapter, you'll definitely want to program this as I explain it. A lot of the concepts are fairly abstract until you see them in action in your code. Then they're very concrete.

Using a GridLayout

Ready to start programming? This time, make a new project workspace, but *don't* use the Applet Wizard. We'll start a fresh application, made from scratch. No, I don't like doing things the hard way. You'll see that we're going to whip up a nicely laid out group of buttons with a lot less effort than using the Dialog editor would require.

Starting the Program

Begin with a titled `Frame` that knows how to go away when it's not wanted, as in Listing 11.1.

LISTING 11.1 A FRAME THAT CLOSES POLITELY

```java
// Fiveinarow.java

import java.awt.*;

public class Fiveinarow
{

    // constants:
        final static byte size = 3;

    // class members:

    public void   main( String[] args )
```

```
    {
        FiveFrame ff = new FiveFrame();
            ff.setTitle( "Can you get 5 In A Row?" );
        ff.resize( 240, 300 );
        ff.show();
    }

}

class FiveFrame extends Frame
{
    public boolean handleEvent( Event e )
    {
        if (e.id == Event.WINDOW_DESTROY )
        {
            dispose();
            System.exit(0);
            return true;
        }
        else
            return super.handleEvent( e );
    }

}
// end of Fiveinarow.java
```

Adding a Grid of Buttons

Now let's add the button grid. First, declare an array of a new button type, the GButton. The declaration should look like this:

```
// class members:
    static GButton[][] btns;
```

That declares a two-dimensional array of GButton objects. Remember that this assigns a type to the btns array, but doesn't actually create an array.

Next, define an empty class that does nothing but extend the Button class. This code goes at the end of the file:

```
class GButton extends Button
{
}

// end of Fiveinarow.java
```

To complete the array of GButtons, between the Frame.resize() and the Frame.show() calls, add this code:

```
        ff.resize( 240, 300 );

        btns = new GButton[size][size];

        for ( int r = 0; r < size; r++ )
        {
            for ( int c = 0; c < size; c++ )
            {
                btns[r][c] = new GButton();
            }
        }

        ff.show();
```

The assignment to btns, new GButton[size][size], is the one that actually creates an array. Actually, this is an array of null pointers. In the nested loops, you actually assign a pointer to a GButton to each element of the array.

That creates the array of GButtons. If you run the program at this point, you won't see them. Next we'll have to show them on the Frame. We'll do this by attaching the GButtons to a Panel, and showing that Panel in the Center of a BorderLayout in the Frame. We'll use a GridLayout in the Panel.

I know that the GridLayout is new to you, but it's so simple to use that I want you to just dive into the code. It's completely straightforward.

The middle four lines in this group handle the layout:

```
ff.resize( 240, 300 );

ff.setLayout( new BorderLayout() );

Panel p1 = new Panel();
p1.setLayout( new GridLayout(size,size) );

ff.add( "Center", p1 );

btns = new GButton[size][size];
```

First, we set a `BorderLayout` for the `Frame`. Then we create a `Panel` and assign it a `GridLayout`. The two parameters are the number of rows and the number of columns you want in the grid. The last line adds the `Panel` in the `Center` region of the `Frame`'s `BorderLayout`.

Now all that remains is to insert the buttons into the panel. Add the new line:

```
p1.add( btns[r][c] )
```

inside the inner loop, as this shows:

```
for ( int c = 0; c < size; c++ )
{
    btns[r][c] = new GButton();
    p1.add( btns[r][c] );
}
```

When you `add()` into a `GridLayout`, the `LayoutManager` fills the first row, from left to right, then the second, and so on. I've used the loop counters `r` and `c` to suggest rows and columns.

When you run this code, you should get a Tic Tac Toe board, like the one shown in Figure 11.1.

FIGURE 11.1 LAUNCHING A TIC TAC TOE BOARD.

The full code is shown in Listing 11.2.

LISTING 11.2 A TIC TAC TOE BOARD

```java
// Fiveinarow.java

import java.awt.*;

public class Fiveinarow
{

    // constants:
        final static byte size = 3;

    // class members:
        static GButton[][] btns;

    public void   main( String[] args )
    {
        FiveFrame ff = new FiveFrame();
          ff.setTitle( "Can you get 5 In A Row?" );
        ff.resize( 240, 300 );

        ff.setLayout( new BorderLayout() );
```

```
        Panel p1 = new Panel();
        p1.setLayout( new GridLayout(size,size) );

        ff.add( "Center", p1 );

        btns = new GButton[size][size];

        for ( int r = 0; r < size; r++ )
        {
            for ( int c = 0; c < size; c++ )
            {
                btns[r][c] = new GButton();
                p1.add( btns[r][c] );
            }
        }

        ff.show();
    }
}

class FiveFrame extends Frame
{
    public boolean handleEvent( Event e )
    {
        if (e.id == Event.WINDOW_DESTROY )
        {
            dispose();
            System.exit(0);
            return true;
        }
        else
            return super.handleEvent( e );
    }

}

class GButton extends Button
{
```

```
}
// end of Fiveinarow.java
```

Grouping in Panels

Next, we'll add a panel of buttons at the bottom, but first we'll make those buttons display *X* and *O* marks when they're clicked. Give it a moment's thought before you look at my solution.

Adding Xs and Os

Start with a new class member to keep track of whose turn it is. Later we'll get fancy, adding check boxes and radio buttons to set the turn. For now, let's just take alternate turns, starting with *X*.

Add the new member shown here:

```
// class members:
    static GButton[][] btns;
    static boolean x_turn = true;
```

Then we'll add an `action()` method to the `GButton` class that does the real work. This will be very short, but it needs a bit of explaining.

First, I'm going to use the *ternary operator*, which will be new to everyone but C programmers:

```
exp_bool ? true_val : false_val
```

The `exp_bool` is evaluated first. If it's `true`, then `true_val` is returned. Otherwise, `false_val` is returned.

Next, I'm using a complex expression to find out if the `GButton`'s label is a null string. This uses the `String.equals()` method:

```
String.equals( "" ); // true for a null string

String s1, s2;
```

. . .
```
    s1== s2; // true if s1 and s2 are THE SAME STRING
```

The `equals()` method returns `true` if the values are equal. The `==` comparison, if you use it on objects, returns `true` only if both objects are the same. It returns `false` if two different strings that happen to have the same contents are compared.

I'm also using chained methods:

```
o1.method1().method2();

// OK if o1.method1() evaluates to o2, this way:

    // ( o1.method1() ).method2()
    //         o2        .method2()
```

In the code, I'm using:

```
getLabel().equals("");
```

This is the same as:

```
String stmp = getLabel();
stmp.equals("");
```

Here's the actual method you should add to the `Gbutton` class:

```
class GButton extends Button
{
    public boolean action( Event e, Object o )
    {
        if ( getLabel().equals("") )
        {
            setLabel( Fiveinarow.x_turn ? "X" : "O" );
            Fiveinarow.x_turn = !Fiveinarow.x_turn;
            return true;
        }
        else
```

```
        return false;
    }
}
```

It checks the button's label to see if it is a null `String`. If it is, either an `"X"` or `"O"`, depending on whose turn it is, is assigned as the `Button`'s label. The `x_turn` variable is reversed so that the other player gets the next turn.

Now when you compile and run, you'll have a working Tic Tac Toe game. Of course, the title asks if you can get Five-in-a-Row, which you can't on a 3-by-3 board. If that frustrates you, change the size constant to `12` and rebuild. Then you'll be able to actually play a game of Five-in-a-Row.

If you do that, by the way, you'll be adding 135 buttons to your layout. (That's 12-by-12 minus 3-by-3.) See why I said this would be quicker than using the dialog editor?

Adding More Buttons on a Panel

Now let's add a pair of `Button` objects in the `South` region. One will say `Restart`, and the other will say `Exit`. This time we can use a `FlowLayout`.

We'll make single-object classes to keep this coding simple, and I'll explain why that is the best way to get the job done.

Adding the Buttons

I'm going to add constructors to the new button classes. These will assign the labels by calling the constructor of the extended class. The extended class is known as `super` in the extending class. If you want to call `super`'s constructor, you use the `super` keyword as if it were a method name, this way:

```
MyClass( whatever, params )
{
    super( other, params );

    // optional code here
}
```

This `super()` call must be the first line in the constructor.

Begin by adding the two classes shown here:

```
class RestartButton extends Button
{
    RestartButton()
    {
        super( "Restart" );
    }

    public boolean action( Event e, Object o )
    {
        for( int r = 0; r < Fiveinarow.size; r++ )
            for ( int c = 0; c < Fiveinarow.size; c++ )
                Fiveinarow.btns[r][c].setLabel( "" );
        Fiveinarow.x_turn = true;

        return true;
    }
}

class ExitButton extends Button
{
    ExitButton()
    {
        super( "  Exit  " );
    }

    public boolean action( Event e, Object o )
    {
        System.exit(0);
        return true;
    }
}

// end of Fiveinarow.java
```

With those in place, the next thing is to create a `Panel`, create the new buttons, `add()` them to the `Panel` and attach the `Panel` to the `Frame`'s `South` region. That's easier to code than explain.

Add this code, just above the `ff.show()` call:

```
Panel p2 = new Panel(); // FlowLayout default
    RestartButton rb = new RestartButton();
    ExitButton xb = new ExitButton();

    p2.add( rb );
    p2.add( xb );
ff.add( "South", p2 );

    ff.show();
```

Now when you run the program you'll get the result shown in Figure 11.2.

FIGURE 11.2 A DIFFERENT PANEL OF BUTTONS ADDED.

The full program is shown in Listing 11.3.

LISTING 11.3 TWO STYLES OF BUTTON PANELS

```
// Fiveinarow.java

import java.awt.*;
```

```
public class Fiveinarow
{

    // constants:
       final static byte size = 3;

    // class members:
       static GButton[][] btns;
       static boolean x_turn = true;

    public void   main( String[] args )
    {
       FiveFrame ff = new FiveFrame();
          ff.setTitle( "Can you get 5 In A Row?" );
       ff.resize( 240, 300 );

       ff.setLayout( new BorderLayout() );

       Panel p1 = new Panel();
       p1.setLayout( new GridLayout(size,size) );

       ff.add( "Center", p1 );

       btns = new GButton[size][size];

       for ( int r = 0; r < size; r++ )
       {
          for ( int c = 0; c < size; c++ )
          {
             btns[r][c] = new GButton();
             p1.add( btns[r][c] );
          }
       }

       Panel p2 = new Panel(); // FlowLayout default
          RestartButton rb = new RestartButton();
          ExitButton xb = new ExitButton();
```

```
                p2.add( rb );
                p2.add( xb );
            ff.add( "South", p2 );

            ff.show();
        }
    }


class FiveFrame extends Frame
{
    public boolean handleEvent( Event e )
    {
        if (e.id == Event.WINDOW_DESTROY )
        {
            dispose();
            System.exit(0);
            return true;
        }
        else
            return super.handleEvent( e );
    }

}

class GButton extends Button
{
    public boolean action( Event e, Object o )
    {
        if ( getLabel().equals("") )
        {
            setLabel( Fiveinarow.x_turn ? "X" : "O" );
            Fiveinarow.x_turn = !Fiveinarow.x_turn;
            return true;
        }
        else
            return false;
    }
```

```
}

class RestartButton extends Button
{
    RestartButton()
    {
        super( "Restart" );
    }

    public boolean action( Event e, Object o )
    {
        for( int r = 0; r < Fiveinarow.size; r++ )
            for ( int c = 0; c < Fiveinarow.size; c++ )
                Fiveinarow.btns[r][c].setLabel( "" );
        Fiveinarow.x_turn = true;

        return true;
    }
}

class ExitButton extends Button
{
    ExitButton()
    {
        super( "  Exit  " );
    }

    public boolean action( Event e, Object o )
    {
        System.exit(0);
        return true;
    }
}

// end of Fiveinarow.java
```

Go ahead and play a game or two. This is a pretty impressive result for just over 100 lines of code, isn't it?

Late Binding and Switches

The way we've been adding `action()` methods to particular objects and having the Abstract Windows Toolkit (AWT) get the right one seems almost magical. You code an `ExitButton` class and its `action()` method gets called when it's clicked. You've got 11 buttons, but the AWT gets the right one. How?

Very, very efficiently, that's how.

The AWT creates a table of `action()` methods. The event loop reads an address from that table and calls it. In C code it would be a table of pointers to pointers. It's slightly slower than an absolute function call.

The alternative is using a `switch` (or multiple `if` statements) that picks the right method. In hand-written assembler, the method table call is one-sixth the size of the switch. Your actual results will depend on the machine that runs your Java, but letting the Java compiler–runtime combination pick the right routine is probably close to an order of magnitude faster than using your own switch.

C++ programmers refer to this as *late binding*. The compiler doesn't know, at compile time, which function will be called so it creates a table that is accessed at runtime. As a general rule, you should always be writing better code if you let the compiler do as much as possible. Using late binding instead of runtime switches is a perfectly good example of this effect.

Using the Checkbox Object

`Checkboxes` are traditionally used as inputs when a simple yes or no, on or off, or other binary choice is required. We'll use a `Checkbox` here as an output device as well. I think you'll agree that this works well. We'll start by taking a quick look at the class, and then we'll put a `Checkbox` to use in our game.

The Checkbox Class

A `Checkbox` extends the `Component` class. The `Checkbox` class has no fields. It has these constructors:

```
Checkbox cb;
CheckboxGroup cbg;

cb = new Checkbox();
    // unlabeled, set to off

cb = new Checkbox( "Label" );
    // labeled, set to off

cb = new Checkbox( "Label", cbg, state );
    // see below under "Using a CheckboxGroup"
```

Grouping `Checkbox` objects in a `CheckboxGroup` changes them into radio buttons, which we'll cover later in this chapter when we get to the `CheckboxGroup`. For now, we'll deal with plain `Checkbox` objects.

The most interesting methods are `getState()` and `setState()`. The former returns a the boolean value (`true` when checked) and the latter is called with a boolean to set the value. Note that if you use radio buttons, only `setState( true )` works. You can't "unpunch" a radio button—`setState( false )` only works for plain `Checkbox` objects.

Using an Input Checkbox

Let's add a `Checkbox` at the top of our game. We'll label it X to move and use it to set the first move. Start by adding a new class static member, which will be a new type we'll create. The line here that shows the `XCheckbox` is new:

```
// class members:
    static GButton[][] btns;
    static boolean x_turn = true;
    static XCheckbox xcb;
```

Then add the XCheckbox to the North region of the Frame. If you put it in a Panel, it will be neatly centered. The middle four lines here do that:

```
ff.setLayout( new BorderLayout() );

Panel p0 = new Panel();
       xcb = new XCheckbox();
    p0.add( xcb );
ff.add( "North", p0 );

Panel p1 = new Panel();
```

Then add a class with a constructor for the XCheckbox at the end of the file. The constructor should add the name and set the state to the value of the x_turn data member. This code will do that:

```
class XCheckbox extends Checkbox
{
   XCheckbox()
   {
      super( "X to move" );
      setState( Fiveinarow.x_turn );
   }
}

// end of Fiveinarow.java
```

Now you can run the program and take a look at your Checkbox. Of course, it's not connected to anything, so checking and unchecking it does nothing.

Output to a Checkbox

Let's begin by having the XCheckbox correctly report the status of the x_turn member. To do this, we'll have to replace the lines that set x_turn with calls to a method that sets x_turn and sets the XCheckbox. This method (add it just before the end of the Fiveinarow class) will do the job:

```
static void setTurn( boolean b )
{
    x_turn = b;
    xcb.setState( b );
}
```

Two lines set x_turn. One is the middle line in the deepest indent in the action() method of the Gbutton class. Change it to call the setTurn() method, as shown here:

```
class GButton extends Button
{
    public boolean action( Event e, Object o )
    {
        if ( getLabel().equals("") )
        {
            setLabel( Fiveinarow.x_turn ? "X" : "O" );
/*HERE*/    Fiveinarow.setTurn( !Fiveinarow.x_turn );
            return true;
        }
        else
            return false;
    }
}
```

The other place this member is set is in the RestartButton class. Change that one to call setTurn(), as shown here:

```
class RestartButton extends Button
{
    RestartButton()
    {
        super( "Restart" );
    }

    public boolean action( Event e, Object o )
    {
```

```
          for( int r = 0; r < Fiveinarow.size; r++ )
              for ( int c = 0; c < Fiveinarow.size; c++ )
                  Fiveinarow.btns[r][c].setLabel( "" );
    /*HERE*/ Fiveinarow.setTurn( true );

          return true;
      }
  }
```

Now when you run the program, the Checkbox will correctly report that it is (or isn't) X's turn to move. The only thing that it won't do is actually process your input. That's the final improvement we have to make before we replace the Checkbox with radio buttons.

Input from the Checkbox

When you click on a Checkbox you reverse its state. The AWT calls the Checkbox's action() method after it sets the new state. So all we need to do is set the x_turn member of the Fiveinarow class to the value of the XCheckbox's state in an action() method. This is the completed XCheckbox class:

```
class XCheckbox extends Checkbox
{
    XCheckbox()
    {
        super( "X to move" );
        setState( Fiveinarow.x_turn );
    }

    public boolean action( Event e, Object o )
    {
        Fiveinarow.x_turn = getState();
        return true;
    }
}
```

That's simple enough, isn't it? Of course, this lets you cheat. When you play the game you can, for example, place 3 Xs in a row. Try it.

Figure 11.3 shows how you can misuse this new capability.

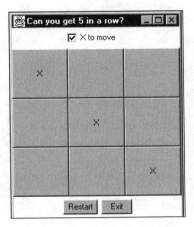

FIGURE 11.3 CHEATING AT TIC TAC TOE.

Listing 11.4 shows the full program to this point.

LISTING 11.4 PARTIAL FIVE-IN-A-ROW PROGRAM

```
// Fiveinarow.java

import java.awt.*;

public class Fiveinarow
{

    // constants:
        final static byte size = 3;

    // class members:
        static GButton[][] btns;
        static boolean x_turn = true;
        static XCheckbox xcb;
```

```
public void   main( String[] args )
{
   FiveFrame ff = new FiveFrame();
     ff.setTitle( "Can you get 5 In A Row?" );
   ff.resize( 240, 300 );

   ff.setLayout( new BorderLayout() );

   Panel p0 = new Panel();
      xcb = new XCheckbox();
      p0.add( xcb );
   ff.add( "North", p0 );

   Panel p1 = new Panel();
   p1.setLayout( new GridLayout(size,size) );

   ff.add( "Center", p1 );

   btns = new GButton[size][size];

   for ( int r = 0; r < size; r++ )
   {
      for ( int c = 0; c < size; c++ )
      {
         btns[r][c] = new GButton();
         p1.add( btns[r][c] );
      }
   }

   Panel p2 = new Panel(); // FlowLayout default
      RestartButton rb = new RestartButton();
      ExitButton xb = new ExitButton();

      p2.add( rb );
      p2.add( xb );
   ff.add( "South", p2 );

   ff.show();
```

```
      }

      static void setTurn( boolean b )
      {
          x_turn = b;
          xcb.setState( b );
      }
}

class FiveFrame extends Frame
{
      public boolean handleEvent( Event e )
      {
          if (e.id == Event.WINDOW_DESTROY )
          {
              dispose();
              System.exit(0);
              return true;
          }
          else
              return super.handleEvent( e );
      }

}

class GButton extends Button
{
      public boolean action( Event e, Object o )
      {
          if ( getLabel().equals("") )
          {
              setLabel( Fiveinarow.x_turn ? "X" : "O" );
              Fiveinarow.setTurn( !Fiveinarow.x_turn );
              return true;
          }
          else
              return false;
```

```
      }
   }

   class RestartButton extends Button
   {
      RestartButton()
      {
         super( "Restart" );
      }

      public boolean action( Event e, Object o )
      {
         for( int r = 0; r < Fiveinarow.size; r++ )
            for ( int c = 0; c < Fiveinarow.size; c++ )
               Fiveinarow.btns[r][c].setLabel( "" );
         Fiveinarow.setTurn( true );

         return true;
      }
   }

   class ExitButton extends Button
   {
      ExitButton()
      {
         super( "  Exit  " );
      }

      public boolean action( Event e, Object o )
      {
         System.exit(0);
         return true;
      }
   }

   class XCheckbox extends Checkbox
   {
```

```
XCheckbox()
{
    super( "X to move" );
    setState( Fiveinarow.x_turn );
}

public boolean action( Event e, Object o )
{
    Fiveinarow.x_turn = getState();
    return true;
}
}

// end of Fiveinarow.java
```

If you know some younger children, they'll be delighted with this little program. You might want to retitle the box Tic Tac Toe and save the finished program at this stage.

Using a CheckboxGroup

The trouble with Tic Tac Toe is that a moderately skilled player will never lose. Two moderately skilled players will always tie. While we add to our Java skill by learning about radio buttons, we'll switch from Tic Tac Toe to Five-in-a-Row, a game of skill that will challenge two intelligent players for hours at a time.

Switch the size constant from 3 to 12 and rebuild. When you run this version, you'll be playing Five-in-a-Row. As with Tic Tac Toe, two players alternate, writing X and O. The goal is to get Five-in-a-Row, vertically, horizontally or diagonally. Figure 11.4 shows a game in progress.

You'll win Five-in-a-Row if you get four in a row with both ends open. As you see in Figure 11.4, O has four in a row. X can block one end, but O will win by playing at the end X doesn't block.

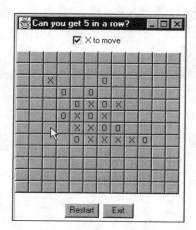

FIGURE 11.4 X CAN'T BLOCK BOTH ENDS.

The basic defensive strategy is to block one end when your opponent reaches three in a row. Knowing this, the offensive goal is to get a pattern in which placing one letter gets you three in a row in two separate directions. Knowing this, the defensive strategy....

Did I hear someone mention radio buttons?

A better version of this game would show a pair of radio buttons, one labeled, X to play and the other, O to play. As I noted above, the Checkbox turns into a radio button when you put it into a CheckboxGroup class.

The CheckboxGroup Class

You collect Checkbox objects in a CheckboxGroup by using the third form of the Checkbox constructor, this way:

```
CheckboxGroup cbg = new CheckboxGroup();

Checkbox cb1 = new Checkbox( "Item 1", cbg, true  );
Checkbox cb2 = new Checkbox( "Item 2", cbg, false );
Checkbox cb3 = new Checkbox( "Item 3", cbg, false );
```

A `CheckboxGroup` is *not* a `Container`. It's just an `Object`. It's purpose is to be sure that only one `Checkbox` at a time is in a `true` state. If you punch one, another one is unpunched.

That's all you need to know to use the `CheckboxGroup` class. Let's install one at the top of our game.

Using an Input CheckboxGroup

We'll need an `OCheckbox` to go along with our `XCheckbox`. Begin by adding it to the static members of the `Fiveinarow` class, this way:

```
// class members:
   static GButton[][] btns;
   static boolean x_turn = true;
   static XCheckbox xcb;
   static OCheckbox ocb;
```

Then you'll create the `CheckboxGroup` and add the `OCheckbox` where you added the `XCheckbox`. Both the constructors will need to pass the `CheckboxGroup` to their class's constructors. The code should look like this:

```
Panel p0 = new Panel();
   CheckboxGroup cbg = new CheckboxGroup();
   xcb = new XCheckbox( cbg );
   ocb = new OCheckbox( cbg );
   p0.add( xcb );
   p0.add( ocb );
ff.add( "North", p0 );
```

Now we'll modify the `XCheckbox` class to call the `Checkbox`'s constructor with the three-parameter form. The constructor becomes:

```
XCheckbox( CheckboxGroup g )
{
   super( "X to move", g, Fiveinarow.x_turn );
}
```

Then copy the XCheckbox class and turn it into the OCheckbox class:

```
class OCheckbox extends Checkbox
{
    OCheckbox( CheckboxGroup g )
    {
        super( "O to move", g, !Fiveinarow.x_turn );
    }

    public boolean action( Event e, Object o )
    {
        Fiveinarow.x_turn = !getState();
        return true;
    }
}
```

Note that there's a ! operator added to each of the lines that use the x_turn member.

Finally, you'll need to improve the setTurn() method. It has to punch the appropriate radio button when it resets the turn. This is the new code:

```
static void setTurn( boolean b )
{
    x_turn = b;
    if ( x_turn )
        xcb.setState( true );
    else
        ocb.setState( true );
}
```

Remember that you have to setState() to true (i.e., punch the button) when the Checkbox object is included in a CheckboxGroup.

With these changes, you can rebuild and run the finished program. Mine's shown here in Figure 11.5.

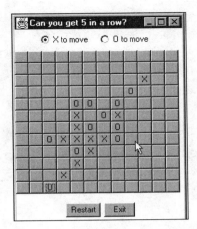

FIGURE 11.5 PLAYING THE COMPLETED 5 IN A ROW GAME.

By the way, did you notice that *O* has this game won?

Listing 11.5 shows the finished Five-in-a-Row program.

LISTING 11.5 THE FINISHED FIVE-IN-A-ROW PROGRAM

```java
// Fiveinarow.java

import java.awt.*;

public class Fiveinarow
{

    // constants:
        final static byte size = 12;

    // class members:
        static GButton[][] btns;
        static boolean x_turn = true;
        static XCheckbox xcb;
        static OCheckbox ocb;

    public void   main( String[] args )
```

```
{
    FiveFrame ff = new FiveFrame();
    ff.setTitle( "Can you get 5 in a row?" );
    ff.resize( 240, 300 );

    ff.setLayout( new BorderLayout() );

    Panel p0 = new Panel();
        CheckboxGroup cbg = new CheckboxGroup();
        xcb = new XCheckbox( cbg );
        ocb = new OCheckbox( cbg );
        p0.add( xcb );
        p0.add( ocb );
    ff.add( "North", p0 );

    Panel p1 = new Panel();
    p1.setLayout( new GridLayout(size,size) );

    ff.add( "Center", p1 );

    btns = new GButton[size][size];

    for ( int r = 0; r < size; r++ )
    {
        for ( int c = 0; c < size; c++ )
        {
            btns[r][c] = new GButton();
            p1.add( btns[r][c] );
        }
    }

    Panel p2 = new Panel(); // FlowLayout default
        RestartButton rb = new RestartButton();
        ExitButton xb = new ExitButton();

        p2.add( rb );
        p2.add( xb );
    ff.add( "South", p2 );
```

```
        ff.show();
    }

    static void setTurn( boolean b )
    {
        x_turn = b;
        if ( x_turn )
            xcb.setState( true );
        else
            ocb.setState( true );
    }
}

class FiveFrame extends Frame
{
    public boolean handleEvent( Event e )
    {
        if (e.id == Event.WINDOW_DESTROY )
        {
            dispose();
            System.exit(0);
            return true;
        }
        else
            return super.handleEvent( e );
    }

}

class GButton extends Button
{
    public boolean action( Event e, Object o )
    {
        if ( getLabel().equals("") )
        {
            setLabel( Fiveinarow.x_turn ? "X" : "O" );
            Fiveinarow.setTurn( !Fiveinarow.x_turn );
```

```
            return true;
        }
        else
            return false;
    }
}

class RestartButton extends Button
{
    RestartButton()
    {
        super( "Restart" );
    }

    public boolean action( Event e, Object o )
    {
        for( int r = 0; r < Fiveinarow.size; r++ )
            for ( int c = 0; c < Fiveinarow.size; c++ )
                Fiveinarow.btns[r][c].setLabel( "" );
        Fiveinarow.setTurn( true );

        return true;
    }
}

class ExitButton extends Button
{
    ExitButton()
    {
        super( "  Exit  " );
    }

    public boolean action( Event e, Object o )
    {
        System.exit(0);
        return true;
    }
}
```

```
}

class XCheckbox extends Checkbox
{
    XCheckbox( CheckboxGroup g )
    {
        super( "X to move", g, Fiveinarow.x_turn );
    }

    public boolean action( Event e, Object o )
    {
        Fiveinarow.x_turn = getState();
        return true;
    }
}

class OCheckbox extends Checkbox
{
    OCheckbox( CheckboxGroup g )
    {
        super( "O to move", g, !Fiveinarow.x_turn );
    }

    public boolean action( Event e, Object o )
    {
        Fiveinarow.x_turn = !getState();
        return true;
    }
}

// end of Fiveinarow.java
```

After you play a few games, give some thought to adding some logic to check for a win. In the next chapter you'll learn to use the drawing tools. Then you could actually draw a nice line showing the five *X*s or *O*s that make up the win.

Of course, after you finish this book you'll want to extend the game so that two players can compete across the Web. Send me a copy when you get it working!

Summary

In this chapter we got our work done by playing games.

We started by using the `GridLayout` to add an array of `Button` objects to a `Panel` in a `BorderLayout`. We started with a 3-by-3 grid, which looks like a Tic Tac Toe game.

Then we added a group of two `Checkbox` objects in the `South` region. A little work on the `action()` method of our grid of buttons gave us a real, two-player Tic Tac Toe game.

We went on to add a `Checkbox` object in the `North` region. We hooked this up first as an output device, using its `setState()` method to make it checked or not depending on whose turn it was. Then we used its `action()` method to trap and act on checks that the user enters in the `Checkbox`.

Finally, we replaced the `Checkbox` with a pair of `Checkbox` objects connected in a `CheckboxGroup` to make radio buttons.

In the next chapter, we'll meet the `Graphics` object. Everything we've done so far has used components that someone has programmed for us. When you understand `Graphics`, you'll be able to draw anything your mind can conceive.

By the way, did you notice that our whole game uses just 161 lines? And that programming a 15-by-15 version of the game would require changing one constant? And that you've just done a polished game for Windows 3.x, 95, and NT, for OS/2, the Macintosh, Solaris, and lots of other Unix versions?

Java's a nice language for GUI programming!

## CHAPTER 12

DRAWING TOOLS

Java includes a rich set of graphics capabilities. Sun's Java Workshop, for example, is a Java development system like Visual J++, but it is wrapped in a Web browser, not a traditional IDE. It's written in Java.

I'm not recommending that we immediately discard our C++ compilers. On the other hand, there really isn't any limit to what you can do in Java.

We'll start by looking at the reasons for using graphics in Java applets. I think you'll agree that there is a huge role for Java graphics in all Web sites.

The we'll look at the `Graphics` class, which we've been using all along, just beneath the surface. Each `Component` has a `paint()` method that uses a `Graphics` object to draw itself. Buttons, for example, know how to look like they are being clicked.

The `Graphics` class has methods for drawing lines, rectangles, ovals, and many more primitive shapes. We'll program a panel display with a raised look using multiple rectangles.

Using ovals, we'll draw a cup. (Add your own Java.) You'll see that the arc, which is nearly incomprehensible in the AWT documentation, is just a partial oval.

We won't cover all the methods in the `Graphics` arsenal. By putting a selection of them into use you'll be able to use the whole class. First, though, we'll need to see how the concepts work.

Along the way, we'll meet the `Color` and `Dimension` classes, which we'll put to use in our drawing.

Java Graphics for Applets

Do we really need graphics programming capabilities in our applets? After all, HTML is very good at supporting graphics, setting background colors, using multiple colors and sizes of text, and so on. Why use Java when we could use a scanner and a good paint program to develop our images? The reason is simple: speed. Before we leave this chapter you'll have programmed a page-wide banner decorated with a cup. This would take tens of kilobytes as a bit map. It takes 3 K in a Java applet.

Your Java-enhanced page will be up on your user's screens while other non-Java pages are slowly loading graphics files. Java won't replace bitmaps—you don't want to try programming a photograph, for example—but for most decorative work (e.g., a logo you want to display on each page), Java will let you provide artwork while you maintain really hot performance over a simple modem connection.

Here we'll find out how it's done.

The Graphics Class

Back in Chapter 9 we looked at the `Container` class. It has a `paintComponents()` method that we postponed. Earlier, we began using Applet Wizard code that includes this method:

```
paint( Graphics g )
```

```
    {
        g.drawString( "...
    }
```

The `Component` class has a `paint()` method, which is overridden by classes that need to display their objects on the screen. Each `paint()` method uses a `Graphics` object.

Each implementation handles the interface between the `Graphics` object and the underlying operating system. On top of this, the individual object's `paint()` methods are implemented so that, for example, a radio button in Windows looks like a Windows' radio button.

We can work with the Java Graphics class as if it is our operating system's API for screen output. Courtesy of individual implementation teams, we're programming OS/2, the Macintosh, and all the rest, all through this class.

Graphics Concepts

Each Component has a `paint()` and a `repaint()` method. Each `Container` has a `paintComponents()` method. These methods do their actual painting with a `Graphics` object that the Abstract Windows Toolkit (AWT) passes to them when it calls these methods.

The AWT works with the underlying operating system to call the painting methods at appropriate times. For example, when one window is closed the underlying windows `paint()` methods get called. A `Container` (e.g., `Window`, `Frame`, `Panel`) calls its `paintComponents()` method. This calls, in turn, the `paint()` methods for the individual components.

Well below the level at which we program, the AWT and the underlying operating system handle details such as allocating memory and mapping the memory into which we paint to actual video memory.

What we see is a `Graphics` object and a `Component`. The `Component` occupies some portion of the screen's real estate. Within that `Component` we can draw with a rich variety of drawing tools provided by the `Graphics` class. (We can write text, too, but that's a subject for Chapter 13.)

We won't worry about peer objects as we program, but you've probably been stumbling over them whenever you look at the online AWT documentation. (Most `Component`'s method lists start with `addNotify()`, which is about peer `Components`.)

Peers are used internally by the AWT to do its drawing work. They keep partially drawn objects off our screens. When a `Component` finishes its painting work in a peer `Component`, it hands back the completed work for display. You don't need to worry about peers to use `Graphics` objects.

The Graphics Class

The `Graphics` class is an abstract class. It has no fields and, because it is abstract, you can't call its constructor to create a new `Graphics` object. Where do `Graphics` objects come from? When you create a `Component`, the AWT builds an appropriate `Graphics` object. Each component has a `paint()` method, which is called by the AWT with a `Graphics` object parameter. You don't call the `paint()` method yourself—let the AWT do that. When the AWT calls `paint()`, it provides the `Graphics` object.

You can force a call to `paint()` by calling the `repaint()` method. If your painting is static (e.g., that handsome logo you want on each page) you'll program the `paint()` method yourself, but let the AWT handle calling it. You'd call `repaint()` in, for example, a drawing program where you were changing the display based on mouse movements.

The methods of the `Graphics` class are what we'll work with. This is a partial list:

- `clearRect()`, `drawRect()`, `fillRect()`
- `drawOval()`, `fillOval()`
- `drawArc()`, `fillArc()`
- `drawBytes()`, `drawString()`
- `drawPolygon()`, `fillPolygon()`
- `setFont()`, `getFont()`
- `getColor()`, `setColor()`

There are more tools in the `Graphics` class, too. You might find the rounded and 3D rectangles useful, for example. When you finish this chapter, you'll want to dive into the online AWT documentation (API, Volume 2, **java.awt**, `Graphics` class). Once you start using the tools, as we'll do here, using any of the rest of them will be no problem.

Building a Framework

We'll program an application that takes advantage of the speed of **JVIEW.EXE**, but we'll inherit from `Applet` to make later conversion simple.

The first challenge is to get a `Graphics` object and see something displayed on the screen. Listing 12.1 shows a framework.

LISTING 12.1 A FRAMEWORK FOR A GRAPHIC LOGO

```
// MLogo.java

import java.awt.*;
import java.applet.Applet;

public class MLogo extends Applet
{
    void main( String[] args )
    {
        MLogo ml = new MLogo();

        MyFrame f = new MyFrame( "Sample Logo App" );
        f.setLayout( new BorderLayout() );

        f.add( "Center", ml );

        f.resize( 500, 200 );

        Panel ps = new Panel();
        ps.add( new OKButton() );
```

```
        f.add( "South", ps );

        f.show();
    }

    public void paint( Graphics g )
    {
        g.drawString( "Marty's Logo Goes Here", 30, 30 );
    }
}

class MyFrame extends Frame
{
    MyFrame( String s )
    {
        super( s );
    }

    public boolean handleEvent( Event e )
    {
        if (e.id == Event.WINDOW_DESTROY )
        {
            System.exit(0);
            return true;
        }
        else
            return super.handleEvent( e );
    }
}

class OKButton extends Button
{
    OKButton()
    {
        super( "   OK   " );
    }
```

```
    public boolean action( Event e, Object o )
    {
        System.exit( 0 );
        return true;
    }
}
// end of MLogo.java
```

Build a new project workspace (mine's named `MLogo` because I'll be building Marty's logo) and enter this code, changing the names to suit yourself.
When you get it running, you should have a display like the one in Figure
12.1.

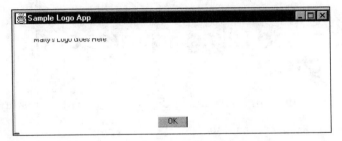

FIGURE 12.1　STARTING THE LOGO APP.

Before we go on, look closely at these lines in the `main()` routine:

```
MLogo ml = new MLogo();

    MyFrame f = new MyFrame( "Sample Logo App" );
    f.setLayout( new BorderLayout() );

        f.add( "Center", ml );
```

The `ml` object is an `MLogo`, which is this program's class extending
`Applet`. An `Applet` object is an extension of the `Panel` class. So when
you `add()` the `ml` object to your `Frame`, you are adding a `Panel`. The
`paint()` method in this `Applet` is found all the way back in `Component`.
An `Applet` is a `Panel`, a `Panel` is a `Container`, and the `Container` is a
`Component`.

The rest of this program provides a button that closes the program and a correct response if you click the `close this window` button in the upper-right corner. It uses the `drawString()` method, just to say something and show that the machinery is all working. This is the subject of the next chapter. For now, the parameters are:

```
Graphics.drawString( String to_draw, int xloc, int yloc );

// xloc and yloc are in pixels
// 0, 0 is the top-left corner
```

All `Graphics` dimensions are given in pixels, measured from the top-left corner.

Drawing and Filling Squares and Rectangles

Ready to start drawing? Try adding this to your `paint()` method:

```
g.drawRect( 40, 40, 80, 30 );
    g.fillRect( 80, 80, 50, 20 );
```

That gives the result shown in Figure 12.2.

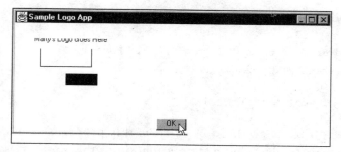

FIGURE 12.2 ADDING A `drawRect()` AND A `fillRect()` METHOD.

The drawRect() and fillRect() Methods

As you can see, `drawRect()` draws the outline of a rectangle. The `fillRect()` method fills the rectangle. Both work in the currently set color, which defaults to black.

The parameters are `ints` for the left and top corner's location and for the width and height. Squares, of course, are rectangles in which height and width are equal.

Now you know everything you need to know about these methods.

Drawings Should Fit

The problem with the method calls we just added is that they are based on absolute coordinates. Try launching your application again and then resize the window. Your rectangles remain stubbornly unchanged. This may be just what you require sometimes, but most of the time you'll want your graphics to accommodate different window sizes.

The `Component` class, which is the abstract base for everything that you can see on the screen, provides a `size()` method. It returns a `Dimension` object. This isn't really an object in the sense that a `Button` or a `Panel` is an object. Rather, it's a use of the object-oriented language to provide multiple return values from a function call.

If you want to know the size of a screen component, you need to know height and width. A `Dimension` object provides fields `Dimension.width` and `Dimension.height`. Once again, I've provided an explanation of a concept that's more complex than the code that embodies it.

Delete the three lines in your current `paint()` method and replace them with the code you see in Listing 12.2.

LISTING 12.2 A FLEXIBLE RECTANGLE

```
public void paint( Graphics g )
{
    int offset = 4; // space left around border
    int lf = offset;
    int tp = offset;

    Dimension d = size();
    int rt = d.width - offset - 1;
    int bt = d.height - offset - 1;

    int wd = rt - lf - 1;
    int ht = bt - tp - 1;

    g.setColor( Color.black );
    g.drawRect( lf, tp, wd, ht );

}
```

This draws a rectangle set in by 4 (offset) pixels from the full size of your
Applet. When you resize your application's Frame (or your browser's
window, if you're running as an applet) the rectangle will stretch or shrink
appropriately, always leaving a 4-pixel border.

Bear in mind that the top-left corner is 0, 0. Starting the rectangle at 4,
4 leaves a 4-pixel-wide border (0, 1, 2, and 3) at the left and top.

The right and bottom sides may take some thought. If your panel is
100 pixels wide, they're numbered 0 through 99. To leave a 4-pixel wide
border, you want to leave 96, 97, 98, and 99 empty, so the rightmost pixel
to draw is 95.

I'll explain that g.setColor() call in the next section.

Drawing a Decorative Panel

Now that we have a nice, stretchy rectangle, let's convert it into a decorative panel. I'm going to use the Color object, which encapsulates a 24-bit

color scheme. Each of the three primary screen colors—red, green, and blue—have an unsigned byte integer that gives them an intensity. 0 is off, and 255 is maximum intensity.

You can construct `Color` objects as shown here:

```
Color black = new Color(   0,   0,   0 );

Color red   = new Color( 255,   0,   0 );
Color green = new Color(   0, 255,   0 );
Color blue  = new Color(   0,   0, 255 );

Color white = new Color( 255, 255, 255 );

Color medium_cyan = new Color( 0, 150, 150 );
```

There are other `Color` constructors. You can using floating point values between 0.0 (off) and 1.0 (maximum) for red, green, and blue. You can also combine the three bytes into a single `int`. (Red, green, and blue are the second, third, and fourth sets of eight bits in the `int`, respectively.)

If you remember from our discussion of HTML, however, you'd be wise to stay away from subtle color variations. Your users will be running a wide range of machines, many of which will have limited colors and some will even be monochrome. What will appear is the user's hardware's best approximation.

The `Color` object also provides a set of convenient constant (`final static`) values that let you write code with named colors, which I'll use here. Again, it's easier to do than to explain.

I'm going to go for a raised effect to make a decorative panel. You do this by simulating a light source. Picture a raised rectangle with a light shining from the northwest. The north and west edges will be bright; south and east will be dark. So we'll draw a few light lines in the north and west, and some dark ones on the south and east edges.

We could draw individual lines with the `drawLine()` method, but the rectangle makes a more convenient line drawing tool, if your lines are horizontal or vertical. For a horizontal line that is 5 pixels thick, you just draw a rectangle with a height of 5.

I'll start this effect with a line width, in the `bwid` variable, of 10. That's way too fat, but it lets you see exactly what's happening. Enter the new `paint()` code shown here:

```
int bwid = 10; // size of visible border

g.setColor( Color.darkGray );
g.fillRect( lf+1, bt-bwid-1, wd-2, bwid ); // S edge
g.fillRect( rt-bwid-1, tp+1, bwid, ht-2 ); // E edge

g.setColor( Color.lightGray );
g.fillRect( lf+1, tp+1, wd-2, bwid ); // N edge
g.fillRect( lf+1, tp+1, bwid, ht-2 ); // W edge

g.setColor( Color.cyan );
g.fillRect( lf+bwid+1, tp+bwid+1,
    wd-2*(bwid+1), ht-2*(bwid+1) );

}
```

When you run this code, you'll get the view shown in Figure 12.3.

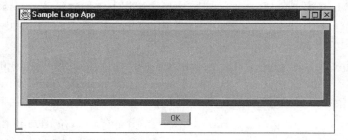

Figure 12.3 Light and dark edges, too wide.

This doesn't look very good, but it shows you what's going on. Do you see how I've handled the southwest and northeast corners? The lighter color goes all the way to the edge; the darker color stops at the edge of the lighter color.

Now set your `bwid` down to 2 and launch the program again. That will give you an attractive, raised-panel effect. Listing 12.3 shows the full program to this point.

LISTING 12.3 RAISING THE DECORATIVE PANEL

```java
// MLogo.java

import java.awt.*;
import java.applet.Applet;

public class MLogo extends Applet
{
    void main( String[] args )
    {
        MLogo ml = new MLogo();

        MyFrame f = new MyFrame( "Sample Logo App" );
        f.setLayout( new BorderLayout() );

        f.add( "Center", ml );

        f.resize( 500, 200 );

        Panel ps = new Panel();
        ps.add( new OKButton() );
        f.add( "South", ps );

        f.show();
    }

    public void paint( Graphics g )
    {
        int offset = 4; // space left around border
        int lf = offset;
        int tp = offset;

        Dimension d = size();
```

```
            int rt = d.width - offset - 1;
            int bt = d.height - offset - 1;

            int wd = rt - lf - 1;
            int ht = bt - tp - 1;

            g.setColor( Color.black );
            g.drawRect( lf, tp, wd, ht );

              int bwid = 2; // size of visible border

            g.setColor( Color.darkGray );
            g.fillRect( lf+1, bt-bwid-1, wd-2, bwid ); // S edge
            g.fillRect( rt-bwid-1, tp+1, bwid, ht-2 ); // E edge

            g.setColor( Color.lightGray );
            g.fillRect( lf+1, tp+1, wd-2, bwid ); // N edge
            g.fillRect( lf+1, tp+1, bwid, ht-2 ); // W edge

            g.setColor( Color.cyan );
            g.fillRect( lf+bwid+1, tp+bwid+1,
                wd-2*(bwid+1), ht-2*(bwid+1) );

        }
    }


class MyFrame extends Frame
{
    MyFrame( String s )
    {
        super( s );
    }

    public boolean handleEvent( Event e )
    {
        if (e.id == Event.WINDOW_DESTROY )
        {
            System.exit(0);
```

```
            return true;
        }
        else
            return super.handleEvent( e );
    }
}

class OKButton extends Button
{
    OKButton()
    {
        super( "    OK    " );
    }

    public boolean action( Event e, Object o )
    {
        System.exit( 0 );
        return true;
    }
}
// end of MLogo.java
```

Drawing and Filling Circles, Ovals, and Arcs

Ready for a cup of Java? Let's use the left third or so of our panel (that's the decorative panel we're drawing inside our `Panel Applet`) for a cup of steaming Joe. We'll start with an oval.

Circles and Ovals

The `drawOval()` and `fillOval()` methods are identical to `drawRect()` and `fillRect()` in their parameters. They place an oval inside the rectangle that your parameters describe.

Add this code at the end of your `paint()` method, and run your program:

```
int wd1 = wd/3;
int ht1 = ht/4;

int lf1 = lf + bwid + 3;
int tp1 = tp + ht1;

g.setColor( Color.black );
g.drawOval( lf1, tp1, wd1, ht1 );

g.setColor( Color.white );
g.fillOval( lf1+1, tp1+1, wd1-2, ht1-2 );

}
```

This draws a black oval outline and then fills the outline with a white oval. The result is shown in Figure 12.4.

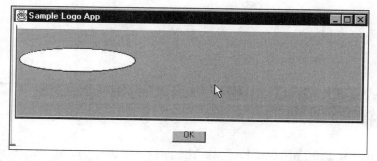

FIGURE 12.4 ADDING A `drawOval()` AND A `fillOval()` METHOD.

Note that we're still using soft-coded values for the rectangles' coordinates. This cup will stretch along with our panel. You'll get a circle when the height and width of the bounding rectangle are equal.

Arcs

Let's go on to the base of the cup. We'll want to draw the bottom half as an oval. The `drawArc()` and `fillArc()` methods are close cousins of the oval methods. Their difference is that two added parameters describe where to start and stop drawing. (In the case of `fillArc()`, they describe where to make the first and second cuts in a pie. What you'll see looks like a slice of pie lifted out.)

If you picture your oval as a clock face, 3:00 is considered 0 degrees. The starting point is given in degrees, measured counterclockwise from 3:00. 45 is 1:30, 90 is 12:00, etc. The ending point is given as the offset from the start, also in degrees measured counterclockwise. You use 90 for a quarter arc, 180 for a half arc, etc. You can specify a positive (i.e., counterclockwise) or a negative (i.e., clockwise) offset. Both of these get the right half of an oval:

```
drawArc( tp, lf, ht, wd, 90, -180 );
    // 180 degrees clockwise, starting at 12:00

drawArc( tp, lf, ht, wd, 270, 180 );
    // 180 degrees counterclockwise, starting at 6:00
```

You can take the bottom half of an oval either of these ways:

```
drawArc( t,l,h,w, 0, -180 );
    // clockwise, from 3:00 to 9:00

drawArc( t,l,h,w, 180, 180 );
    // counterclockwise, from 9:00 to 3:00
```

Again, it's easier to code than to explain. For the bottom of the coffee cup, add these lines to the end of `paint()`:

```
int wd2 = (2*wd1)/3;
int ht2 = (2*ht1)/3;

int lf2 = lf1 + (wd1 - wd2)/2;
```

```
    int tp2 = tp1 + ht/2;

    g.setColor( Color.black );
    g.drawArc( lf2, tp2, wd2, ht2, 0, -180 );

}
```

When you run the program now, you'll get the cup of Java shown in Figure 12.5.

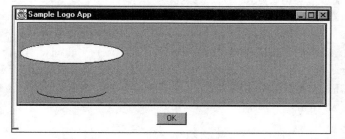

FIGURE **12.5** THE CUP TAKES SHAPE.

You can use `drawLine()` to make sides for this cup. The `drawLine()` method takes four integer parameters: the *x* and *y* coordinates of the starting and ending points, respectively. These lines draw the diagonals in a square from 0, 0 to 100, 100:

```
drawLine( 0, 0, 100, 100 );
    // northwest to southeast

drawLine( 100, 0, 0, 100 );
    // northeast to southwest
```

Add these lines to `paint()` to draw sides on your cup:

```
    g.drawLine( lf1, (tp1 + ht1/2),
        lf2, (tp2 + ht2/2) );

    g.drawLine( lf1+wd1-1, (tp1+ht1/2),
        lf2+wd2-1, (tp2 + ht2/2) );

}
```

This gives you the result you can see in Figure 12.6.

FIGURE 12.6 SIDES ADDED TO THE CUP.

There's only one small problem. A backpacker will recognize the classic lines of the Sierra cup, here. It's an all-purpose metal cup, which you can cook in. It's an absolutely terrible cup for coffee. The metal burns your lips.

I'm going to lose those sides and suggest the shape by drawing another arc. I've struck an average between top and bottom to get a middle arc. Then I pushed the middle arc down just a bit, to suggest a slightly curved side to my cup.

Here's the last code to add to `paint()` to get the art shown in Figure 12.7.

```
/* These didn't look good
g.drawLine( lf1, (tp1 + ht1/2),
    lf2, (tp2 + ht2/2) );

g.drawLine( lf1+wd1-1, (tp1+ht1/2),
    lf2+wd2-1, (tp2 + ht2/2) );
*/

int lf3 = (lf1 + lf2) / 2;
int tp3 = (tp1 + tp2) / 2;
int wd3 = (wd1 + wd2) / 2;
int ht3 = (ht1 + ht2) / 2;

tp3 += ht/20;
```

```
    g.drawArc( lf3, tp3, wd3, ht3, 0, -180 );
}
```

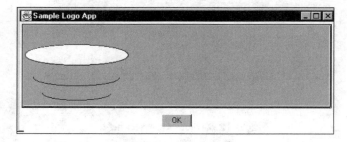

FIGURE 12.7 MY FINAL CUP.

Note that I've used /* ... */ to comment out the lines. You'll probably want to try different values for the offset of tp3. My 5% adjustment pleases me, but I'm not you. The completed program is in Listing 12.4.

LISTING 12.4 THE COMPLETED WORK OF ART

```
// MLogo.java

import java.awt.*;
import java.applet.Applet;

public class MLogo extends Applet
{
    void main( String[] args )
    {
        MLogo ml = new MLogo();

        MyFrame f = new MyFrame( "Sample Logo App" );
        f.setLayout( new BorderLayout() );

        f.add( "Center", ml );

        f.resize( 500, 200 );
```

```
    Panel ps = new Panel();
    ps.add( new OKButton() );
    f.add( "South", ps );

    f.show();
}

public void paint( Graphics g )
{
    int offset = 4; // space left around border
    int lf = offset;
    int tp = offset;

    Dimension d = size();
    int rt = d.width - offset - 1;
    int bt = d.height - offset - 1;

    int wd = rt - lf - 1;
    int ht = bt - tp - 1;

    g.setColor( Color.black );
    g.drawRect( lf, tp, wd, ht );

    int bwid = 2; // size of visible border

    g.setColor( Color.darkGray );
    g.fillRect( lf+1, bt-bwid-1, wd-2, bwid ); // S edge
    g.fillRect( rt-bwid-1, tp+1, bwid, ht-2 ); // E edge

    g.setColor( Color.lightGray );
    g.fillRect( lf+1, tp+1, wd-2, bwid ); // N edge
    g.fillRect( lf+1, tp+1, bwid, ht-2 ); // W edge

    g.setColor( Color.cyan );
    g.fillRect( lf+bwid+1, tp+bwid+1,
        wd-2*(bwid+1), ht-2*(bwid+1) );

    int wd1 = wd/3;
```

```
int ht1 = ht/4;

int lf1 = lf + bwid + 3;
int tp1 = tp + ht1;

g.setColor( Color.black );
g.drawOval( lf1, tp1, wd1, ht1 );

g.setColor( Color.white );
g.fillOval( lf1+1, tp1+1, wd1-2, ht1-2 );

int wd2 = (2*wd1)/3;
int ht2 = (2*ht1)/3;

int lf2 = lf1 + (wd1 - wd2)/2;
int tp2 = tp1 + ht/2;

g.setColor( Color.black );
g.drawArc( lf2, tp2, wd2, ht2, 0, -180 );

/* These didn't look good
g.drawLine( lf1, (tp1 + ht1/2),
    lf2, (tp2 + ht2/2) );

g.drawLine( lf1+wd1-1, (tp1+ht1/2),
    lf2+wd2-1, (tp2 + ht2/2) );
*/

int lf3 = (lf1 + lf2) / 2;
int tp3 = (tp1 + tp2) / 2;
int wd3 = (wd1 + wd2) / 2;
int ht3 = (ht1 + ht2) / 2;

tp3 += ht/20;

g.drawArc( lf3, tp3, wd3, ht3, 0, -180 );
    }

}
```

```
class MyFrame extends Frame
{
   MyFrame( String s )
   {
      super( s );
   }

   public boolean handleEvent( Event e )
   {
      if (e.id == Event.WINDOW_DESTROY )
      {
         System.exit(0);
         return true;
      }
      else
         return super.handleEvent( e );
   }
}

class OKButton extends Button
{
   OKButton()
   {
      super( "   OK   " );
   }

   public boolean action( Event e, Object o )
   {
      System.exit( 0 );
      return true;
   }
}
// end of MLogo.java
```

Getting a Handle on Your Cup

You're on your way. This is easy programming, isn't it? Java's `Graphics` class provides the methods you need.

So here I'm going to let you go off on your own. Make the artistic decisions first. (I use old-fashioned technology, pencil and paper, for this.) Where should the handle go? How are you going to show it?

Putting it in place will probably take two arcs. You may want to draw a bunch, separated by a pixel each, to get the right thickness.

Good luck, and have fun!

Summary

We started by looking at the reasons for graphics programming in applets that will be embedded in HTML pages. For many types of graphics, such as the logo we've been building, a Java applet is tiny compared to the equivalent bitmapped graphic image. My complete `MLogo.class` is just 3 K.

Then we looked at the underlying concept. `Graphics` objects are built by each component and the AWT hands them to you as a parameter of the `paint()` method, which you override to do your own graphics work.

After building a framework, we went on to program rectangles with the `drawRect()` and `fillRect()` methods. You used the `size()` method of the `Component` to size a decorative panel to fit the `Applet`. This coding technique allows for resizing by the user.

We went on from a decorative panel to a coffee cup, built with ovals and arcs, which are partial ovals. Combining a `drawOval()` outline with a `fillOval()` white space gave us the top of our cup. Two half ovals made with `drawArc()` calls sketched the middle and bottom of our cup.

We also tried to use `drawLine()` to make sides, but they didn't look very good. After that, I left the handle of the cup up to you.

In Chapter 13, we're going to get on to fancy font work.

13

A THING OF BEAUTY

In this chapter we're going go look at more ways to make your applets a joy forever. I claim no talent as an artist, but I can still get professional results in Java. Those of you with a flair for the artistic should be able to get exciting results.

Whatever your artistic talent, by the end of this chapter you'll have more capabilities and, I'd guess, some ideas you'll want to implement. There's more power in Java than we can explore here, but this will get you going.

We'll start with a good look at fonts. If you're already a fontmeister, you'll learn how Java implements baselines, ascents, and descents. If you thought those terms came from a ski slope, you'll learn what they mean, too. We'll use `Font` and `FontMetrics` objects to get complete control.

Then we'll go on to the `Polygon` class. This is the describe-it-yourself shape class. I'll drop a lightning bolt onto my logo. You'll see that it adds lots of visual excitement, but it doesn't cost more than a fraction of a second in download time.

Before we leave, we'll look at the `GridBagLayout` class. That's the one that lets you lay out your forms as fussily as you can with the Dialog editor but preserve the `LayoutManager`'s ability to handle a variety of screen sizes and aspect ratios.

You can do lots more with Java than we'll cover here. In fact, if you really want to write your own Web browser, Java's the right language. I've picked the areas I think it makes the most sense to use Java in lieu of graphics in HTML.

Let's get started with font work.

Fonts

We've already been using the default font when we use the `drawString()` method of the `Graphics` class. That method uses the currently selected font to draw the string. When you call `drawString()`, you specify *x* and *y* coordinates, along with the `String`, but these are *not* the top-left coordinates of a bounding rectangle.

We'll begin by setting a large font size and drawing both text and lines so you can see exactly what's going on.

Setting a Font

You set a font with `Graphics.setFont()`. This takes a `Font` object as its parameter. You create a `Font` object by specifying a font name, style, and size.

The `Font` class has `final static` values for styles:

- `Font.PLAIN`
- `Font.BOLD`
- `Font.ITALIC`

You can or (the | operator) `BOLD` and `ITALIC` together, for a fourth choice.

The font sizes are given in points. There are 12 points in a pica and 6 picas in an inch. (Actually, that's only an approximation of the truth about these printers' measures. The real truth is different in North America from in Europe. Get a good book on typesetting if you want to learn more.) Seventy-two-point type is one inch tall.

Of course, you could reasonably ask what is meant by the font's height. We'll dive into all this, and we'll use Java to do it.

Let's start by setting a large font. You'd do that this way:

```
Font fnt = new Font( "TimesRoman", Font.PLAIN, 60 );

g.setFont( fnt );
fnt = g.getFont();
```

The first line creates a "TimesRoman" font, plain style, 60 points high. Sort of. The second line sets this font as the active font. The third line is a necessary part of all your font work.

The problem is that you have no idea what fonts are available on your users' computers. Your setFont() request is a lot fuzzier a request than you're writing in most programming. Interpret it as, "Please set a font that's as close to this request as possible."

"TimesRoman" means a font with *serifs*, those little squiggles that make text like this nice and readable.

"Helvetica" is a *sans serif* font. It's boring text, like this.

On a Windows PC, you'll probably get New Times Roman and Arial when you specify "TimesRoman" and "Helvetica".

All of which is simply to explain the third line. It looks for the actual truth about the font in use. It may not be the font you asked for.

Now, let's use this font in our logo application.

Locating Text

I'm going to write text at 200, 120 in my logo program (MLogo.java, as it was at the end of the last chapter). But I want to see exactly where Java puts the text, so first I'll draw a tee on its side, with the intersection at 200, 120. I've done this like this:

```
g.drawLine( 200, 120, 400, 120 ); // Baseline
g.drawLine( 200, 60, 200, 140 );  // Left side
```

Then I can use `drawString()` to write text at 200, 120. In Listing 13.1, the `drawArc()` call is the former last line in the `paint()` method. The comment and the other lines are new.

LISTING 13.1 A LOOK AT THE TEXT'S LOCATION

```
g.drawArc( lf3, tp3, wd3, ht3, 0, -180 );

// Logo Text

Font fnt = new Font( "TimesRoman",
    Font.PLAIN, 60 );

g.setFont( fnt );
fnt = g.getFont();

g.drawLine( 200, 120, 400, 120 ); // Baseline
g.drawLine( 200, 60, 200, 140 );  // Left side

g.drawString( "A x d g", 200, 120 );
}
```

Add these lines (varied to suit your space) and run. Figure 13.1 shows the result.

The horizontal line is the font's *baseline*, the imaginary line that the letters rest on. It's the *y* coordinate in the `drawString()` call. The *ascent* of a letter is its height above the baseline. The *descent* is mostly zero, but letters such as *g* and *p* have *descenders*, parts that drop below the baseline.

You'll meet one more typesetting term. *Advance* is the distance from the start of one letter to the start of the next. In practice, you won't worry too much about the advance of individual letters unless you're working on a typesetting program.

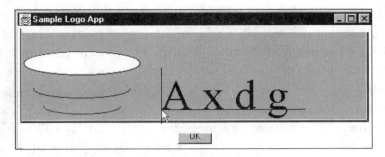

FIGURE 13.1   TEXT LOCATION, ASCENT, AND DESCENT.

The FontMetrics Class

You could just write your logo, using `setFont()` and `drawString()`, but if you did, the user wouldn't be able to resize the window. Occasionally, the user's window size would match your intention and the result would look good. Frequently your logo would be grossly oversized or undersized. What you want is to fit a logo in the available space.

I'm going to write *Marty's Logo* on the right side of my coffee cup. I want it to turn out like Figure 13.2.

FIGURE 13.2   THE EFFECT I WANT.

I'll use two lines, with the first word starting at the coffee cup and the other ending at the right edge. In most cases, the limiting dimension is height, so I'll pick a size that neatly fits both words.

You do this by taking a rough stab, picking a test size. Then you get your font in the test size. With an actual font, you total the font's maximum ascent and descent. In this case I'll multiply by two because we've got a two-line logo. I'll also allow a bit of extra space to leave a border and to leave space between the words vertically. For now, I'm going to trust that the resulting size isn't too wide for the available space.

The `FontMetrics` class tells you everything you need to know about your font's measurements. It will tell you the width of a *W* or of an *i*. It will tell you what the average ascent and descent is. The methods `getMaxAscent()` and `getMaxDescent()` will tell you what those maxima are. This is what you want to know.

You don't create a *new* font metrics object. You ask a `Font` object to give you its metrics with a `getFontMetrics()` call. That's done like this:

```
fnt = g.getFont(); // get current font

FontMetrics fm = fnt.getFontMetrics();
```

Then you use the methods of the `FontMetrics` object to find out how tall a line must be to fit both maximum ascent and descent:

```
int line_size = fm.getMaxAscent() + fm.getMaxDescent();
```

That line size is the absolute minimum you need. It allows no *leading*, the space between lines. (The term *leading* goes back to the days when spacers made from actual lead were inserted between lines of metal type.) You'll want to allow some leading and a little extra space for the top and bottom.

Once you have the actual height your font will use (number of lines times the sum of line size plus leading, plus a bit for looks) you can see how that compares to the space you've actually got. Then you can adjust the font size, this way:

```
// test_size is point size in use in the test font

int actual_size = ... ;
    // available panel height

int this_size = ... ;
    // compute line size plus leading plus border
    // for the test font
```

```
int correct_size = test_size *
   ( actual_size / this_size );
   // got 90, but test uses 100? multiply by 90/100
```

I've done that calculation to get a good font size, as Listing 13.2 shows. This code entirely replaces the test lines we just used in the paint() method.

LISTING 13.2 SIZING THE FONT

```
// Logo Text

  int test_size = 60;
Font fnt = new Font( "TimesRoman",
   Font.BOLD | Font.ITALIC, test_size );

g.setFont( fnt );
fnt = g.getFont(); // This is the one we really got!

FontMetrics fm = getFontMetrics( fnt );

// Divide height into 2 Ascents and 2 Descents

int psize = size().height -
   2*( offset + bwid + 1 );
int fsize = ( test_size * psize ) /
   ( 2 * (fm.getMaxAscent() + fm.getMaxDescent()) );

fnt = new Font( "TimesRoman",
   Font.BOLD | Font.ITALIC, fsize );
g.setFont( fnt );

fnt = g.getFont();
fsize = fnt.getSize();

g.drawString( (new Integer( fsize )).toString(),
   size().width/2, (size().height*2)/3 );

}
```

That last line is one that tests this code. The `fsize` variable is the size of the actual font, after we've set it. In the first `drawString()` argument, I use it to create an `Integer` object so I can call the `toString()` method. That converts to the text equivalent of the number. The next two arguments put the *x* location at half way across the full width and two-thirds of the way down, respectively.

Enter this code and launch the new program. You'll get a result that looks like Figure 13.3. When you resize, you'll get the new size reported, and the report will be in the new size. It's fun to play with.

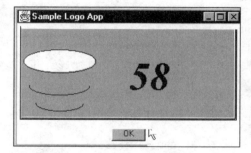

FIGURE 13.3 REPORTING THE SIZE IN THE REPORTED SIZE.

Using the stringWidth() Method

The reason we don't often need to use the advance values for individual letters is that we have the very convenient `stringWidth()` method of the `FontMetrics` class. This computes the total advance for a `String`. If you want to know how long, in pixels, the string "`Logo`" is, this will do:

```
Font fnt = getFont();
FontMetrics fm = fnt.getFontMetrics();

int wid = fm.stringWidth( "Logo" );
```

I've used that method to position the word *Logo* next to the right edge. As you can see in Listing 13.3, I've also allowed for some border pixels to keep the word from touching the border lines.

As you see in the listing, begin by commenting out that nice display of the number. We're writing the actual logo text now. If you don't answer to "Marty," your logo shouldn't look exactly like mine, of course.

LISTING 13.3

```
/*
g.drawString( (new Integer( fsize )).toString(),
    size().width/2, (size().height*2)/3 );
*/

int brdr = 5 + bwid + offset;

fm = getFontMetrics( fnt );
g.drawString( "Marty's",
    size().width/3 + 3,
    brdr + fm.getMaxAscent() );

g.drawString( "Logo",
    size().width - brdr - fm.stringWidth("Logo"),
    size().height - brdr - fm.getMaxDescent() );

}
```

When I run that, I get the result shown in Figure 13.4.

FIGURE 13.4 SHOWING THE ACTUAL LOGO TEXT.

Make sure you try resizing your window, to see how this stays in place.

It Still Needs Work

It's your turn to write some of this code! Try resizing your window until it's really tall and skinny. Figure 13.5 gives you an example.

FIGURE 13.5 THE LOGO DOESN'T FIT.

What you need to do is be sure that *Marty's* (or whatever your logo says) fits in length. After you get the first version of the correctly sized font, ask for the stringWidth() of your longer word and compare that to the space available. Don't change anything if it's too short—a bigger font won't fit the height available—but make another proportional adjustment if it's too long.

Good luck!

At the end of each major section I've been including full listings, which readers tell me helps them track down the bugs that come from not being exactly sure where to put things. To save space, in this chapter we'll end with full listings of the paint() method because the rest of the program does not change. Refer to Listing 12.4 if you need to look at other parts of the code.

Listing 13.4 shows the full paint() routine through this point. Yours should have the length-checking code you added.

LISTING 13.4 THE FULL paint() METHOD

```
public void paint( Graphics g )
{
    int offset = 4; // space left around border
    int lf = offset;
    int tp = offset;

    Dimension d = size();
    int rt = d.width - offset - 1;
    int bt = d.height - offset - 1;

    int wd = rt - lf - 1;
    int ht = bt - tp - 1;

    g.setColor( Color.black );
    g.drawRect( lf, tp, wd, ht );

    int bwid = 2; // size of visible border

    g.setColor( Color.darkGray );
    g.fillRect( lf+1, bt-bwid-1, wd-2, bwid ); // S edge
    g.fillRect( rt-bwid-1, tp+1, bwid, ht-2 ); // E edge

    g.setColor( Color.lightGray );
    g.fillRect( lf+1, tp+1, wd-2, bwid ); // N edge
    g.fillRect( lf+1, tp+1, bwid, ht-2 ); // W edge

    g.setColor( Color.cyan );
    g.fillRect( lf+bwid+1, tp+bwid+1,
        wd-2*(bwid+1), ht-2*(bwid+1) );

    int wd1 = wd/3;
    int ht1 = ht/4;

    int lf1 = lf + bwid + 3;
    int tp1 = tp + ht1;

    g.setColor( Color.black );
```

```
            g.drawOval( lf1, tp1, wd1, ht1 );

            g.setColor( Color.white );
            g.fillOval( lf1+1, tp1+1, wd1-2, ht1-2 );

            int wd2 = (2*wd1)/3;
            int ht2 = (2*ht1)/3;

            int lf2 = lf1 + (wd1 - wd2)/2;
            int tp2 = tp1 + ht/2;

            g.setColor( Color.black );
            g.drawArc( lf2, tp2, wd2, ht2, 0, -180 );

            /* These didn't look good
            g.drawLine( lf1, (tp1 + ht1/2),
                lf2, (tp2 + ht2/2) );

            g.drawLine( lf1+wd1-1, (tp1+ht1/2),
                lf2+wd2-1, (tp2 + ht2/2) );
            */

            int lf3 = (lf1 + lf2) / 2;
            int tp3 = (tp1 + tp2) / 2;
            int wd3 = (wd1 + wd2) / 2;
            int ht3 = (ht1 + ht2) / 2;

            tp3 += ht/20;

            g.drawArc( lf3, tp3, wd3, ht3, 0, -180 );

    // Logo Text

            int test_size = 60;
            Font fnt = new Font( "TimesRoman",
                Font.BOLD | Font.ITALIC, test_size );

            g.setFont( fnt );
            fnt = g.getFont(); // This is the one we really got!
```

```
FontMetrics fm = getFontMetrics( fnt );

// Divide height into 2 Ascents and 2 Descents

int psize = size().height -
    2*( offset + bwid + 1 );
int fsize = ( test_size * psize ) /
    ( 2 * (fm.getMaxAscent() + fm.getMaxDescent()) );

fnt = new Font( "TimesRoman",
    Font.BOLD | Font.ITALIC, fsize );
g.setFont( fnt );

fnt = g.getFont();
fsize = fnt.getSize();

/*
g.drawString( (new Integer( fsize )).toString(),
    size().width/2, (size().height*2)/3 );
*/

int brdr = 5 + bwid + offset;

fm = getFontMetrics( fnt );
g.drawString( "Marty's",
    size().width/3 + 3,
    brdr + fm.getMaxAscent() );

g.drawString( "Logo",
    size().width - brdr - fm.stringWidth("Logo"),
    size().height - brdr - fm.getMaxDescent() );
}
```

Polygons

I don't know if it's the fact that a stylized lightning bolt was the old flow-chart symbol for a communications link or because the lightning bolt reminds you of how you feel after too many cups of Java, but the lightning symbol is popular on Web pages. We'll add one of our own.

My logo code and lightning bolt together add about 1 K to the **.class** file that your users will be downloading. That doesn't take a second with a pokey 14.4 modem or even a slow connection through a service like CompuServe.

(Hello, *Infoworld*? How about that "IW Electric" bitmap? Steal this code, please!)

The Polygon Class

A `Polygon` is any object made from multiple straight line segments. You could describe a rectangle with a `Polygon`. It would work, but it wouldn't be very convenient. Where `Polygon` objects come into their own is with irregular figures.

To describe a `Polygon`, you provide an array of *x* coordinates and a companion array of *y* coordinates. This code describes a `Polygon` that happens to be a square from 0, 0 to 100, 100:

```
int[] xpts = new int[5];
int[] ypts = new int[5];

x[0] =   0; y[0] =   0; // Start at  0,   0
x[1] = 100; y[1] =   0; // draw to 100,   0
x[2] = 100; y[2] = 100; // draw to 100, 100
x[3] =   0; y[3] = 100; // draw to   0, 100
x[4] = x[0]; y[4] = y[0]; // close the square

Polygon psquare = new Polygon( xpts, ypts, 5 );
```

The third parameter to the constructor is the number of points in the coordinate arrays.

Note that there is no rule in Java saying that a `Polygon` has to be a closed figure. If your end point is *not* your starting point, you'll have an unclosed shape. I recommend you make a practice of very explicitly closing your `Polygon` (e.g., `x[n] = x[0]`) when you want a closed figure. If you don't do that, you'll have shot yourself in the foot the first time you decide to move the `Polygon`'s starting point just a bit.

As always, the full details are available online in the Abstract Windows Toolkit (AWT), Volume 2, **java.awt package**, `Polygon` class. Without checking, you'd probably guess that you could write code like:

```
Polygon poly = ... // assign values

g.drawPolygon( poly );
g.fillPolygon( poly );
```

You'd be right, too. Now let's do it.

Building a Polygon

Look at the code in Listing 13.5 to see how I've built a resizable lightning bolt. I started by taking some vertical dimensions from `size().height` and some horizontal dimensions from `size().width`.

I'm giving you a finished lightning bolt. As you might guess, my first few bolts didn't have much voltage. You have to start with a pencil sketch, number the points, and then drop in approximate values. You can refine them with little adjustments, like those the `bbit` variable provides here.

Listing 13.5 also shows that after you set up the arrays of points, creating and drawing the polygon takes just three lines of code.

LISTING 13.5 A RESIZABLE LIGHTNING BOLT

```
// Add a lightning bolt graphic

    int btop = size().height / 4;
    int bqtr = 0; // btop / 2;
    int bmid = btop * 2;
    int bbtm = btop * 3;
```

```
        int blft = size().width / 2;
        int brgt = ( blft * 11 ) / 6;
        int bctr = ( blft + brgt ) / 2;
        int bbit = ( brgt - blft ) / 20;

        // Make a lightning bolt
        int[] xpts = new int[7];
        int[] ypts = new int[7];

        xpts[0] = bctr + 2*bbit; ypts[0] = btop;
        xpts[1] = bctr +   bbit; ypts[1] = bmid;
        xpts[2] = brgt;          ypts[2] = btop + bqtr;
        xpts[3] = bctr - 2*bbit; ypts[3] = bbtm;
        xpts[4] = bctr -   bbit; ypts[4] = bmid;
        xpts[5] = blft;          ypts[5] = bbtm - bqtr;
        xpts[6] = xpts[0];       ypts[6] = ypts[0];

        Polygon bolt = new Polygon( xpts, ypts, 7 );

        g.setColor( Color.blue );
        g.fillPolygon( bolt );
    }
```

Figure 13.6 shows the lightning bolt that this code creates.

FIGURE 13.6   LIGHTNING STRIKES!

Try resizing your window now. It looks good, doesn't it?

Give the Bolt Some Java

Now I'll use a little trick to add some visual excitement without doing much work. It's a trick that you can use all over your Java graphics. (You can achieve excess pretty quickly, this way, if you get carried away.)

I'm going to predraw the graphic in one color and then shift it just a bit and redraw in another color. When you do this, you'll see the graphic improve its excitement level. It begins to look like it's wired on too much caffeine. That's just what the Web needs, right?

Figure 13.7 shows the result.

FIGURE 13.7 WIRED LIGHTNING.

This code is all that you need to do this:

```
Polygon bolt = new Polygon( xpts, ypts, 7 );

g.setColor( Color.white );
g.fillPolygon( bolt );

for ( int i = 0; i < 7; i++ )
{
    xpts[i] -= 4; ypts[i] -= 3;
}

g.setColor( Color.blue );
g.fillPolygon( new Polygon(xpts, ypts, 7) );
}
```

The first time I painted the bolt I used white. Then I switched back to blue for the second painting. The second one paints over most of the first.

Don't worry about forgetting to switch those colors. About half the time you do it wrong you'll decide you like the mistake better than what you had in mind.

Listing 13.6 shows the full paint() method, doing the complete logo (except for checking the text length, which you've added to your version).

LISTING 13.6 MARTY'S LOGO, COMPLETE

```
public void paint( Graphics g )
{
    int offset = 4; // space left around border
    int lf = offset;
    int tp = offset;

    Dimension d = size();
    int rt = d.width - offset - 1;
    int bt = d.height - offset - 1;

    int wd = rt - lf - 1;
    int ht = bt - tp - 1;

    g.setColor( Color.black );
    g.drawRect( lf, tp, wd, ht );

    int bwid = 2; // size of visible border

    g.setColor( Color.darkGray );
    g.fillRect( lf+1, bt-bwid-1, wd-2, bwid ); // S edge
    g.fillRect( rt-bwid-1, tp+1, bwid, ht-2 ); // E edge

    g.setColor( Color.lightGray );
    g.fillRect( lf+1, tp+1, wd-2, bwid ); // N edge
    g.fillRect( lf+1, tp+1, bwid, ht-2 ); // W edge

    g.setColor( Color.cyan );
```

```
g.fillRect( lf+bwid+1, tp+bwid+1,
    wd-2*(bwid+1), ht-2*(bwid+1) );

int wd1 = wd/3;
int ht1 = ht/4;

int lf1 = lf + bwid + 3;
int tp1 = tp + ht1;

g.setColor( Color.black );
g.drawOval( lf1, tp1, wd1, ht1 );

g.setColor( Color.white );
g.fillOval( lf1+1, tp1+1, wd1-2, ht1-2 );

int wd2 = (2*wd1)/3;
int ht2 = (2*ht1)/3;

int lf2 = lf1 + (wd1 - wd2)/2;
int tp2 = tp1 + ht/2;

g.setColor( Color.black );
g.drawArc( lf2, tp2, wd2, ht2, 0, -180 );

/* These didn't look good
g.drawLine( lf1, (tp1 + ht1/2),
    lf2, (tp2 + ht2/2) );

g.drawLine( lf1+wd1-1, (tp1+ht1/2),
    lf2+wd2-1, (tp2 + ht2/2) );
*/

int lf3 = (lf1 + lf2) / 2;
int tp3 = (tp1 + tp2) / 2;
int wd3 = (wd1 + wd2) / 2;
int ht3 = (ht1 + ht2) / 2;

tp3 += ht/20;
```

```
      g.drawArc( lf3, tp3, wd3, ht3, 0, -180 );

// Logo Text

    int test_size = 60;
   Font fnt = new Font( "TimesRoman",
      Font.BOLD | Font.ITALIC, test_size );

   g.setFont( fnt );
   fnt = g.getFont(); // This is the one we really got!

   FontMetrics fm = getFontMetrics( fnt );

   // Divide height into 2 Ascents and 2 Descents

   int psize = size().height -
      2*( offset + bwid + 1 );
   int fsize = ( test_size * psize ) /
      ( 2 * (fm.getMaxAscent() + fm.getMaxDescent()) );

   fnt = new Font( "TimesRoman",
      Font.BOLD | Font.ITALIC, fsize );
   g.setFont( fnt );

   fnt = g.getFont();
   fsize = fnt.getSize();

   /*
   g.drawString( (new Integer( fsize )).toString(),
      size().width/2, (size().height*2)/3 );
   */

   int brdr = 5 + bwid + offset;

   fm = getFontMetrics( fnt );
   g.drawString( "Marty's",
      size().width/3 + 3,
      brdr + fm.getMaxAscent() );
```

```
    g.drawString( "Logo",
        size().width - brdr - fm.stringWidth("Logo"),
        size().height - brdr - fm.getMaxDescent() );

// Add a lightning bolt graphic

    int btop = size().height / 4;
    int bqtr = 0; // btop / 2;
    int bmid = btop * 2;
    int bbtm = btop * 3;

    int blft = size().width / 2;
    int brgt = ( blft * 11 ) / 6;
    int bctr = ( blft + brgt ) / 2;
    int bbit = ( brgt - blft ) / 20;

    // Make a lightning bolt
    int[] xpts = new int[7];
    int[] ypts = new int[7];

    xpts[0] = bctr + 2*bbit; ypts[0] = btop;
    xpts[1] = bctr +   bbit; ypts[1] = bmid;
    xpts[2] = brgt;          ypts[2] = btop + bqtr;
    xpts[3] = bctr - 2*bbit; ypts[3] = bbtm;
    xpts[4] = bctr -   bbit; ypts[4] = bmid;
    xpts[5] = blft;          ypts[5] = bbtm - bqtr;
    xpts[6] = xpts[0];       ypts[6] = ypts[0];

    Polygon bolt = new Polygon( xpts, ypts, 7 );

    g.setColor( Color.white );
    g.fillPolygon( bolt );

    for ( int i = 0; i < 7; i++ )
    {
        xpts[i] -= 4; ypts[i] -= 3;
    }
```

```
        g.setColor( Color.blue );
        g.fillPolygon( new Polygon(xpts, ypts, 7) );
    }
```

GridBagLayout

Ready to leave the artwork and get back to laying out forms? Actually, the artwork is more fun, but we've got to tend to business, too.

The most sophisticated of the `LayoutManager`-based classes is the `GridBagLayout`. It's the most powerful, but it's not the simplest. The basic concept is that your layout is a grid and each component is rectangular, but any component can take as many rows and columns as it needs or wants. A component's *display area*, the rows and columns it occupies, can be further adjusted by assigning *insets* (spacing at the edges), selecting an *anchor* (center or one of the four primary compass points), and selecting stretch-to-fit (or not) both horizontally and vertically.

The GridBag Classes

Two classes implement a gridbag layout: `GridBagLayout` and `GridBagConstraints`. You attach a `GridBagLayout` to a container as you do any other layout:

```
GridBagLayout gbl = new GridBagLayout();

// assume _this_ is a Container
setLayout( gbl );
```

The `GridBagConstraints` class has lots of public fields and a `clone()` method. You set the fields and then call the `GridBagLayout`'s `setConstraints()` method to attach a clone of the fields to a `Component` within the `GridBagLayout`. Here's an example:

```
GridBagLayout gbl = new GridBagLayout();
setLayout( gbl );

Button b1, b2, b3;
```

```
b1 = new Button( " B1 " );
b2 = new Button( " B2 " );
b3 = new Button( " B3 " );

add( b1 );
add( b2 );
add( b3 );

GridBagConstraints gbc = new GridBagConstraints();

// set fields for b1, then:
gbl.setConstraints( b1, gbc );

// set fields for b2, then:
gbl.setConstraints( b2, gbc );

// set fields for b3, then:
gbl.setConstraints( b3, gbc );
```

I've no taste for typing **GridBagConstraints** repeatedly, so I'll create a GBCC cover class. You can do that trivially:

```
class GBCC extends GridBagConstraints
{
    // GBCC is an easy way to type:
    // GridBagConstraints.Constant
}
```

With that class, you simplify the typing:

```
gbc.fill = GBCC.HORIZONTAL;

    // same as:

gbc.fill = GridBagConstraints.HORIZONTAL;
```

With that in mind, I'll refer to GBCC.<constant> to name the final static fields in the GridBagConstraints class.

GBCC.HORIZONTAL is one of the possible values for the GBCC.fill field. The others are GBCC.VERTICAL, GBCC.BOTH, and GBCC.NONE. These specify the stretch-to-fit direction(s).

GBCC.weightx and GBCC.weighty specify weights in the appropriate dimension. If one Button has twice the GBCC.weightx value of another Button, it will be twice as wide.

You can anchor a field in GBCC.CENTER or to a side, such as GBCC.NORTH. These are values you assign to the GBCC.anchor field.

Here's an example:

```
GridBagLayout gbl = new GridBagLayout();
setLayout( gbl );

Button b1, b2, b3;

b1 = new Button( " B1 " );
b2 = new Button( " B2 " );
b3 = new Button( " B3 " );

add( b1 );
add( b2 );
add( b3 );

GBCC gbc = new GBCC();

gbc.weighty = 1;

gbc.fill = GBCC.VERTICAL;
gbc.anchor = GBCC.WEST;
gbc.weightx = 3;
gbl.setConstraints( b1, gbc );

gbc.weightx = 2;
gbl.setConstraints( b2, gbc );

gbc.anchor = GBCC.CENTER;
gbl.setConstraints( b3, gbc );
```

This example specifies VERTICAL stretch for b1, anchored to the WEST side of its display area. It's weight is 1.5 times the weight of b2 and b3. Button b3 will be stretched vertically in the center of its display area. Now let's try some examples.

Create an Empty Frame

Begin by creating a new project workspace. Mine's called GBTest. The code in Listing 13.7 creates a nearly empty frame that responds correctly when you click the close button in the upper-right corner or click the **OK** button.

LISTING 13.7 A NEARLY EMPTY FRAME

```
// GBTest.java

import java.applet.Applet;
import java.awt.*;

public class GBTest extends Applet
{
    public void main( String args[] )
    {
        MyFrame f = new MyFrame( "GBTest" );
        f.resize( 400, 300 );

        GBTest g = new GBTest();
        f.add( "Center", g );

        g.init();

        f.show();
    }

    public void init()
    {
        CloseButton okb = new CloseButton( "   OK   " );
```

```
            add( okb );

         }
      }
   class MyFrame extends Frame
   {
      MyFrame( String s )
      {
         super( s );
      }

      public boolean handleEvent( Event e )
      {
         if ( e.id == Event.WINDOW_DESTROY )
         {
            System.exit(0);
            return true;
         }
         else
            return super.handleEvent( e );
      }

   }

   class CloseButton extends Button
   {
      CloseButton( String s )
      {
         super( s );
      }

      public boolean action( Event e, Object o )
      {
         System.exit(0);
         return true;
      }
   }
```

```
class GBCC extends GridBagConstraints
{
    // use for GBCC.Constants
}

// end of GBTest.java
```

With a skeleton, we can start to build a `GridBagLayout` form.

Adding the GridBagLayout

Let's start with four `Button` objects and a `TextArea` above the **OK** button. You can set the component's constraints before you add it to the form, or add it first and then set the constraints. I'm using the add-first method.

Listing 13.8 shows the code to add a `GridBagLayout`, four new `Button` objects, and a `TextArea` above the **OK** button. Then it creates a `GridBagConstraints` object and uses it to set constraints for each component. Note that `gridwidth GBCC.REMAINDER` is set for each of the last three components: `button 4`, the `TextArea`, and the **OK** button.

LISTING 13.8

```
public void init()
{
    GridBagLayout gbl = new GridBagLayout();
    setLayout( gbl );

    Button b1 = new Button( " B1 " );
    Button b2 = new Button( " B2 " );
    Button b3 = new Button( " B3 " );
    Button b4 = new Button( " B4 " );

    add( b1 );
    add( b2 );
    add( b3 );
    add( b4 );
```

```
TextArea ta = new TextArea();
add( ta );

CloseButton okb = new CloseButton( "   OK   " );
add( okb );

GBCC gbc = new GBCC();

gbl.setConstraints( b1, gbc );
gbl.setConstraints( b2, gbc );
gbl.setConstraints( b3, gbc );

gbc.gridwidth = GBCC.REMAINDER;
gbl.setConstraints( b4, gbc );
gbl.setConstraints( ta, gbc );
gbl.setConstraints( okb, gbc );

}
```

The REMAINDER width specifies that the component takes the rest of the
width of the row. By implication, it also specifies that the next component
starts a new row.

The result is shown in Figure 13.8. Now, let's use this start to examine
some of the constraints we can set.

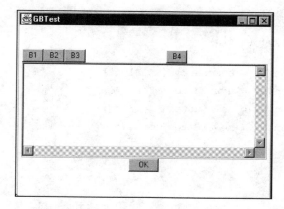

FIGURE 13.8 MOSTLY DEFAULT CONSTRAINTS.

The first three buttons are laid out in columns that are as wide as needed to fit the button. The fourth button is centered in its width, which we specified as REMAINDER.

Arranging the Form

Let's start by specifying that each component gets the same weight. Listing 13.9 highlights the one line you need to add to do this. Figure 13.9 shows the result.

LISTING 13.9 SPACING THE TOP ROW BUTTONS

```
TextArea ta = new TextArea();
add( ta );

CloseButton okb = new CloseButton( "   OK   " );
add( okb );

GBCC gbc = new GBCC();
  gbc.weightx = 1;            // ADD THIS LINE!

gbl.setConstraints( b1, gbc );
gbl.setConstraints( b2, gbc );
gbl.setConstraints( b3, gbc );
```

Because all the components on the first line have the same weight, they are given equal widths, as you see in Figure 13.9.

For the next examples, let's switch the fill field to BOTH so our buttons are stretched to fill their entire display areas, vertically and horizontally. This is seldom useful with buttons, but it will help you see exactly what space the GridBagLayout allocates to each component.

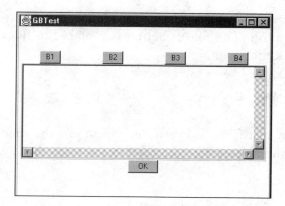

FIGURE 13.9   ALL COMPONENTS HAVE EQUAL WIDTHS.

We'll start with two rows of equal buttons. Listing 13.10 shows the code changes, and Figure 13.10 shows the result.

LISTING 13.10   FULL STRETCH IN TWO COLUMNS

```
GBCC gbc = new GBCC();
gbc.weightx = 1;
  gbc.fill = GBCC.BOTH;                  // NEW!

gbl.setConstraints( b1, gbc );

  gbc.gridwidth = GBCC.REMAINDER;        // NEW!
gbl.setConstraints( b2, gbc );

  gbc.gridwidth = 1;                     // NEW!
gbl.setConstraints( b3, gbc );

gbc.gridwidth = GBCC.REMAINDER;
```

You see that the buttons are now stretched to the full extent of the space available. In the code, note that I've reset the `gridwidth` field back to 1 for Button `b3`. Without that line, `b3` would also have `REMAINDER` for the `gridwidth` field.

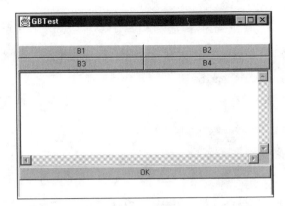

FIGURE 13.10 WIDE-BODY BUTTONS.

Final Form Layout

At this point, you should experiment with the `GridBagConstraints` until you are comfortable with them. Try different weights, fills, anchors, and so on.

I'm going to leave this form with the **OK** button reduced to normal size and centered, and the second row of top buttons similarly adjusted. Take a look at Figure 13.11 and see if you can duplicate it, before you look at Listing 13.11, which shows the full program.

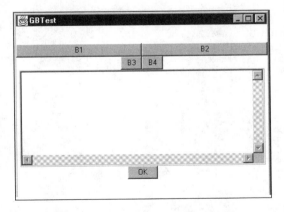

FIGURE 13.11 GRIDBAG EXPERIMENTING.

LISTING 13.11

```java
// GBTest.java

import java.applet.Applet;
import java.awt.*;

public class GBTest extends Applet
{
    public void main( String args[] )
    {
        MyFrame f = new MyFrame( "GBTest" );
        f.resize( 400, 300 );

        GBTest g = new GBTest();
        f.add( "Center", g );

        g.init();

        f.show();
    }

    public void init()
    {
        GridBagLayout gbl = new GridBagLayout();
        setLayout( gbl );

        Button b1 = new Button( " B1 " );
        Button b2 = new Button( " B2 " );
        Button b3 = new Button( " B3 " );
        Button b4 = new Button( " B4 " );

        add( b1 );
        add( b2 );
        add( b3 );
        add( b4 );

        TextArea ta = new TextArea();
```

```
        add( ta );

        CloseButton okb = new CloseButton( "    OK    " );
        add( okb );

        GBCC gbc = new GBCC();
        gbc.weightx = 1;
        gbc.fill = GBCC.BOTH;

        gbl.setConstraints( b1, gbc );

        gbc.gridwidth = GBCC.REMAINDER;
        gbl.setConstraints( b2, gbc );

        gbc.gridwidth = 1;
        gbc.fill = GBCC.NONE;
        gbc.anchor = GBCC.EAST;
        gbl.setConstraints( b3, gbc );

        gbc.gridwidth = GBCC.REMAINDER;
        gbc.anchor = GBCC.WEST;
        gbl.setConstraints( b4, gbc );

        gbc.anchor = GBCC.CENTER;
        gbl.setConstraints( ta, gbc );

        gbc.fill = GBCC.NONE;
        gbl.setConstraints( okb, gbc );

    }
}
class MyFrame extends Frame
{
    MyFrame( String s )
    {
        super( s );
    }
```

```
    public boolean handleEvent( Event e )
    {
        if ( e.id == Event.WINDOW_DESTROY )
        {
            System.exit(0);
            return true;
        }
        else
            return super.handleEvent( e );
    }

}

class CloseButton extends Button
{
    CloseButton( String s )
    {
        super( s );
    }

    public boolean action( Event e, Object o )
    {
        System.exit(0);
        return true;
    }
}

class GBCC extends GridBagConstraints
{
    // use for GBCC.Constants
}

// end of GBTest.java
```

Before you put a gridbag-based form on the Web, you might consider this: each class you use generates a separate **.class** file. As convenient as that GBCC class is for development, you might want to change all the GBCCs in your code back to GridBagConstraints and then delete the GBCC class.

Summary

We've covered some topics here, loosely related by the fact that they all help you produce better-looking Java programs. We began with fonts.

The essential reality of fonts is that you can't be certain what fonts will be available on your users' hardware, so methods such as `setFont()` are really requests instead of orders. You have to use `getFont()` after a `setFont()` to see what really happened.

After setting (and checking to see what was set) a font, we looked at the font's dimensions, courtesy of the `FontMetrics` class. The baseline is the location specified in the `drawString()` method. The font's ascent (rise above the baseline) and descent (on letters like *p* and *g*) combine to determine the height of the font. The `stringWidth()` method provides a handy substitute for dealing with the advance of individual characters.

After you learned all about fonts, you used that knowledge to put a two-line text logo into the graphic panel we prepared in Chapter 12. Then we went on to use the `Polygon` class to add a lightning bolt.

`Polygons` are built from arrays of *x* and *y* point locations. If you make sure that the last point is the same as the first, they're closed geometric forms. `drawPolygon()` and `fillPolygon()` work just as they do for other shapes.

Finally, we took a look at the `GridBagLayout` class and the associated `GridBagConstraints` class. These let you lay out your forms flexibly but with almost no limit on what you can achieve, provided you're content with a basic horizontal and vertical arrangement.

This ends Part II. In Part III, we'll look into some advanced programming topics. Chapter 14 kicks off the advanced topics with a look at Java exception handling.

## PART III

ADVANCED JAVA PROGRAMMING

Exceptions Are the Rule

Welcome to Part III, where we'll cover some basic advanced Java programming. Does *basic advanced* sound like a contradiction or an oxymoron? It does to me.

There's a certain method to this madness. Throwing and catching exceptions, which we'll cover here, is an advanced programming concept. It only arrived recently in C++, and it still isn't part of most programming languages.

Multithreading and the concurrency issues that it raises aren't part of any other major programming language. Java is the first language in large-scale use that directly incorporates multithreaded operations.

These are definitely advanced topics, but they're also basic in the sense of being fundamental to, part of the foundation of, Java. You can't create a URL, for example, without catching the `MalFormedURLException` that this can throw. Or, to do animation at 20 times per second, you create a thread that displays the image and then goes to sleep for a twentieth of a second. You can't put a thread to sleep unless you're ready to catch an exception.

So far, we haven't used exceptions, but exceptions are the rule in Java. Lots of the library methods throw exceptions, and you can't even compile your program if you don't handle them correctly. In C++, you can ignore exceptions if you so choose. You can't do that in Java.

There's good news and bad news. The bad news is that exception handling is no fun. You'll never point to your screen and say to a passerby, "Isn't that a cool exception handler!" No video. No audio. Exception handling is a programming technique. Now the good news: this may be the easiest part of Java to learn. The Java syntax for exception handling is clean and simple. So are the basic concepts, which we'll look at in the first section here.

After you've learned to handle Java's exceptions, we'll go on to defining our own exceptions. Because exceptions are just another Java class, defining your own by extending an existing class is just like extending any other class. You already know how.

Then we'll take up multiple exception handling. Java does this with grace. You'll like it.

The next-to-last section of this chapter will cover throwing exceptions out of a method. That's done when a method wants to throw an exception, but it wants to tell the compiler that the exception should be passed upstairs to a calling routine. Again, it's very cleanly done.

Finally, we'll cover the `finally` statement block. You won't need to use it often, but it's invaluable when you do need it. And it's as cleanly done as the rest of exception handling.

Let's begin at the beginning.

Basic Exception Handling

In this section, we'll cover the theory first, and then we'll put it into practice with some code that catches an exception. As with many other parts of

Java, the concepts require a fair amount of explanation. The coding, however, is simple once you understand the concepts.

The Theory of Exception Handling

There are three parts in exception handling:

- The `try` block
- The `catch` block
- The `finally` block

The `finally` block is optional and used infrequently. We'll cover it in the final section of this chapter. The other two are common. The code will look something like this:

```
try
    {
        // code to try
    }
catch ( SomeTypeOfException ex )
    {
        // code to handle exception
    }
```

Exceptions are things that won't happen often but that you need to think about. For example, you could handle reading a sequential file by putting the read-a-full-buffer code into the `try` block and handling the end-of-file-reached condition as an exception.

The `catch` block catches an `Exception` object thrown by the `try` block. The `Exception` object is a member of a class that extends the `Throwable` class. `Exception` objects hold any data or methods that might be useful in handling the exception. If, for example, your `file read` code threw an exception when it read less than a full block, the `catch` block would want to know how many bytes were read.

The `throwable` class is also extended by Java `Error` objects. Unlike exceptions, errors are not recoverable. Syntactically, they are just like exceptions, so we can ignore them here. Java's internal exceptions, like `MalFormedURLException` all end with the word *Exception*. Errors end with *Error*.

Handling Exceptions in Code

In Java, most work dealing with files requires a `URL` object, which behaves very much like a disk drive identifier. The fact that the drive it identifies may be halfway around the world doesn't mean much to the code. One constructor (the one you'll probably use) takes a `String` that names the `URL` in the normal fashion:

```
URL msft = new URL ( "http://microsoft.com" );
```

But that won't work with outside a `try`/`catch` pair because the constructor can throw the `MalFormedURLException`. Try the code in Listing 14.1 to see the error, reported in Figure 14.1.

LISTING 14.1 FAILING TO CATCH AN EXCEPTION

```
// Exceptions.java

import java.net.*;

public class Exceptions
{
    public void main( String[] args )
    {
        URL msft = new URL( "http://microsoft.com" );
    }
}
// end of Exceptions.java
```

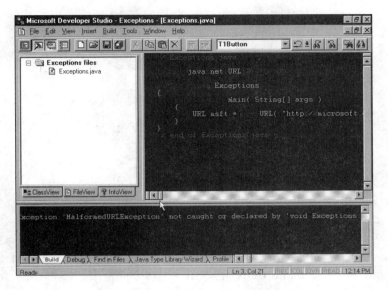

FIGURE 14.1 COMPILER CATCHES MISSING EXCEPTION HANDLER.

Your code has to handle the exceptions that might be thrown. If you look up the constructor `URL.URL()` (Java API, Volume 1, package **java.net**, `URL` class) you'll see that the exceptions it throws are part of the definition. Your code has to handle them. You can pass them out of the current function, which we'll cover later in this chapter under "Throwing Exceptions." For now, let's take the common action: catch the exception where it could be thrown.

Change the `main()` method so that it includes the `URL.URL()` call in a `try` block, and then handle the exceptions in a `catch` block. Listing 14.2 shows a null but perfectly acceptable `catch` block. This code will compile cleanly (and do absolutely nothing).

LISTING 14.2 CATCHING THE EXCEPTION

```
// Exceptions.java

import java.net.*;

public class Exceptions
```

```
{
   public void main( String[] args )
   {
      try
      {
         URL msft = new URL( "http://microsoft.com" );
      }
      catch ( MalFormedURLException e )
      {

      }
   }
}
// end of Exceptions.java
```

The catch block works like a function that takes the Exception as a parameter. The name (here it's just e) following the Exception class name is the name you'd use within the catch block. Its scope is the catch block.

The catch block is called as a function is, with the Exception object as an argument. If the Exception is not thrown, the catch block is skipped. Execution resumes at the first statement after the catch block.

Most authorities describe the try and catch blocks just as I've done. Actually, a single statement is a perfectly acceptable block. If you'd like to save lines (not to mention typing time), the code could be written this way:

```
try URL msft = new URL( "http://microsoft.com" );
catch ( MalFormedURLException e );
```

I usually use actual blocks except for code that's so typically one-lined that the try/catch pair become idiomatic. In Chapter 15, we'll put our threads to sleep, this way:

```
// th is a Thread

try th.sleep( 50 );
catch( InterruptedException e );

// sleep for 50 milliseconds
```

If a `catch` block for the `Exception` thrown exists, the compiler is happy. What the `catch` block does is up to you. In the case of a string constant in `URL.URL`, doing nothing may be acceptable. During a `sleep()`, the `InterruptedException` is a wake up call from another thread. If the argument to `URL.URL` were a string that the user entered, a more elaborate treatment would be needed.

Defining Your Own Exceptions

Now that we've used Java's exceptions, let's create our own. Again, we'll cover the theory and then try it in practice.

The Theory of Defining New Exceptions

We did the ground breaking in the last section. This has become simple. To create your own exceptions, you extend an existing exception class.

You create and throw the exception in a `try` block, as in:

```
try
    {
        ... do some stuff
        if ( something exceptional occurs )
            throw new MyException();
        else
            // business as usual
    }
    catch ( MyException e )
    {
        ... handle exception
    }
    ... more of whatever class

} // end of whatever class

class MyException extends Throwable
```

```
{
}
```

You can create a constructor or constructors for your exception, just as you would with any other class. Add any data members that will be useful in the `catch` block, and put any code that you'll need in the exception class if you want to eliminate details from the `catch` block.

Creating New Exceptions in Code

Let's build a practical class that uses exceptions. I want an array of objects, but for many applications you can't anticipate how many entries you'll have in an array, so let's make a `GrowableArray` class. We'll create it with a starting size and an increment. For example, you could create a word processor that worked on an array of `Paragraph` objects. You might start with a default 1,000-element array, and then add 100 new elements whenever the array is filled.

It's logical to code this array's `add()` method to simply add an object (which is what will happen most of the time) and to handle the out-of-space condition as an exception:

```
public void add( Object o )
    {
        try
        {
            // add the new object
        }
        catch ( )
        {
            // exception if no space
            // grow array here
        }
    }
```

Fortunately, Java does array bounds checking, so it will throw an exception for us. We'll use that one to be sure you've got the hang of these exceptions. First, however, I'll add a routine I've wanted to use ever since we started to use `println()`.

Library Code

I've been nothing but frustrated with the lack of a function that simply waits for a keypress. When you're debugging or writing short test routines, it's great to be able to simply use a `println()` or two to see what's going on. Then you throw in a `keyWait()` so you can look at the result and press a key when you've understood it.

Unfortunately for my purposes, the basic keyboard `read()` method serves lots of devices, including the keyboard. For the other ones it has to be able to throw an `IOException` (device not available, end of file, etc.). The `keyWait()` is trivial now that you know about `try` and `catch` blocks. It's this:

```
try System.in.read();
catch ( IOException e );
```

Do you understand that the second line is a null statement? Look at the blocks written this way:

```
try
{
    System.in.read();
}
catch
{
    ; // null statement
}
```

While we're at it, I like to tuck little routines like that into a `Lib` class. If you make it a static, you can call it this way:

```
Lib.keyWait();
```

My full `Lib` class looks like this:

```
class Lib
{
    public static void keyWait()
    {
        try System.in.read();
        catch ( IOException e );
    }
}
```

Please don't make a giant `Lib` class that has every trick you ever invented. Keep a text file that organizes your `Lib` routines and copy one routine at a time into a program-specific `Lib` class. The goal is to have what you need and nothing else.

The Growable Array

The key to writing a `GrowableArray` class is keeping an array of `Object` objects. I call mine `objects`. Then keep an `int` that points to the next empty spot in the array. The basics of the code are easy:

```
add(Object o)
{
    objects[next_object] = o
    next_object++;
}
```

Don't check the array for size! Java will check that assignment and throw an `ArrayIndexOutOfBoundsException` when you come to the end. Don't put in your own bounds check because that would just duplicate the work that Java will do anyway. Let the Java check work for you. This is the right way to code the `add()` method:

```
add(Object o)
    {
        try
        {
```

```
            objects[next_object] = o;
            next_object++;
        }
        catch ( ArrayIndexOutOfBoundsException e )
        {
            // expand the array, then add
        }
    }
```

For testing, I'm creating an array that's only five long initially and that adds only three new elements when it runs out of space. Remember that when you pass an `Object` to a function, such as our `add()` function, you're passing a reference, not the `Object` itself. The exact form of an `Object` reference is implementation-dependent, but it's probably only a few bytes (maybe six or eight). In a real application, you'd start with a thousand or so and add a hundred at a time, but that would be tedious to test.

For testing, I've also added `println()` reports in the `add()` method. Listing 14.3 shows the full program to this point.

LISTING 14.3   ADDING TO A GROWABLEARRAY

```java
// Exceptions.java

import java.io.*;

public class Exceptions
{
    static GrowableArray ga;

    public void main( String[] args )
    {
        ga = new GrowableArray( 5, 3 );

        for ( int i = 0; i < 10; i++ )
        {
            System.out.println( i );
```

```
            ga.add( new Object() );
        }

        Lib.keyWait();
    }
}

class GrowableArray
{
    int used;
    int size;

    int start_size;
    int increment;

    Object[] objects;

    GrowableArray( int ssize, int incr )
    {
        used = 0;
        start_size = ssize;
        increment = incr;

        objects = new Object[ssize];
        size = ssize;
    }

    void add( Object o )
    {
        try
        {
            objects[used] = o;
            used++;
        }
```

```
      catch (ArrayIndexOutOfBoundsException e)
      {
          Object[] newobj = new Object[ size + increment ];

          for ( int i = 0; i < used; i++ )
             newobj[i] = objects[i];

          size = size + increment;
          objects = newobj;

          objects[used] = o;
          used++;
          System.out.print( "Grew objects to " );
          System.out.print( size );
          System.out.println( "." );
      }
   }
}


class Lib
{
   public static void keyWait()
   {
      try System.in.read();
      catch ( IOException e );
   }
}

// end of Exceptions.java
```

Create your own version and run it. When you do, you should get a report like the one shown in Figure 14.2.

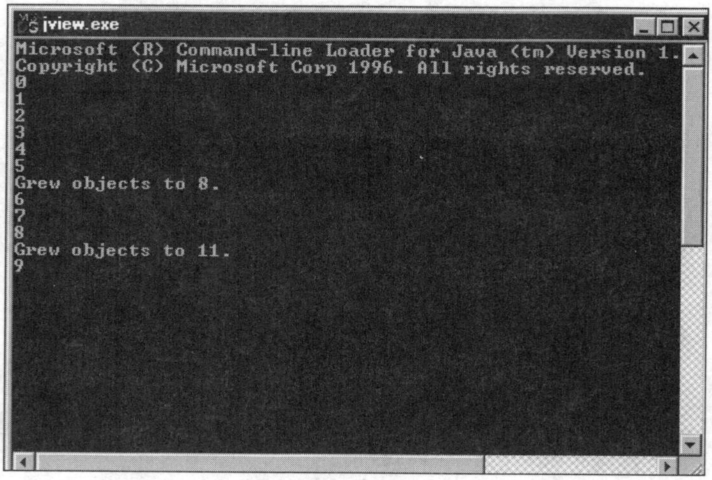

FIGURE 14.2 THE ARRAY GROWS AS EXPECTED.

Reading the Array

Now we're ready to add a method that returns an `Object` from the array. This time, we can't depend on the built-in array bounds checking. That won't catch a request for an object within the size of the array that hasn't been assigned with an `add()` yet. We'll need our own index check. Begin with a class that extends `Throwable`. You frequently don't need members or methods, as in this example:

```
class IndexTooBig extends Throwable
{
}
```

Then create a `get()` method. It should throw an exception when appropriate. This is the idea:

```
try
{
    if ( i < used )
        return objects[i];
    else
```

```
            throw new IndexTooBig();
    }
```

Then to handle the problem, my `catch` uses `println()` to make a little report. In production code, of course, you'll want to fix the problem or give the user another shot.

Listing 14.4 shows the full program. I've added a short set of test cases and some appropriate `println()` calls to the main line, and commented out the old debugging `println()` calls.

LISTING 14.4 THROWING YOUR OWN EXCEPTIONS

```java
// Exceptions.java

import java.io.*;

public class Exceptions
{
    static GrowableArray ga;

    public void main( String[] args )
    {
        ga = new GrowableArray( 5, 3 );

        for ( int i = 0; i < 10; i++ )
        {
            // System.out.println( i );
            ga.add( new Object() );
        }

        int[] tests = { 3, 9, 14 };
        Object got;

        for ( int i = 0; i < 3; i++ )
        {
            got = ga.get( tests[i] );
            System.out.print( i );
```

```
            if ( got != null )
                System.out.println( ": an Object" );
            else
                System.out.println( ": null" );
        }

        Lib.keyWait();
    }
}

class GrowableArray
{
    int used;
    int size;

    int start_size;
    int increment;

    Object[] objects;

    GrowableArray( int ssize, int incr )
    {
        used = 0;
        start_size = ssize;
        increment = incr;

        objects = new Object[ssize];
        size = ssize;
    }

    void add( Object o )
    {
        try
        {
            objects[used] = o;
            used++;
        }
        catch (ArrayIndexOutOfBoundsException e)
```

```
        {
            Object[] newobj = new Object[ size + increment ];

            for ( int i = 0; i < used; i++ )
                newobj[i] = objects[i];

            size = size + increment;
            objects = newobj;

            objects[used] = o;
            used++;
            System.out.print( "Grew objects to " );
            System.out.print( size );
            System.out.println( "." );
        }
    }

    Object get( int i )
    {
        try
        {
            if ( i < used )
                return objects[i];
            else
                throw new IndexTooBig();
        }
        catch ( IndexTooBig e )
        {
            System.out.println( " Index " +
                new Integer(i).toString() + " too big." );
            return null;
        }
    }
}

class IndexTooBig extends Throwable
{
```

```
   }

   class Lib
   {
      public static void keyWait()
      {
         try System.in.read();
         catch ( IOException e );
      }
   }

// end of Exceptions.java
```

When you run this code, you should get an OK for cases zero and one but an error report for two. Did you notice that I've checked for indexes that are too large but not for ones that are negative? It's often true that when one thing can go wrong, other problems can occur, too. For that we need multiple exception handlers associated with a single `try` block.

Multiple Exceptions

It's easier to handle two or more exceptions than it was to handle the first. You just have to add more `catch` blocks, one for each exception that might be thrown.

This is what the code looks like:

```
try
{
   // lots of possible exceptions
   // in this block
}
catch( FirstTypeOfException e1 )
{
   // handle FirstTypeOfException
}
catch( NextTypeOfException e1 )
```

```
{
    // handle NextTypeOfException
}

... // as many catch blocks as needed

catch( LastTypeOfException e1 )
{
    // handle LastTypeOfException
}
```

In our `GrowableArray` class, negative indexes will generate the built-in exception, so we don't need another check in the `try` block. We just add another `catch` block, like this:

```
try
{
    if ( i < used )
        return objects[i];
    else
        throw new IndexTooBig();
}
catch ( IndexTooBig e )
{
    System.out.println( " Index " +
        new Integer(i).toString() + " too big." );
    return null;
}
    catch( ArrayIndexOutOfBoundsException e )
{
    System.out.println( " Index " +
        new Integer(i).toString() + " is negative." );
    return null;
}
```

Are you surprised that the same variable name, e, can be defined twice here? As with a method parameter, the name is local to each `catch` block.

(You can nest `try` and `catch` blocks inside another `catch` block, of course. If you do, you'll have to invent a second variable name.)

Listing 14.5 shows the full program, including an additional test case added to the `main()` routine. Figure 14.3 shows the result you should get.

LISTING 14.5 USING MULTIPLE CATCHERS

```java
// Exceptions.java

import java.io.*;

public class Exceptions
{
    static GrowableArray ga;

    public void main( String[] args )
    {
        ga = new GrowableArray( 5, 3 );

        for ( int i = 0; i < 10; i++ )
        {
            // System.out.println( i );
            ga.add( new Object() );
        }

        int[] tests = { 3, 9, 14, -3 };
        Object got;

        for ( int i = 0; i < 4; i++ )
        {
            got = ga.get( tests[i] );
            System.out.print( i );
            if ( got != null )
                System.out.println( ": an Object" );
            else
                System.out.println( ": null" );
        }
```

```
        Lib.keyWait();
    }
}

class GrowableArray
{
    int used;
    int size;

    int start_size;
    int increment;

    Object[] objects;

    GrowableArray( int ssize, int incr )
    {
        used = 0;
        start_size = ssize;
        increment = incr;

        objects = new Object[ssize];
        size = ssize;
    }

    void add( Object o )
    {
        try
        {
            objects[used] = o;
            used++;
        }
        catch (ArrayIndexOutOfBoundsException e)
        {
            Object[] newobj = new Object[ size + increment ];

            for ( int i = 0; i < used; i++ )
                newobj[i] = objects[i];
```

```java
            size = size + increment;
            objects = newobj;

            objects[used] = o;
            used++;
            System.out.print( "Grew objects to " );
            System.out.print( size );
            System.out.println( "." );
        }
    }

    Object get( int i )
    {
        try
        {
            if ( i < used )
                return objects[i];
            else
                throw new IndexTooBig();
        }
        catch ( IndexTooBig e )
        {
            System.out.println( " Index " +
                new Integer(i).toString() + " too big." );
            return null;
        }
        catch( ArrayIndexOutOfBoundsException e )
        {
            System.out.println( " Index " +
                new Integer(i).toString() + " is negative." );
            return null;
        }
    }
}

class IndexTooBig extends Throwable
{
```

```
}

class Lib
{
    public static void keyWait()
    {
        try System.in.read();
        catch ( IOException e );
    }
}

// end of Exceptions.java
```

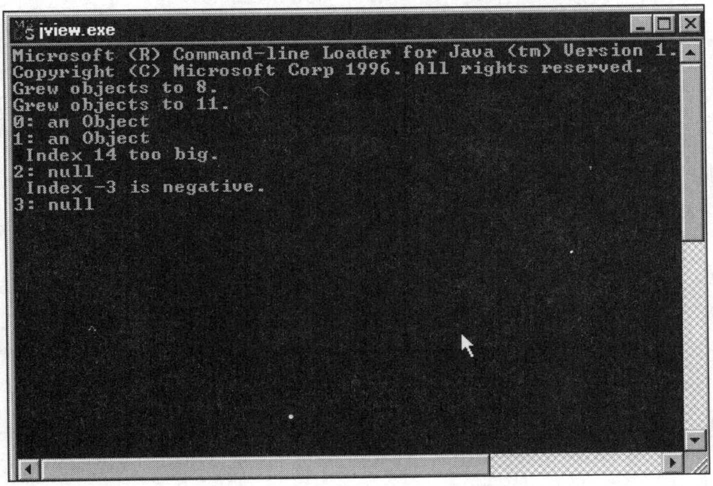

FIGURE 14.3 MULTIPLE EXCEPTIONS CORRECTLY REPORTING.

Now we're ready for the long pass.

Throwing Exceptions

You've already learned to use the `throw` verb to throw an exception. If this were football, that would be the little screen pass. Just flip it a few feet over the head of that big dude from the other team. Now we're going to talk about `throws`, the big-time, all-the-way-down-the-field pass.

We'll look at the theory, and then we'll put it into practice.

Handling Long throws

You can do one of two things when you `throw` an `Exception`. You can put the `throw` in a `try` block, as we've done here and handle it with a `catch` block. The compiler won't let you `throw` one you don't `catch`.

The alternative is to `throw` the exception back to the calling program. You do this by adding the keyword `throws` after the parameters to the method that is doing the throwing, this way:

```
type method( params ) throws WhateverException
{
    ... // do whatever
        throw new WhateverException();
    ... //
}
```

When you `throw` the exception, control leaves, as if you had used a `return` statement. The method that called the one that `throws` the exception must be prepared to handle it, as if it had done the `throw`. (It probably uses a `try` and `catch` pair, but it to can use `throws` to kick the `Exception` on up the line. Sooner or later, somebody must `catch` it, though.)

A Sample throw

As an example, let's cut back to a very simple, stripped-down version of the code we've been using. It will `throw` any value greater than 10.

If you enter and run the code in Listing 14.6, you should get a report saying that 14 is not kosher.

LISTING 14.6 THROWING ONE BACK TO A CALLER

```java
// Exceptions.java

import java.io.*;

public class Exceptions
{
    public void main( String[] args )
    {
        try
        {
            qback( 1 );
            qback( 14 );
        }
        catch ( IndexTooBig e )
        {
            System.out.print( "Bad value: " );
            System.out.println( e.bummer );
        }
    }

    static void qback( int i ) throws IndexTooBig
    {
        if ( i > 10 )
            throw new IndexTooBig( i );
    }
}

class IndexTooBig extends Throwable
{
    int bummer;

    IndexTooBig( int i )
    {
        bummer = i ;
    }
```

```
}
```

```
// end of Exceptions.java
```

Note that here I've used a data member in the exception to return the bad value. That meant adding a constructor that would assign the offending value to the data member. This lets the `catch` block have some information to work with, other than the simple fact that something went wrong in a called routine.

Finally, we come to the last exception handler, `finally`.

Finally

The `finally` clause is, appropriately enough, the last one on the subject of exception handling. We noted briefly at the outset that you can end a `try` and `catch` group with a `finally` block.

Actually, a `try` block could be followed by a `finally` without any `catch` blocks, if you like. Normally, though, the `finally` will trail `catch` blocks.

The `finally` block is always executed before exiting from a `try` and `catch` group. Did I say *always*? Make that ALWAYS! If your `try` block encounters no exceptions and ends with a `return` statement, the `return` will detour through the `finally` block on its way out of the method.

Now let's get to the code:

Programming a finally Block

A `finally` block is written this way:

```
try
{
    // code to try
}
catch( Exception e )
```

```
    {
        // catch code
    }
    finally
    {
        // finally code
    }
```

Bear in mind that you can have from any number of catch blocks in the group or none at all.

A Final Example

Listing 14.7 shows a sample with which you can experiment.

LISTING 14.7   TESTING THE FINALLY BLOCK

```
// Exceptions.java

import java.io.*;

public class Exceptions
{
    public void main( String[] args )
    {
        try
        {
            qback( 1 );
            qback( 14 );
        }
        catch ( IndexTooBig e )
        {
            System.out.print( "Bad value: " );
            System.out.println( e.bummer );
        }
```

```
        try System.in.read();
        catch( IOException e );
    }

    static void qback( int i ) throws IndexTooBig
    {
        try
        {
            if ( i > 10 )
                throw new IndexTooBig( i );
            return;
        }
        finally
        {
            System.out.print( "Finally: " );
            System.out.println( i );
        }

        // System.out.println( "This never appears" );

    }
}

class IndexTooBig extends Throwable
{
    int bummer;

    IndexTooBig( int i )
    {
        bummer = i ;
    }
}

// end of Exceptions.java
```

The normal flow of control would be from the try block to the code following the last associated catch block, if the try block didn't throw an exception. If your work is done in the `try` block, you can `return` from there, too.

Similarly, the normal flow is from the `catch` to the code following the last `catch`, or to the `finally`. So what about that `println()` that I've commented out?

Uncomment it and try to compile. The compile will fail with an "unreachable code" error. That's because the `try` block exits with either a `throw`, which returns control almost immediately to the caller, or a `return`, which does the same.

Both of these exits, however, exit through the `finally` block, as you see when you run the example. So a `finally` block is used when you really, truly, always want to do something.

In Java, lots of cleanup is done for you. When you exit a function, for example, its local variables are discarded. This happens after you `return`, but before the actual return. The `finally` block lets you put your own code in this hidden exit space.

Summary

Exceptions are new to most programmers, so in that sense they're an advanced programming topic. At the same time, handling exceptions is basic to Java programming. Happily, it's simple to do.

We started by using a basic `try` and `catch` pair to handle the `Exception` objects that Java's built-in routines throw. This lets us do critical things like using input/output routines and using a `Thread`'s `sleep()` method.

We went on to create our own `Exception` objects and `throw` them ourselves. This is just like creating any other Java object, with the one difference being that only objects that extend the `Throwable` class can be thrown.

Then we went on to use multiple `catch` blocks to handle different exceptions. We used one example in which we had a `catch` for a built-in Java `Exception` and another for our own `Throwable` object.

Next, we used the `throws` keyword in a method's definition to let us throw an exception without needing a `try` and `catch` group in the throwing routine. That pushed the `catch` responsibility back to the calling routine—it didn't eliminate it.

Finally, we went on to the `finally` block. This can end a group started with a `try` block. Code in the `finally` block is executed after the `try` block and any `catch` block that gets control. It is always executed, even if the other code tries to exit with a `throw` or a `return` to a higher-level routine.

That completes the exception-handling work. It's a beautifully done part of Java, I think. Even if it is entirely new to you, once you see how it works, it feels right. And this brings us to our final Java topic: multithreading.

In Chapter 15, we'll learn how to do several things at once.

MULTITHREADED PROGRAMS

There's lots of power in the Java language, and the `Thread` class really shows its strength. If you want to write your own operating system, you've got all the power you need.

Why? I mentioned in Chapter 14 that the file I/O classes in combination with the URL object makes opening a file anywhere on the Web as easy as opening a file on a local disk, but there's a huge difference.

When you read from a local disk, you can reasonably assume that the read will take a millisecond or two. Your program can wait until the data is available. On the Web, reading may take several seconds or even minutes. You need to be able to do something else while you are waiting for the data. And you need to be able to get back to the data as soon as it's available.

In short, you need to be able to handle chores that would otherwise be the province of the operating system. A general-purpose OS, such as one of the Windows operating systems, just doesn't know enough about your particular application to decide what should be done first and that these other things should be done while we're waiting for data. You have to know the application to decide.

In this chapter we'll cover the basics of multithreaded operations, beginning with launching a thread. After we've launched one thread, we'll launch multiple, simultaneous threads. Then we'll pause to take a look at the built-in Visual J++ debugging capabilities, and we'll create smart buttons that control threads. From there we'll take a quick look at how to synchronize multiple threads. I'll concentrate on the `synchronized` keyword, which will keep most programs out of trouble.

We'll take a look at the multithreading source code the Applet Wizard generates, finishing the topic we started back in Chapter 7. It uses multiple `Image` objects to achieve animation. Then we'll do our own animation but not with `Image` objects. Anytime you can avoid downloading multiple graphics files from the Web, your applets will be more likely to please your users. Finally, we'll close with a few words on daemons.

Let's dive right into our first multithreaded program.

Launching a Thread

The `Thread` class provides all the behaviors you need to run multiple threads in an application. Its methods include `start()`, `stop()`, `suspend()`, `resume()`, and `sleep()`. They all do exactly what their names promise. Except for `sleep()`, they don't even need arguments. The `sleep()` method requires a `long` argument, which is the number of milliseconds before the `Thread` is sent a wake-up call.

The one thing the `Thread` class doesn't know is what you want your `Thread` to do. For that, you override the `run()` method with one that does your work.

Launching a Single Thread

Listing 15.1 shows what you need to create and launch a `Thread`. This one says "Hello, Thread Word!" repeatedly.

LISTING 15.1 LAUNCHING OUR FIRST THREAD

```java
// Threads.java

import java.applet.Applet;
import java.awt.*;

public class Threads extends Applet
{
   public void main( String[] args )
   {
      MyThread mt = new MyThread();

      System.out.println( mt.isAlive() );
      mt.start ();
   }
}

class MyThread extends Thread
{
   int times = 10;

   public void run()
   {
      for ( int i = 0; i < times; i++ )
         System.out.println( "Hello, Thread World!" );
   }
}
// end of Threads.java
```

When you run this program, it will print its message as many times as you specify. It's always a good idea, by the way, to limit your Thread's run() in some way so that it will definitely stop after reaching some pre-set limit. You can expand the limit as you proceed with debugging and remove the limit when you are confident that your Thread won't run out of control.

A Thread will run even after the user closes the Web page that is running your applet. System.exit() is needed to close all Thread objects unless your run() method comes to completion or you otherwise stop() the Thread.

What's Going on Here?

Starting a Thread is completely different from in-line procedural coding. You are launching a program (a "programlet"?) that runs simultaneously with the program that launches the Thread, as well as with any other Thread objects that are running.

A Thread is considered alive if it is running. Consider the following:

```
// MyThread's run() never completes

MyThread mt = new MyThread();

    // mt.isAlive() returns false

mt.start()

    // mt.isAlive() returns true

mt.suspend()

    // still alive

mt.resume()

    // still alive

mt.stop()

    // mt.isAlive() returns false
```

The main() routine that launches the Thread is still running, along with the Thread's run() code. Add the new lines to main() that are shown in Listing 15.2, and predict the result before you run the program.

LISTING 15.2 SHOWING SIMULTANEOUS OPERATION

```java
// Threads.java

import java.applet.Applet;
import java.awt.*;

public class Threads extends Applet
{
   public void main( String[] args )
   {
      MyThread mt = new MyThread();

      System.out.println( mt.isAlive() );
      mt.start ();

        for ( int i = 0; i < 30; i++ )              // NEW!
            System.out.println( mt.isAlive() );     // NEW!
   }

}

class MyThread extends Thread
{
   int times = 10;

   public void run()
   {
      for ( int i = 0; i < times; i++ )
         System.out.println( "Hello, Thread World!" );
   }
}

// end of Threads.java
```

If you run this code repeatedly you'll get different results almost every time. The main() routine starts by reporting false. Then you get a mixture of Hello reports from the Thread and true reports from main().

Mostly, I get a few reports in a row from each, rather than a neat, alternating shuffle. Eventually, you'll get nothing but `false` reports after the thread has run to completion. You may need to increase the count in `main()` from 30 to a higher number to see the final `false` reports.

The point to remember is that your `Thread` runs, and the program that launched it also runs.

Launching Multiple Threads

What does it take to launch multiple threads? Nothing more than it took to launch a single thread. We'll try it, using differently named threads.

If you don't provide a name, the first `Thread` you launch is named `Thread-1`, the next is `Thread-2`, etc. You can provide a name, this way:

```
MyThread mt = new MyThread( "Judith" );
    // creates a Thread named "Judith"
```

If you look at the online documentation (API, Volume 1, **java.lang** package, `Thread` class) you'll see a rather long list of constructors. It documents individually each of the possibilities that I would describe more succinctly as follows:

```
Thread.Thread( [G] [R] [S] )

    G — optional ThreadGroup
    R — optional Runnable
    S — optional String

All combinations OK except:
    Thread.Thread( G )
```

You can supply any of those arguments, but they must be in the order given here, and you can't use the `ThreadGroup` by itself. We'll just use the `String` parameter, which is the name you give the `Thread`. You'll see an example of the `Runnable` parameter when we get to the Applet Wizard code. Consider the code in Listing 15.3. It creates and launches two threads, which then talk to us, as you see in Figure 15.1.

LISTING 15.3 LAUNCHING MULTIPLE THREADS

```java
// Threads.java

import java.applet.Applet;
import java.awt.*;

public class Threads extends Applet
{
    public void main( String[] args )
    {
        MyThread jack = new MyThread( "jack", "Jill" );
        MyThread jill = new MyThread( "jill", "Jack" );

        jack.start();
        jill.start();

        while ( jack.isAlive() || jill.isAlive() );

        try System.in.read();
        catch ( java.io.IOException e );
    }

}

class MyThread extends Thread
{
    int times = 10;
    String greeting;

    MyThread( String name, String greet )
    {
        super( name );
        greeting = greet;
    }

    public void run()
    {
```

```
        for ( int i = 0; i < times; i++ )
            System.out.println( "Hi, " + greeting + "!" );
    }
}

// end of Threads.java
```

The `main()` program starts `jack`, then `jill`. Then it waits until both `Thread` objects run to completion. Finally it pauses, which lets me take the screen shot shown in Figure 15.1. Take a look at who speaks first.

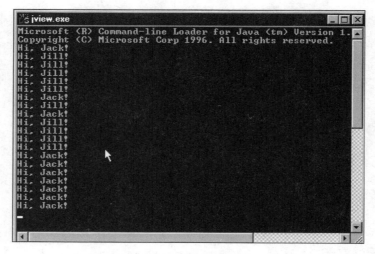

FIGURE 15.1 JACK AND JILL GREET EACH OTHER.

Even though she started second, Jill's first greeting arrived before Jack's. (Other runs were different, of course.) Again, the important point is that these `Thread` objects are running independently.

The Debugger

Our next program will attach threads to buttons, which lets you start and stop running threads with button clicks. Before we go on with it, let's take a quick look at the debugger.

Visual J++ supports a powerful debugger, inherited from Visual C++. Just as pressing **Ctrl+F5** will build and execute, pressing **F8** will build and run the debugger. This loads the program, the debugger, your classes' symbol tables, and debug-related toolbars. Figure 15.2 shows the added toolbars.

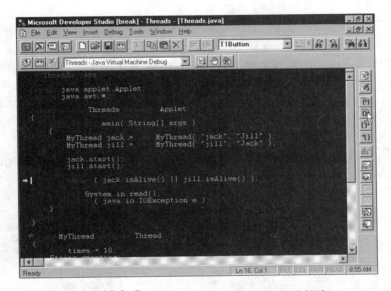

FIGURE 15.2 TOOLBARS ADDED TO SUPPORT DEBUGGING.

The standard debug toolbar lets you single-step your program; step over, into, or out of subroutines; examine variables; and set breakpoints.

Figure 15.3 shows a Quick Watch. Clicking the **Quick Watch** button lets you type in the name of any variable and examine it. I've asked for `jack.greeting` here. Obviously, the debugger supports object-oriented programming.

Some programmers love debuggers with this power and consider them indispensable tools. Others never use them. I subscribe to both camps, depending on the language. In Assembler, I couldn't live without a powerful debugger. In C++, I don't use a debugger.

In Java, I don't use the debugger very often. The JVIEW window provides a very convenient place to write values of misbehaving variables. If you're used to using the Developer Studio's debugger for Visual C++ work, you'll probably keep right on using it for Java.

If you haven't yet made up your mind what is right for you, make a serious effort to master the debugger. You may find it indispensable. Even if you decide that it doesn't fit your style, you'll run into the occasional problem where it will be invaluable.

The only problems that regularly make me want a powerful debugger are multithread-related problems. Unfortunately, the debugger does not yet have a particularly good idea about how to follow multiple threads. To use it, you have to move the suspect code into the main branch of the program, debug it there, and then move it back into a thread. This, of course, doesn't help if the problem comes from the run-time interrelationship of your threads.

On the whole, however, I think the debugger is far more powerful than any reasonable person would expect in a 1.0 language release.

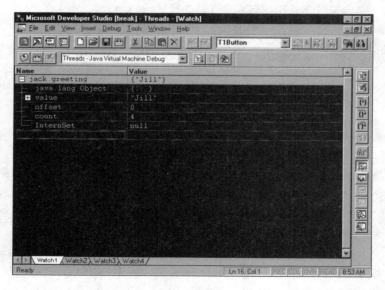

FIGURE 15.3   CHECKING A **Thread** OBJECT'S DATA MEMBER.

Creating Smart Buttons

So far, we've created buttons like the OKButton, which knows how to shut the program down. What if you want your buttons to work on objects that your program has created? You need to give the buttons access to any objects they need to manipulate. This is simple when you can pass the objects as part of the buttons' constructors.

Suppose you want a button to compose a message based on some object's name. You can get that to work this way:

```
// main() or init() code

    MyThread jack = new MyThread( "jack", "Jill" );
    StartButton sb = new StartButton( jack );


    . . .


class StartButton extends Button
{
    MyThread mythread;

    action( Event e, Object o )
    {
        // use mythread.getName() here
    }
}
```

When you pass the object to the button's constructor, you're passing a reference, not the actual object. With that reference, the button can use the object's data members and methods (assuming the protection allows this).

I've used this technique to build an application that sports three buttons. Two of them start and stop different threads, and the third closes the application. The BorderLayout provides an easy, useful arrangement. Figure 15.4 shows this application in operation.

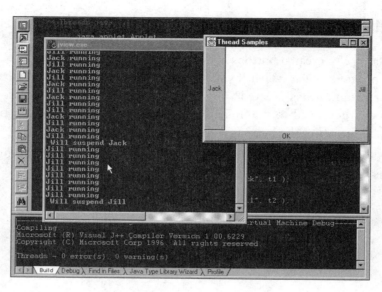

FIGURE **15.4**   WATCHING JACK AND JILL RUNNING.

The button labeled Jack starts and stops a thread that writes Jack run-ning to the JVIEW window in a long-running loop. The button labeled Jill does the same thing, but it reports Jill running, of course. You can see in Figure 15.4 that I had both threads running, then clicked **Jack**, followed quickly by a click on **Jill**.

The program that does this is listed in full in Listing 15.4. Here, we'll consider some of the key parts.

First, this is the thread class:

```java
class MyThread extends Thread
{
    final static int times = 10000;

    boolean running;

    MyThread( String s )
    {
        super( s );
    }
```

```
public void run()
{
    for ( int i = 0; i < times; i++ )
    {
        System.out.println( getName() + " running" );
        try sleep(100); catch( InterruptedException e );
    }
}

}
```

You can see that I've added a `boolean` that we can flip to `true` when the thread is running. The `run()` code introduces the `sleep()` method. It sleeps for the specified time, unless something `throws` the `InterruptedException`, which could also wake it up. . In this case, I've asked for a 100-millisecond delay (a tenth of a second).

The `times` data member will turn the thread off (by letting it run to completion) after 10,000 iterations. This field started at 10 when I wrote the original version. It grew by one zero at a time as I proved to myself that I wasn't releasing escapee threads on an unsuspecting computer.

Now let's look at the `FlipButton` class. This is the one that starts and stops both Jack and Jill. This is the code:

```
class FlipButton extends Button
{
    MyThread mt;

    FlipButton( String s, MyThread m )
    {
        super( s );
        mt = m;
    }

    public synchronized boolean action( Event e, Object o )
    {
        if ( !mt.isAlive() )
        {
```

```
            mt.start();
        }
        else if ( mt.running )
        {
            System.out.println( " Will suspend " +
                mt.getName() );
            mt.suspend();
        }
        else
        {
            System.out.println( " Will resume " +
                mt.getName() );
            mt.resume();
        }

        mt.running = !mt.running;

        return true;
    }
}
```

The data member mt is the MyThread object passed from the main() or init() routine of the application or applet. The constructor passes the name string to the Button class constructor. Then it saves the MyThread reference in mt.

The action() method is declared as a synchronized function. We'll get into this in the next section. This method checks to see if the MyThread is alive. If not, it starts it. Otherwise, it suspends a running thread or resumes a suspended thread. It reverses the value of the "running" boolean to get ready for the next button click. It also writes a note on each flip into the JVIEW window. It uses the attached MyThread object's getName() method to report the name of the Thread being affected. Each instance of FlipButton will be attached to a different thread, so it will report a different name.

The rest of the code repeats items you've seen before, such as the use of an extended Frame class to handle the WINDOW_DESTROY message and an OKButton to turn the program off. It's shown in full in Listing 15.4.

LISTING 15.4 THE SMART BUTTON APPLICATION

```java
// Threads.java

import java.applet.Applet;
import java.awt.*;

public class Threads extends Applet
{
    public void main( String[] args )
    {
        Threads app = new Threads();
        MyFrame f = new MyFrame( "Thread Samples" );
        f.add( "Center", app );
        f.resize( 300, 200 );

        f.setLayout( new BorderLayout() );

        MyThread t1 = new MyThread( "Jack" );
        t1.setPriority( Thread.MIN_PRIORITY );

        MyThread t2 = new MyThread( "Jill" );
        t2.setPriority( Thread.MAX_PRIORITY );

        FlipButton jack = new FlipButton( "Jack", t1 );
        f.add( "West", jack );

        FlipButton jill = new FlipButton( "Jill", t2 );
        f.add( "East", jill );

        OKButton okb = new OKButton();
        f.add( "South", okb );

        f.show();
    }
}

class MyFrame extends Frame
{
```

```
    MyFrame( String s )
    {
        super( s );
    }

    public boolean handleEvent( Event e )
    {
        if ( e.id == Event.WINDOW_DESTROY )
        {
            System.exit(0);
        }
        return true;
    }
}

class FlipButton extends Button
{
    MyThread mt;

    FlipButton( String s, MyThread m )
    {
        super( s );
        mt = m;
    }

    public synchronized boolean action( Event e, Object o )
    {
        if ( !mt.isAlive() )
        {
            mt.start();
        }
        else if ( mt.running )
        {
            System.out.println( " Will suspend " +
                mt.getName() );
            mt.suspend();
        }
```

```
      else
      {
          System.out.println( " Will resume " +
              mt.getName() );
          mt.resume();
      }

      mt.running = !mt.running;

      return true;
   }
}

class OKButton extends Button
{
   OKButton()
   {
      super( "   OK   " );
   }

   public boolean action( Event e, Object o )
   {
      System.exit(0);
      return true;
   }
}

class MyThread extends Thread
{
   final static int times = 10000;

   boolean running;

   MyThread( String s )
   {
      super( s );
   }
```

```
    public void run()
    {
       for ( int i = 0; i < times; i++ )
       {
          System.out.println( getName() + " running" );
          try sleep(100); catch( InterruptedException e );
       }
    }


}

// end of Threads.java
```

Before we get to animation, we'll look closely at the synchronized keyword.

Synchronizing Resource Access

When you write multithreaded code, you have to constantly bear in mind the effects of one thread interrupting another and of multiple threads accessing the same data or code. In our smart button example, the FlipButton's action() method changes the thread's status with a suspend() or resume(), and then it flips the boolean member.

What happens if it gets interrupted? You could have a situation in which the data member doesn't record the actual state of the thread. In the sample program, it doesn't really matter very much if running is mismatched, but you might have another thread that needs to know the status of Jack or Jill.

If Jack, for example, is waiting between having issued the thread.suspend() and flipping the running member's value, the querying thread will find that Jack is running, when in fact, it's suspended.

This is where synchronized is used. Something that is synchronized cannot be entered by a second thread until the first thread has finished using it. This helps ensure that operations that compose a single unit of work are performed together.

Synchronizing Data

You can lock data items in any block of instructions. Assume you are processing a `key_value` data member. You want exclusive control of this member while you perform three vital steps. This will give you the control you need:

```
synchronized ( key_value )
    { step1(); step2(); step3() }
```

You can use this technique to synchronize data members or whole objects.

Be careful about the timing of a synchronizing block. If the steps in updating it are processing steps, you're fairly safe, but if the steps in updating it involve user interaction, you'll run into trouble. Inevitably, the user will begin entering data, then call a co-worker for additional information, and then go to lunch while waiting for a return call, all the while holding the lock.

The right technique is to gather all information from the user working on a copy of the object. Then, when the user presses **Enter** or clicks **OK**, lock your object and update from the available data.

Synchronizing Classes

When Java loads a class, it creates an object member of the `Class` class. You can write lots of Java without knowing this (we have), and you can write lots of Java ignoring this (you will), but a `Class` can do some interesting things.

A method can find out what class it is, like this:

```
Class c = getClass();
```

If you want to know the name of a class, you can do it this way:

```
    Class c = getClass();
    System.out.println( c.getName() );

    // or just:
```

```
        System.out.println( ( getClass() ).getName() );
```

Online, look up Java API, Volume 1, **java.lang** package, `Class` class, for more details. For now, the important function is `getClass()`. This code lets you lock all of a class's static data members:

```
synchronize( getClass() )
{
    // update static class members here
}
```

Coordinating Threads

The problems and solutions in coordinating threads would by themselves fill a good-sized book. The term *operating systems* would be prominent in the title.

If you don't want to write your own operating system, however, Java gives you simple solutions. Suppose you want the `jack` and `jill` threads to speak, then wait for a response. (The `jill` thread won't say, `Hi, Jack!` twice in a row.) A fallible but very simple approach is to use the `Thread.yield()` method, like this:

```
// code in Thread-based class:

    public void run()
    {
        for ( int i = 0; i < times; i++ )
        {
            System.out.println( getName() + " running" );
/* HERE */  yield();
            try sleep(100); catch( InterruptedException e );
        }
    }
```

As its name suggests, the `yield()` method gives up control. If you removed the `sleep()`, here, this would fairly reliably allow `jack` to say, `Hi, Jill!` after each time `jill` says, `Hi, Jack!`

For complete reliability, you'll have to use more code. You could include a reference to `jack` as a member of `jill`, and vice versa. Then add a counter that records the number of times the thread has spoken. At startup, have the thread check to see if both counters are zero or if its partner has already spoken.

If its partner hasn't spoken, note that this thread is the initiator (use a `boolean` object member) and speak. Speaking is `println()`, followed by incrementing the counter, in a `synchronized` method. If its partner has spoken, note that this thread is the responder, and then speak.

From then on, the initiator will `yield()` if its counter is higher than the responder's counter. The responder will `yield()` if the two counters are equal. You'll have a conversation strictly built with alternating `Hi, Jack!` and `Hi, Jill!` comments.

With a technique such as this, you can include as much `sleep()` between speaking as you like, but remember not to put the `sleep()` in a `synchronized` block or method.

Multi-Image Animation

Back in Chapter 7, when we covered the Applet Wizard's code, I asked you to not get the multithreaded applet code. It wouldn't have made sense then, but it will now. The multithreaded code generated by the Wizard is very specific. It assumes that you'll be using multiple images and repainting the screen several times each second to display these images.

The effect is elegant animation. The cost, unless your Images are tiny, is very long downloads over the 'Net. (Of course, the costs for an application—the `Image` source is local disk files—can be minimal and the result compelling.)

The .GIF Files

The Applet Wizard will generate code, which we'll get to in the next section, and a series of .GIFs in the directory **project\images**. They are

IMG00001.GIF through **IMG0018.GIF**. You can use them over a blue background to have clouds gently floating in the sky.

You can work with them in the bitmap editor. Figure 15.5 shows this editor opened automatically when I used **Files/Open** and then chose **images\img0001.gif**. (Select the file of type **Image Files**.)

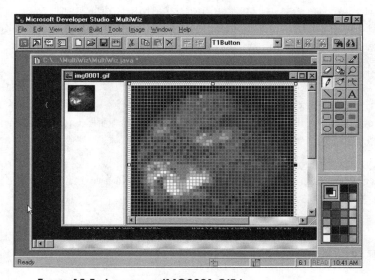

FIGURE 15.5   LAUNCHING **IMG0001.GIF** IN THE BITMAP EDITOR.

The .java Files

I named my project **MultiWiz**. As before, you get a `Frame` file, which is the same as the one we covered in Chapter 7. You also get **MultiWiz.java**, which has many differences. We'll cover these here. While we're at it, you'll see how you can do your own animation using multiple .GIFs or other `Image` source files.

I hope that you take a good look at the next section before you get started on multiple `Image` animation. Web pages that don't make me wait for long downloads are the ones I like.

Now let's look at the code. After the expected `imports` statements, **MultiWiz.java** declares its class with an `implements` keyword:

```
public class MultiWiz extends Applet implements Runnable
```

`Runnable` is an interface. It declares just one function, `run()`, with no arguments. (The simpler an interface, the more likely it is to be implemented. This is as simple as it gets.) We've used the `Thread` object's `run()` methods.

The optional `Runnable` argument to the `Thread.Thread` constructor can specify another `Runnable` object, an object that implements the `Runnable` interface. When you add a `Runnable` to the `Thread` constructor, you change the `Thread` from calling its own `run()` method to calling the `Runnable`'s `run()` method. This lets the `MultiWiz.java` code use its own `run()`, rather than creating a class that extends `Thread` and putting the `run()` method in that class.

MultiWiz.java adds several new data members:

```
Thread      m_MultiWiz = null;

private Graphics m_Graphics;
private Image    m_Images[];
private int      m_nCurrImage;
private int      m_nImgWidth  = 0;
private int      m_nImgHeight = 0;
private boolean  m_fAllLoaded = false;
private final int NUM_IMAGES = 18;
```

The constructor code, the `getAppletInfo()` method, `init()` and `destroy()` are the same as the ones we've already discussed. The changes start with `displayImage()`:

```
private void displayImage(Graphics g)
{
    if (!m_fAllLoaded)
        return;

    g.drawImage(m_Images[m_nCurrImage],
            (size().width - m_nImgWidth)  / 2,
            (size().height - m_nImgHeight) / 2, null);
}
```

When you work with `Image` objects, you generally don't want to use `drawImage()` until your `Image` is fully loaded. (See the `Image` class in API, Volume 2, **java.awt** package.) When you use multiple `Image` objects for animation, you have to wait until they are all loaded.

The work of the `displayImage()` method is done by the `Graphics` class `drawImage` method. (This is a very smart method. It understands .GIFs, .BMPs, and lots of other image source types. You'll never have to worry about actually putting pixels on the screen.) It uses one of an array of `Image` objects, as specified by `m_nCurrImage`. (Microsoft's programmers are veterans of the "Hungarian notation" they use in C++ work. A more Java-styled name would be `currentImage`.)

The `paint()` method uses the proper technique of displaying a message until all the images are loaded. Then it sets up a `Rectangle` for the `Image`, clears it, and uses the `displayImage()` method to show the image. This is the code:

```
public void paint(Graphics g)
{
    // ANIMATION SUPPORT:
    //      The following code displays a status message until
    //      all the
    // images are loaded. Then it calls displayImage to display
    // the current
    // image.
    //-----------------------------------------------------------
    if (m_fAllLoaded)
    {
        Rectangle r = g.getClipRect();

        g.clearRect(r.x, r.y, r.width, r.height);
        displayImage(g);
    }
    else
        g.drawString("Loading images...", 10, 20);

    // TODO: Place additional applet Paint code here
}
```

The `start()` method creates and launches a new `Thread`, being careful to check that it hasn't already done this. Remember, your applet's `start()` and `stop()` methods will be called by the browser when the user scrolls away from and back to your applet on the current page. The code is straightforward:

```
public void start()
{
    if (m_MultiWiz == null)
    {
        m_MultiWiz = new Thread(this);
        m_MultiWiz.start();
    }
    // TODO: Place additional applet start code here
}
```

The `stop` method takes care of the critical detail of stopping the thread. Remember, a thread will keep running even after an applet is stopped by the user changing HTML pages in the browser. You have to stop it yourself, this way:

```
public void stop()
{
    if (m_MultiWiz != null)
    {
        m_MultiWiz.stop();
        m_MultiWiz = null;
    }

    // TODO: Place additional applet stop code here
}
```

The `run()` method has become a long one. Its heart is a `while` loop:

```
while (true)
    {
        try
```

```
   {
       displayImage(m_Graphics);
       m_nCurrImage++;
       if (m_nCurrImage == NUM_IMAGES)
           m_nCurrImage = 0;

       // TODO:  Add additional thread-specific code here
       Thread.sleep(50);
   }
   catch (InterruptedException e)
   {
       // TODO: Place exception-handling code here in case an
       //       InterruptedException is thrown by
       //       Thread.sleep(),
       //       meaning that another thread has interrupted
       //       this one
       stop();
   }
}
```

The basic technique is to display image[n] and then increment n, wrapping around to 0 when you reach the end of the list. (If you were coding this, you'd catch Java's ArrayIndexOutOfBounds exception, wouldn't you? That check against NUM_IMAGES is a C programming technique.) A fair amount of code in run() concerns the MediaTracker object. A MediaTracker's basic job is to oversee the Web download process, letting you know when an Image, for example, is completely available. This class is documented in Volume 2, **java.awt**. This is the Image loading code:

```
MediaTracker tracker = new MediaTracker(this);
    String strImage;

    // For each image in the animation, this method first con
    // structs a
    // string containing the path to the image file; then it begins
    // loading the image into the m_Images array.  Note that the
    // call to
    // getImage will return before the image is completely loaded.
```

```
//------------------------------------------------------------
for (int i = 1; i <= NUM_IMAGES; i++)
{
    strImage = "images/img00" + ((i < 10) ? "0" : "") + i +
               ".gif";
    if (m_fStandAlone)
        m_Images[i-1] = Toolkit.getDefaultToolkit().getImage(
                            strImage);
    else
        m_Images[i-1] = getImage(getDocumentBase(), strImage);

    tracker.addImage(m_Images[i-1], 0);
}


try
{
    tracker.waitForAll();
    m_fAllLoaded = !tracker.isErrorAny();
}
catch (InterruptedException e)
{
    // TODO: Place exception-handling code here in case an
    //       InterruptedException is thrown by Thread.sleep(),
    //       meaning that another thread has interrupted this
    //       one
}

if (!m_fAllLoaded)
{
    stop();
    m_Graphics.drawString("Error loading images!", 10, 40);
    return;
}
```

The run() method also calls the repaint() method, which triggers the actual screen painting. Remember that the this object here is the one that extends Applet. The full code is in Listing 15.5.

Listing 15.5 MultiWiz.java—Code from the Applet Wizard

```java
// MLR: Listing reformatted to book's width
import java.applet.*;
import java.awt.*;
import MultiWizFrame;

public class MultiWiz extends Applet implements Runnable
{
    Thread     m_MultiWiz = null;

    private Graphics m_Graphics;
    private Image     m_Images[];
    private int       m_nCurrImage;
    private int       m_nImgWidth  = 0;
    private int       m_nImgHeight = 0;
    private boolean   m_fAllLoaded = false;
    private final int NUM_IMAGES = 18;

    // STANDALONE APPLICATION SUPPORT:
    //      m_fStandAlone will be set to true if applet is
    //      run standalone
    //-------------------------------------------------------------
    boolean m_fStandAlone = false;

    public static void main(String args[])
    {
        MultiWizFrame frame = new MultiWizFrame("MultiWiz");

        // Must show Frame before we size it so insets()
        // will return valid values
        //-------------------------------------------------------------
        frame.show();
        frame.hide();
        frame.resize(frame.insets().left +
                     frame.insets().right  + 320,
                     frame.insets().top   +
```

```
                      frame.insets().bottom + 240);

    MultiWiz applet_MultiWiz = new MultiWiz();

    frame.add("Center", applet_MultiWiz);
    applet_MultiWiz.m_fStandAlone = true;
    applet_MultiWiz.init();
    applet_MultiWiz.start();
       frame.show();
}

public MultiWiz()
{
    // TODO: Add constructor code here
}

public String getAppletInfo()
{
    return "Name: MultiWiz\r\n" +
           "Author: Martin Rinehart\r\n" +
             "Created with Microsoft Visual J++ " +
             "Version 1.0";
}

public void init()
{
     // If you use a ResourceWizard-generated "control
     // creator" class to arrange controls in your
     // applet, you may want to call its CreateControls()
     // method from within this method. Remove the
     // following call to resize() before adding the call
     // to CreateControls(); CreateControls() does its
     // own resizing.
     //---------------------------------------------------------
    resize(320, 240);

    // TODO: Place additional initialization code here
```

```
    }

    public void destroy()
    {
        // TODO: Place applet cleanup code here
    }

    private void displayImage(Graphics g)
    {
        if (!m_fAllLoaded)
            return;

        g.drawImage(m_Images[m_nCurrImage],
                (size().width - m_nImgWidth)   / 2,
                (size().height - m_nImgHeight) / 2, null);
    }

    public void paint(Graphics g)
    {
        // ANIMATION SUPPORT:
        //      The following code displays a status
        //      message until all the
        // images are loaded. Then it calls displayImage to
        // display the current image.
        //----------------------------------------------------------
        if (m_fAllLoaded)
        {
            Rectangle r = g.getClipRect();

            g.clearRect(r.x, r.y, r.width, r.height);
            displayImage(g);
        }
        else
            g.drawString("Loading images...", 10, 20);

        // TODO: Place additional applet Paint code here
    }
```

```java
public void start()
{
   if (m_MultiWiz == null)
   {
      m_MultiWiz = new Thread(this);
      m_MultiWiz.start();
   }
   // TODO: Place additional applet start code here
}

public void stop()
{
   if (m_MultiWiz != null)
   {
      m_MultiWiz.stop();
      m_MultiWiz = null;
   }

   // TODO: Place additional applet stop code here
}

public void run()
{
   m_nCurrImage = 0;

      // If re-entering the page, then the images have
      // already been loaded.  m_fAllLoaded == TRUE.
      //--------------------------------------------------------- .
      if (!m_fAllLoaded)
   {
      repaint();
      m_Graphics = getGraphics();
      m_Images    = new Image[NUM_IMAGES];

      MediaTracker tracker = new MediaTracker(this);
      String strImage;
```

```
            // For each image in the animation, this method
            // first constructs a string containing the path
            // to the image file; then it begins loading the
            // image into the m_Images array.  Note that the
            // call to getImage will return before the image
            // is completely loaded.
            //-----------------------------------------------------
        for (int i = 1; i <= NUM_IMAGES; i++)
        {
                strImage = "images/img00" +
                    ((i < 10) ? "0" : "") + i + ".gif";
            if (m_fStandAlone)
                    m_Images[i-1] =
                        Toolkit.getDefaultToolkit().
                        getImage(strImage);
            else
                    m_Images[i-1] = getImage(
                        getDocumentBase(), strImage);

                tracker.addImage(m_Images[i-1], 0);
        }

        try
        {
            tracker.waitForAll();
            m_fAllLoaded = !tracker.isErrorAny();
        }
        catch (InterruptedException e)
        {
                // TODO: Place exception-handling code here
                //       in case an InterruptedException is
                //       thrown by Thread.sleep(), meaning
                //       that another thread has interrupted
                //       this one
        }

        if (!m_fAllLoaded)
```

```
        {
            stop();
                m_Graphics.drawString(
                    "Error loading images!", 10, 40);
            return;
        }

        m_nImgWidth  = m_Images[0].getWidth(this);
        m_nImgHeight = m_Images[0].getHeight(this);
    }
repaint();

while (true)
{
    try
    {
        displayImage(m_Graphics);
        m_nCurrImage++;
        if (m_nCurrImage == NUM_IMAGES)
            m_nCurrImage = 0;

            // TODO:  Add additional thread-specific
            // code here
        Thread.sleep(50);
    }
    catch (InterruptedException e)
    {
            // TODO: Place exception-handling code here
            //       in case an InterruptedException is
            //       thrown by Thread.sleep(), meaning
            //       that another thread has interrupted
            //       this one
        stop();
    }
  }
}
```

```
    // TODO: Place additional applet code here

}
```

Non-Image Animation

For only a small fraction of the download time needed for multi-Image animation, you can do animation with Java's other graphic capabilities. The idea is only slightly different. You draw a picture and then increment a location pointer or separate *x* and *y* location pointers.

Each time the picture is redrawn, the location is changed slightly. A little experimenting with timing of the repaint() work and the distance incremented should provide a good compromise between smooth operation and speed. I'll provide a listing here that takes the lightning bolt from Chapter 13 and throws it across the screen. I call it **Thor**.

Before you look at this code, a couple of notes on how you should really do it. Each Component has a move() method that is much more efficient than redrawing, but you shouldn't use move() if you also use a LayoutManager.

What you want to do is use a Canvas that is positioned by the LayoutManager. Then you can draw on the Canvas using its paint() method. Unfortunately, this book is coming to a close long before the list of fascinating new Java topics is coming to a close. By now, though, you should be able to dive into the **java.awt** package in Volume 2 on your own. Good luck!

Figure 15.6 shows the lightning bolt, frozen in time on the printed page. It's moving right and downward. Printing isn't a good medium for moving images, I'm afraid.

Listing 15.6 shows the lightning bolt code modified and surrounded with buttons in a BorderLayout. The **Throw** button that you see at the top of Figure 15.6 starts and stops the lightning bolt's motion. It starts fully displayed at the left and then moves steadily off the screen to the right.

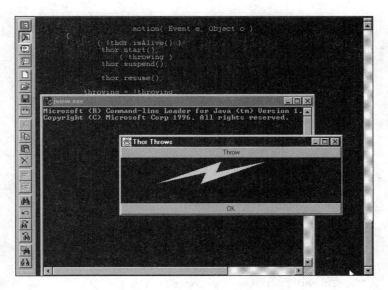

Figure 15.6 ANIMATION, FROZEN IN PRINT.

One of the nice things about graphics is that the part that doesn't show doesn't hurt, either. You'll see in the code that I modify the left argument until it is at the right edge. The effect is that the lightning bolt disappears gracefully. Internally, the Java Virtual Machine takes care of clipping the nonvisible parts of the image so we don't have to do it.

LISTING 15.6 THROWING THE LIGHTNING BOLT

```
// Thor.java

import java.applet.Applet;
import java.awt.*;

class Thor extends Applet // implements Runnable
{
    final static int nsteps = 50;

    int lft;    // current bolt location
    int top;
```

```
   int step = 0;

   public void main( String[] args )
   {
       MyFrame f = new MyFrame( "Thor Throws" );
       f.resize( 400, 150 );
       f.setBackground( Color.black );

       Thor app = new Thor();
       f.add( "Center", app );

       OKButton okb = new OKButton();
       f.add( "South", okb );

       app.init();

       ThorThread tt = new ThorThread( app );
       // tt.setPriority( Thread.MAX_PRIORITY );

       ThrowButton tb = new ThrowButton( tt );
       f.add( "North", tb );

       f.show();
   }

   public void init()
   {
      lft = 0;
      top = 0;
   }

   public void paint( Graphics g )
   {
      drawBolt( g );
   }

   void toss()
   {
```

```
        // step varies from 0 to nsteps

        int w = size().width;
        int h = size().height;

        int lstart = 0;
        int lstop = w;

        int tstart = 0;
        int tstop = h / 2;

        if ( nsteps < step )
            step = 0;

        lft = lstart +
            ( (lstop - lstart) * step ) / nsteps;
        top = tstart +
            ( (tstop - tstart) * step ) / nsteps;
        step++;
        repaint();
    }

public void drawBolt( Graphics g )
{
// Draw a lightning bolt graphic

        int blft = lft;
        int brgt = blft + size().width / 2 ;
        int bctr = ( blft + brgt ) / 2;
        int bbit = ( brgt - blft ) / 20;

        int btop =   top;
        int bbtm = btop + size().height / 2;
        int bmid = ( btop + bbtm ) / 2;

        // Make a lightning bolt
        int[] xpts = new int[7];
        int[] ypts = new int[7];
```

```
        xpts[0] = bctr + 2*bbit;  ypts[0] = btop;
        xpts[1] = bctr +   bbit;  ypts[1] = bmid;
        xpts[2] = brgt;           ypts[2] = btop;
        xpts[3] = bctr - 2*bbit;  ypts[3] = bbtm;
        xpts[4] = bctr -   bbit;  ypts[4] = bmid;
        xpts[5] = blft;           ypts[5] = bbtm;
        xpts[6] = xpts[0];        ypts[6] = ypts[0];

        Polygon bolt = new Polygon( xpts, ypts, 7 );

        g.setColor( Color.yellow );
        g.fillPolygon( bolt );
    }
}

class MyFrame extends Frame
{
    MyFrame( String s )
    {
        super( s );
    }

    public boolean handleEvent( Event e )
    {
        if ( e.id == Event.WINDOW_DESTROY )
        {
            System.exit( 0 );
            return true;
        }
        else
            return super.handleEvent( e );
    }
}

class ThorThread extends Thread
{
    Thor thor;
```

```
    ThorThread( Thor t )
    {
        super( "Thor" );
        thor = t;
    }

    public void run()
    {
        for ( int i = 0; i < 1000; i++ )
        {
            thor.toss();

            try sleep( 50 );
            catch ( InterruptedException e );
        }
    }
}

class ThrowButton extends Button
{
    ThorThread thor;
    boolean throwing = false;

    ThrowButton( ThorThread t )
    {
        super( "Throw" );
        thor = t;
    }

    public boolean action( Event e, Object o )
    {
        if ( !thor.isAlive() )
            thor.start();
        else if ( throwing )
            thor.suspend();
        else
            thor.resume();
```

```
        throwing = !throwing;

        return true;
    }
}

class OKButton extends Button
{
    OKButton()
    {
        super( "   OK   " );
    }

    public boolean action( Event e, Object o )
    {
        System.exit( 0 );
        return true;
    }
}

// end of Thor.java
```

You can see that I've used a `Thread`, unlike the Applet Wizard code. Both methods work. Using a `Thread` seems more straightforward to me. Take your pick.

When you get this running, fiddle with the size and the speed until you get something you like, and then take advantage of the computer.

If `Thor` threw a lightning bolt, (the cartoon kind) it would fatten and shorten from the force of the throw. In flight, it would stretch and finally snap back to its original form. Apply a "squish" factor and a "stretch" factor to the point coordinates of the lightning bolt and you can play with these effects easily.

Have fun with it.

Demons, dmons, and Daemons

In UNIX, the daemon (pronounced *demon*) is a hard-working fixture of almost every installation. A daemon is a job that detaches itself from any monitor and runs on its own. Daemons commonly wake up at predetermined intervals to perform some function. Fetching the latest mail every hour or two is a common daemon chore.

Java also has daemon, or dmon, threads. The documentation likes to talk about *dmons*. The `Thread` methods have names like `isDaemon()`. I think it may be premature to use Java daemons.

Daemons are tremendously useful. I'd launch several useful daemons, including ones to fetch the mail and others to maintain regular communication with my editors so I don't have to actually run a mail program very often.

But daemons can't be launched from an applet, and a Java daemon needs a Java Virtual Machine host. Right now, Windows operating systems (with the possible exception of NT) don't feature direct support for something like a daemon. Until they do, this capability isn't really cross-platform, as I like all my Java work to be.

I've no doubt that within a year or two of the day I've written this, we'll all have daemons handling most of the routine chores on our PCs. After all, stopping what you're doing to connect to an ISP and download your mail is a pretty dumb use of human time, isn't it?

Java and the Web open up a world of new opportunities. Visual J++ lets you code things that you wouldn't dream about with older tools.

Summary

By now you've learned that Java thrives on threads. When you started this chapter, threads were *terra incognito*. Java is the first major language to offer direct multithreaded programming support. (If you've programmed UNIX C, you've been able to use threads but certainly not with the rich set of capabilities that Java incorporates directly into the language.)

We started by launching a single thread. You saw that this was really the second thread of execution. The main program continued running in its thread, while the second thread ran independently.

Then we launched two threads. Because threads are objects, you can create as many as you like with no more trouble than creating objects of any class.

We paused for a brief look at the debugger. Those of you who know the Developer Studio already know about the full-featured debugger. The rest of you should at least give it an extended workout.

After that, we made smart buttons—buttons that control individual threads. We did it by passing threads to the buttons when we created the buttons. Then the button's `action()` methods could directly call the thread's `suspend()`, `resume()`, and other methods.

After that we took a look at synchronizing threads. The `synchronized` keywords let you lock methods and, for specific blocks of code, data members or objects. The `Thread.yield()` method lets one thread yield to others. In combination with data members, these tools let you synchronize your threads.

Then we went on to examine the Applet Wizard's multithreaded code, which is specifically for `Image`-based animation. It generates multiple .GIF files, which are loaded into an array of `Image` objects. These are displayed by a thread, pausing to `sleep()` between images, giving excellent animation but at the expense of possibly lengthy download times.

Then you looked at a demonstration of animation without `Image` objects. I used a similar technique, having a thread redraw an image that moved slightly with each drawing, again with a bit of `sleep()` between drawings. I hope that in your applets you'll use a little `Image`-based animation and a lot of non-`Image` animation.

Finally, I closed with a brief discussion of daemons, or *dmons*, as Java sometimes calls them. They're not really a cross-platform tool at this time, but I expect that situation to change rapidly.

Well, that's it!

You're on your own now. You've come a long way since you first stared at that intimidating jet cockpit, and we asked, "Where's the Cessna?"

Almost without noticing, you've made yourself at home in the cockpit and have rebuilt the Cessna back into a jet fighter.

Along the way, you've seen that Java only appears to be a simple language for writing applets. It's actually a massively powerful language for writing everything from operating systems to major applications, and it's excellent for Web applets.

We haven't begun to see the first crop of Java applications. When we do, they'll be exciting. I hope some of them are yours.

INDEX